BICYCLING HOME

My Journey to Find God

BICYCLING HOME

My Journey to Find God

VIRGINIA MUDD

SUNSTONE PRESS

SANTA FE

Sunstone books may be purchased for educational, business, or sales promotional use.
For information please write: Special Markets Department, Sunstone Press,
P.O. Box 2321, Santa Fe, New Mexico 87504-2321.

Book and Cover design › Vicki Ahl
Body typeface › Adpbe Garamond Pro
Printed on acid-free paper
∞
eBook 978-1-61139-

———————————————————————————————

Library of Congress Cataloging-in-Publication Data

Mudd, Virginia, 1949-
   Bicycling home : my journey to find God / by Virginia Mudd.
     pages cm
   ISBN 978-0-86534-997-1 (softcover : alk. paper)
   1. Mudd, Virginia, 1949- 2. Christian biography--United States. I. Title.
   BR1725.M73A3 2014
   277.3'082092--dc23
   [B]
                                        2014016479

———————————————————————————————

WWW.SUNSTONEPRESS.COM
SUNSTONE PRESS / POST OFFICE BOX 2321 / SANTA FE, NM 87504-2321 /USA
(505) 988-4418 / ORDERS ONLY (800) 243-5644 / FAX (505) 988-1025

Dedication

To Thomas Merton
To the journey Home
To the One I love

CONTENTS

PREFACE

My journey to find God is an adventure story, a mystery story, and a love story. Growing up in Southern California in a relatively unreligious family, this story is never one I would have imagined for myself. But it unfolded mysteriously, step by step, teaching me to trust and say yes to what life and God call me to.

I had no intention of writing a book based on the volumes of letters and journals that chronicled the ten years of my inner and outer journey to discover myself and to find God. But just as my call to find God came to me unbidden, so did the urge to write this book, an urge so persistent and increasingly strong that I came to feel it was God's idea—something I had to do.

Thirty-four years after my journey to find God began, I finally said yes and committed myself to the new journey of retracing the path that took me to my goal in order to offer the story to others. In spite of my willingness, it was, and still is, difficult to share such a personal story. My intimate experiences of God and Christ—poured out in the pages of my private journals—were meant for me and God alone, to understand and to track what was happening to me. However, by now I know better than to say no to God, no matter how uncomfortable or vulnerable an assignment might feel.

While my particular spiritual journey turned out to be most intimately connected with Christ and Christianity, I have come to consider myself a spiritually independent Christian. I know there are many routes to one's spiritual home, and I have always been inspired and guided by the wisdom teachings of other spiritual traditions. And I've found the experiences of mystics of old and of modern times to be enlightening and uplifting. I'd always thought mystics were unusual or especially gifted people. But spiritual teacher Tessa Bielecki says: "A mystic is not a special kind of person, but everyone is, or ought to be, a special kind of mystic…. Mysticism is loving, experiential awareness of God…as natural to us as breathing." And Matthew Fox says: "Deep down, each one of us is a mystic." Many of us experience a deep connection with this awareness of something greater than ourselves, whether we call it God, Source, Love, Allah, Great Spirit, Tao, Indwelling Presence, the Universe, Reality, Life, or something else. The truth of this "common mysticism," and the loving, creative power it taps into and releases into the world, is what I hope to convey and encourage through telling my story.

Thomas Merton, much-revered author, mystic, and my greatest teacher, writes: "If we experience God in contemplation, we experience Him not for ourselves alone but also for others." And so I share this story I have been blessed to live. I hope that what I learned and experienced during those ten years of struggle and joy in my search for God may help make the world a more compassionate, just, peaceful, and joyful place. May you be inspired and encouraged to take and trust your own inner journey home to wholeness, inner peace, and happiness.

1

MY WORST FEAR

"Hey, you lost your wallet!"

I was pedaling at a ponderously slow pace up a long grade on my fully loaded touring bicycle. My thirty pounds of gear felt more like thirty baby elephants. I had just passed a man standing by an old beige pickup truck parked at the side of this quiet, rural road. His dark hair scrambled around unshaven, fleshy cheeks and sloppy mustache; his belly bulged over his pants. I'd caught a waft of beer as I passed.

"Hey...your wallet!" he called out again.

Shit! My heart lurched and I felt suddenly chilled on this warm day. It was May 7, 1984, my first day on the road. I was not even fifty miles into the 1,500-mile solo bike trip I was taking from my home in the San Francisco Bay Area to the home of my heart, the Grand Teton Mountains in Jackson Hole, Wyoming.

It had already been an awful morning. I'd said a wrenching and tearful goodbye to my beloved Paul when he dropped me off on a country road a few miles north of Davis, California.

Setting out for the Tetons

"I'll see you in Wyoming, Love," he'd called after me as I turned over the first pedal strokes of my journey. Paul and I had agreed he would drive my camper truck, Sparky, to Wyoming to meet me, and we would drive back to the Bay Area together. I'd taken a quick last look as I rolled away. Paul was standing next to Sparky. His maroon sweater blended beautifully with the truck's new paint job—a royal blue body with yellow and orange stripes wrapped around it. The black shape of an eagle was painted on the hood—the shadow of that great bird I imagined flying over the truck for guidance and protection. A hot air balloon was painted on the driver's door. What adventures would I have before I would see those special parts of my life again?

Maybe that lingering image of what I was leaving behind had been slowing me down. I probably hadn't exceeded ten miles per hour all morning—I wanted to be doing at least twelve—and on this grade it was more like five. I'd put in enough miles on long bike journeys to know that bike touring could be hard, even with a congenial companion. But this time I was traveling on my own, already feeling lonely and miserable. And now had I managed to lose the one absolutely crucial possession, other than my bike, that I needed to complete my journey?

...*lost your wallet.* The guy's voice echoed in my head. By some odd circumstance the purse must have slipped out of my handlebar pack and fallen on the road. I couldn't go on without it. I turned my cumbersome load slowly around and headed back downhill. I was fifty feet away from the pickup, closing the gap quickly, when I thought to look in my pack. Squeezing the brake lever to slow my descent and steering unsteadily with my right hand, I fumbled with the zipper on the handlebar bag. As I glided steadily closer and closer, I suddenly saw with relief, and horror, that my purse was still snug inside. I'd been tricked. How could I have been so naïve, so stupid? I could now see that the guy's fly was open, his intent frighteningly obvious. How could I get my bike turned around and up the grade fast enough to avoid being grabbed? I felt like I was rolling towards an inevitable fate.

All my life, whenever a situation had seemed hopeless to me, or a challenge insurmountable, I'd been more inclined to respond as a wimp than a warrior, to give up rather than rear up like a stallion and fight. I suspect this came more from being an unwell child—or at least being treated like one—than from any specific incident in which I might have decided that losing was easier than trying to win. I had been told that at birth my right hand looked more like a chicken claw than a hand, and even with exercises my right side was still considerably shorter than my left. A serious illness in infancy had left me with some other significant physical problems; poor circulation and nerve damage to my right side had numbed certain areas of my body, especially part of my right hand, and my eyesight was compromised by a retinal scar. From the age of five I'd been frequently shepherded by my mother from Los Angeles to New York to see pediatricians as well as her own doctors, the finest specialists in the medical profession: neurologists, internists, psychologists, optometrists, orthopedists. I was tested and poked and peered at and hovered over by men in white coats as my mother stood somberly at my bedside. At home I did special exercises, went to more doctors, and had to take naps everyday. Even at nine years old when I went off to camp, I was confined to the infirmary at rest hour to ensure complete quiet.

Even though I felt pretty normal, all the doctors and fuss convinced me that something was seriously wrong with me. Added to that, I could see that my mother was always looking at me, scrutinizing me as though trying to decide if I would make it as an acceptable member of the family. I became more and more self-conscious and unsure of myself. I fell down often, bruising and bloodying my knees. In grade school I was in a constant state of humiliation in gym class. No way could this klutz vault over the "horse" or do graceful somersaults. I twisted and sprained my ankles regularly. When I was a college freshman, I sprained both ankles on the same day and had to be driven to the infirmary in an ambulance because I couldn't walk. The only physical activity I could do with ease and confidence was ride my horse, which I did with wild abandon, much to my mother's consternation.

Convinced that I was weak and incapable, I retreated into my own world. I kept my mouth shut instead of saying what I thought or felt, and dutifully went along with my mother's plans for me, whatever they were. I was too scared to confront her. I couldn't imagine saying, "Mother, I feel fine. I'm not tired. I don't want to take a nap! I won't! You can't make me!" I always admired my older sister, Tory. She was athletic, strong and strong-minded. She stood up for herself to my parents and wasn't afraid to express an unpopular opinion to them.

I remember one time when she blew up at my mother during dinner. I was about seventeen, my sister twenty. She and her boyfriend had arrived the night before, after an exhausting car trip from the Midwest. They had brought with them their beloved dog, Dum Dum, a cute collie-beagle mix. He was as much a part of their family as any child could be.

Dum Dum had an accident in the house because someone had forgotten to let him outside to pee, so he was relegated to the backyard, which was right outside the dining room. Neither Tory nor Dum Dum were used to this kind of separation. When we congregated for dinner that night, the dog immediately took up whining and barking and complaining about being away from his parents in a strange place. During one of Dum Dum's loudest bouts of crying, my mother said, "Poor Dum Dum." Maybe she had a tone of sarcasm in her voice, but whether the comment was genuine or feigned sympathy, it smacked Tory square in the heart.

She exploded not only with protest about Dum Dum's exile but also with her "furious truth" about how she felt about my mother in general.

My mother sat at one end of the Queen Anne mahogany table in stony silence; my father at the other end. The volume of my sister's rage increased. Tory tells me that at one point she looked across the table at me and could see only the top of my head, because I was sliding out of my chair and disappearing under the table. It didn't occur to me to enter the fray and say, "But Mother, she's right. It wasn't his fault that he peed in the house. And he's lonely out there."

In spite of my low self-confidence, as I moved into my adult life, I kept finding that I was capable and competent in a variety of projects and jobs. At eighteen I was the head receptionist in a Washington congressional office, and later the head of my local Congressman's district office. I played a leadership role in several political campaigns. I co-founded an early childhood education center. By the time I was thirty-two I'd served on several community boards, and met the substantial challenge of starting a successful restaurant, and bicycled more than 3,000 miles from one side of the United States to the other.

But now here I was, on a deserted California road, evidently about to become a victim of rape. Being sexually molested had been my worst fear for this solo trip, and now on my very first day, that and maybe worse seemed dead ahead. As I braked harder I could feel the monumental struggle within me between the child convinced she was incapable and the young woman who had proven again and again that she could accomplish whatever she set out to do. When I was no more than thirty feet away, I heard him say, "Do you want some pussy?" That very word and his lustful sneer turned my stomach with overwhelming fear and revulsion.

At that moment something rose up inside me. Instead of feeling paralyzed and surrendering to my fate, a great determination kicked in. I began a gradual left turn. I was going so slowly I was afraid I didn't have enough momentum to keep the bike upright. I pushed hard on the pedals and headed my unwieldy bike back uphill. My abdomen tightened as I pulled hard on the handlebars. My thigh muscles burned with each downward thrust. Would he come after me? "Turn around," he called out, "before I have to catch you." Oh, God. I pedaled on with all the strength I could muster, expecting at any moment to feel huge, hairy arms and beer-breath on my neck. It took me an eternity of three minutes to reach the top of the grade. He must have been too fat and too drunk to handle the exertion of running after me or getting into his truck and catching up.

Heart beating frantically, I accelerated hard on the downhill side. A defiant little voice inside me jeered, *You couldn't catch me if you tried, creep.* As the distance between us grew and still no beige pickup appeared in my rearview mirror, I fervently thanked God—the God who had called me on this journey in the first place.

I was thirty-five years old and had recently come to the heartbreaking end of a marriage and divorce. I was in the midst of a frustrating love relationship, and I'd just finished a two-year, spirit-crushing stint as manager of my own restaurant. I was at a turning point, and I didn't know where I was headed. I'd seen many things in my life ending but no beginnings. Yet more puzzling and disconcerting than any of these uncertainties was the fact that I had become utterly obsessed with the desire to *find God*. In fact, I had been on the quest to find God for the previous five years. I thought I'd found Him in Paul, the man I'd fallen deeply in love with and who'd played a major part in setting me on this spiritual journey. When it became clear that the relationship was only a step on that path, I had really no idea where to go or even what exactly I was looking for. I read spiritual books hoping for clues or step-by-step instructions for finding God. Sometimes during those years I was so preoccupied with life's demands I forgot about this yearning, but mostly this longing for God had been driving me all my waking hours like a lead foot on an interior throttle. And now here I was out in the middle of nowhere with little but my bike and the sense that this solo trip to the Grand Tetons was something I was supposed to do, and that it was related to my search for God.

Before this odd calling, God had not been much a part of my adult life, and precious little of my young life. But I do clearly recall having a sense of God when I was about six years old. Sometimes when I was supposedly taking my afternoon nap, I'd lie there looking at the ceiling where I could distinctly see a figure, an elegant, grandfatherly man. Somehow I knew that was God above me. He always wore a freshly pressed, white tuxedo, and I remember thinking, "How can He always look so neat when He must be so busy?" He had shoulder-length white hair and a long Rip Van Winklish beard. He was impressive but not in the least unapproachable. While He never looked at me directly, I could feel His kindness, and I always felt welcomed and loved. Of course I never told anyone about these naptime visions.

My family had little use for God or religion. My father proudly declared that he was an atheist, and my three brothers echoed his proclamation. Whenever they got together on this subject, they were like a gang of schoolboys, reveling in jokes about God and anyone who believed in Him. God—if He existed—was, of course, male. My mother, not surprisingly, kept quiet on the subject because it was not her place to be anything but supportive to the male family members. I don't know what she believed in her heart, but every year she did go to the Christmas Eve service at St. James Episcopal Church, "for the music," as she put it, and Tory and I always went with her.

Despite God's insignificant position in the family, Tory and I were enrolled in Sunday school, which we attended sporadically, and we were confirmed in the Episcopal Church. I assumed that was what children of a certain age were supposed to do. At the boarding school we were sent to for high school, all students were expected to attend a church of their choice every Sunday. I switched off between "Congo" (Congregational) and "Pisco" (Episcopalian), learning the liturgies of each, following the program as solemnly as any, politely dissolving the wafers or Wonder bread in my mouth without chewing, demurely sipping wine or grape juice. I don't know how much personal prayer —if any—I engaged in, but I could recite the Nicene Creed, and I knew many prayers, ritual responses, and psalms by heart. Every Sunday evening the whole school gathered in the front rooms of the main building to sing hymns, accompanied by old Miss S. on the upright. Over my four years there, I grew to love that ritual. The words and music were comforting and nourishing.

But once I was out of high school, I didn't give a thought to God or to my own spiritual life. It wasn't that I was *anti*-God; He just had no place or purpose or function in my life. Not until I found myself in crisis did my life radically change in relation to God, and I was set on this mysterious path I felt compelled—driven—to follow.

It started with scrambled eggs. I was visiting my mother's house with my husband, the man I married after my first year in college. It was March 15, 1976, and we were having breakfast at that same deeply polished mahogany Queen Anne dining table. It was neatly laid with pretty white linen placemats, matching napkins, and sparkling silverware. A crystal glass of fresh orange juice sat in the upper right corner of my placement. Lipton tea brewed in my favorite silver teapot sat next to the silver salt and peppershakers at the head of my place setting. Breakfast included thin white buttered toast, strips of crispy bacon, and pale yellow, runny scrambled eggs. I wolfed down everything on my plate and said, "Yes, please," when offered a second helping of eggs, then quickly downed those as well. For me this was very weird behavior.

For the past year, since reading Frances Moore Lappé's *Diet for a Small Planet* and countless other books about diet and nutrition, I had become a "health nut." My bookshelves were lined with vegan, macrobiotic and vegetarian cookbooks. I was extraordinarily healthy and aware of my body. I was quite thin for the first time in my life. My husband and I had determined a year earlier to lose some weight. I started out weighing 140 lbs. at 5 feet, 7 inches. I counted calories with meticulous accuracy—900 calories a day. I gradually—sensibly—lost a few pounds. I'd started to exercise—running every day in the hills behind our house. By the time I hit 115 pounds, I felt more than accomplished and pleased with my new look. I loved to feel my bones, even my organs, as they throbbed and hummed within me. I became so intrigued with my skeletal structure, which I'd never seen before, that I wanted to see more of it. The game went from eating my allotted 900 calories to seeing if I could eat only 850...800...maybe even 750.

I always ate in a very methodical, ritualistic manner. I had a small portion of muesli with apple juice in the morning (no dairy, thanks), an undressed salad for lunch, and some sort of whole grain dish for dinner like brown rice and veggies or a barley mushroom casserole. I used carob instead of chocolate, picked only whole grains and natural sweeteners, and tested numerous seaweed varieties. I always measured carefully and ate slowly with utmost care and awareness.

When I weighed 105, it appeared to others that I was ill or anorexic, but I felt more alive and vibrant than I ever had. I had absolute control over my eating, my body, and my habits. Everything that related to food—shopping, preparing, serving, feeding myself—had the quality of a sacred ritual. Then came those scrambled eggs.

"Well," I thought, "I *am* a little underweight, and I am pretty excited about the upcoming political fundraising dinner my husband and I are hosting, so it's understandable." I told myself, "I can afford a little slip-up." But my odd behavior over mediocre scrambled eggs remained a disturbing presence, like a little toothache that wouldn't go away.

A few days later I had another "little slip-up" as I browsed upon the tasty hors d-oeuvres I'd made for our dinner guests, and I had no problem at all snacking randomly on the leftovers either. From then on my precise eating habits seemed to drift away from me like fall leaves from a tree. Except for dinnertime with my husband, my regular mealtimes fell by the wayside too. Instead of my precisely regulated eating habits, I'd buy a cookie while shopping and eat it on the way home, or slice off a 500-calorie chunk of cheese for myself while making dinner, or grab a handful of raisins when I walked by the pantry, or maybe I'd help myself to seconds from the dinner casserole, or drop an overly generous scoop of ice cream over the dessert strawberries.

My "little slip-ups" became habitual and the sense of urgency to eat escalated as though I were caught on some kind of amusement park ride that kept going faster and faster while I tried to hold on. Before long I found I *had* to have something in my mouth, to taste the flavors, to chew on something, to swallow. At first I limited my bingeing to "good" food—whole wheat bread, cheese, nuts, natural sweets, honey ice cream. But within a few months, the power of my craving to have food in my mouth burst through those natural limits, and I was onto whatever was handy. I couldn't pass the refrigerator without opening it and putting *something* in my mouth: whole loaves of zucchini bread (sometimes straight from the freezer), several scoops of ice cream (if not the whole pint), bags of chips, jumbo sandwiches. Afterwards I would lie on the kitchen couch with my stomach so stuffed and hurting it felt like I'd swallowed a basketball. Then I would eagerly anticipate dinner when I could legitimately begin the process all over again.

My mantra changed from *Eat to Live* to *Live to Eat*. To make matters worse, since I was cooking for the local daycare center I had co-founded, I was around food all day long. Cheese toasts, veggie burgers, peanut butter/apple butter sandwiches, zucchini bread with cream cheese, juice. I tasted and re-tasted everything I made for those little kiddies, and cleaned their plates of leftovers directly into my mouth when they came back to me for washing. No need for a compost bucket while I was there!

The final addition to this excruciating condition was that I was constantly creating and cooking elaborate gourmet dishes for fundraising events I was catering, and for trial menu items for the restaurant my husband and I were opening. So from morning to night I wallowed in food. For a foodaholic, I was truly in hog heaven. Only it was a living hell.

For over a year I carried in secret the terror and panic, the guilt and shame of being so totally out of control. Occasionally, when I was particularly terrified, I'd casually say something to my husband like, "Oh, gee, I wish I hadn't eaten so much. Lately I haven't had very good eating habits." And he'd say something like, "Oh, I know what you mean, I do that too sometimes." I didn't scream at the top of my lungs what my inner self was crying out: *Help! Help! I can't stop eating and I am sooo scared! What's happening to me?*

I went on in silence, not even a word to my journal. I couldn't bear to have an empty stomach, yet I always felt unbearably empty inside no matter how stuffed I was. I was terrified of gaining weight. Every new morning, I'd vow that today it was going to be different; maybe something had changed overnight in a dream, in a vision, and I'd be back to normal. This never happened. I gained weight. By summer I was an alarming— to me—112 pounds. I decided the only remedy was to fast, not just short, three-day cleansers, but big-time, ten-day fasts. I did this twice during that same year, hoping desperately that this would break the habit that was now firmly entrenched within me. It didn't. And as if to make up for the food I'd missed, I'd consume ever-greater quantities of food after the fast was over, so that I'd soon surpass the weight I'd been at the start of the fast. By the spring of 1977, a year after I'd gulped down my mother's scrambled eggs, I weighed 123 pounds, but over the year of feasting and fasting and frantically running and biking off calories, I'd probably gained closer to fifty pounds.

My fear of being fat was all-consuming. It was the only thing I thought about in my waking hours. If I were fat, my husband would leave me, men wouldn't look at me, people would scorn or ignore me. It was an unbelievable nightmare. One day as I was biking home, I became aware that I was mentally, emotionally, and physically numb. I was so burdened by the food inside me that I couldn't tell if *I* were there or not. I felt devoid of energy. I don't know how I even managed to pedal; I felt nothing, like a zombie. Something had to change.

I resolved to do *something*. Maybe, I thought hopefully, bingeing was my body's way of dealing with the absence of some vital, missing vitamin or mineral. I went to a holistic health center, and after a lengthy and intricate examination, I received an impressive computer printout detailing the subtleties of my burdened body. Alas, there was no missing vitamin. (How could there be with all the food I was eating?) What the consultants were most interested in, however, was not all the numbers and percentages, but that I had not had a menstrual period for nearly six years. It troubled them considerably more than it did me. For a couple of years after I'd married, I'd taken a particular birth control pill that inhibited my menstrual flow until I changed to non-drug contraceptive options. I'd been off that flow-inhibiting drug for several years, but never returned to a normal monthly cycle. They gave me a referral to someone whom I assumed would prescribe a nifty drug to start my flow again, and I made an appointment.

Several days later I took the BART train to Berkeley for my appointment. Expecting an RN in whites, I was caught completely off-guard when the "doctor" opened the door to her house. "Hi. I'm Linne." She smiled warmly at me. "Come on in." She wore maroon cords and sneakers. Her long, straight, dark brown hair lay over the back of her white sweatshirt. She led me into her small bedroom and asked me to go ahead and sit on a large pillow on the floor so we could begin our first session. After a full year of uncontrollable bingeing, I was too stunned and desperate to resist the fact that I was now in therapy.

I never had the courage to tell Linne I was completely in the grip of food. I told her the reason for my being there was to restart my menstrual cycle. But it didn't matter to her what we talked about, because in her view all roads led to the core of any problem, and we would eventually track down the root cause of whatever was my dysfunction.

Our sessions were like descending into the bowels of a cavern with only a tiny flashlight in hand. I never knew if I could retrace my steps or find another exit. With Linne's gentle but firm prodding, I would shine the light on parts of myself I'd never known—like intense feelings. I told her that as a child my mother was always saying, "Keep your voice down, dear." What she really meant was, "Stuff every strong emotion that comes from your heart or belly or you'll be sorry. It's not ladylike." Prior to therapy my range on the keyboard of emotions hovered around a quiet middle C. As I cracked open my unconscious past, it was shocking and scary to discover feelings of uncertainty, confusion, resentment, frustration, loneliness, and anger. Of all the emotions I was unearthing, anger was the most frightening to me. No one in my childhood family or my marriage ever expressed anger. It either wasn't felt or wasn't allowed. I was afraid to feel angry or to act on that anger by raising my voice or using strong language. I was especially reluctant to express anger toward my husband, fearing he would either hit me or leave me. I had no reason to believe either would happen, but we both avoided conflict; not a harsh word had passed between us in the eight years of our marriage.

Once I started therapy I was depressed a good deal of the time. I cried regularly. One evening when my husband came home from work, he found me huddled between the stereo speakers with the music at full volume, dissolved in tears. "Do you really think you're getting better?" he wondered aloud. Of course, it was the agonizing question I asked myself too, but there seemed only one way to any answer, if there was one, and that was to go on with investigating my scary interior life.

Once I began to connect with and express my inner feelings and emotions, my married life got very messy. Some shit necessarily hit the fan, and it didn't hit just once but many times over several years as we muddled and crashed our way into a new world of honestly expressing the feelings we knew so little about and had so little practice in conveying. My husband hadn't wanted me to "rock the boat" by expressing difficult feelings that might threaten the stability of our marriage. But it was too late for me to turn back, to shut the door I had opened, even if only a crack. I wanted to be able to know what I felt, and what he felt. I wanted us to *express* what we felt, even if it wasn't pleasant or harmonious.

During the two years I worked with Linne—sitting on the large burgundy pillow in her tiny bedroom—I gradually learned to trust the process of deep inner investigation. Uncovering and exploring repressed memories and emotions left a pile of soggy Kleenex on the floor at the end of every hour. Somehow I always emerged from the cavern with a sense of healing and some insights. I could see that I was so shy and reluctant to speak up because growing up I never felt like my opinions or ideas or feelings were heard or that they mattered. I could see why I loved the animals in my life so much because they not only gave me much needed love, but they could also *receive* the love I had to give. I could see that I'd developed a strong sense of self-sufficiency and independence because there were very few people I could trust to genuinely respond to me. The quaint motto, "Children should be seen and not heard" fit perfectly—except for me I'd felt neither seen nor heard.

I began to understand why I had developed certain strategies during childhood to take care of my needs for security, acceptance and love. I began to take incremental steps toward being more trusting, more open, more willing to express my mind and heart to others. I learned that this process of inner investigation—often torturous and frightening—is a process of purification common to all spiritual traditions, requiring considerable courage and faith. The work with Linne opened a door into my inner world and set me on the path that would not only eventually heal the challenges that sent me to her but would change my life.

Several years later I would read some of the writing of Carl Jung and his followers to understand more of my psychological processes. Marion Woodman, in *The Pregnant Virgin*, would explain that my very precise food rituals had to do with the urge to leave girlhood behind and enter into independent, adult womanhood. She would also perfectly describe what would eventually happen to me. In writing about addiction—and in particular food addicts—she wrote: "Truth is what they search for, and painful and perverse as the way may be, the addiction is their way to truth. It is the opening to themselves. Profoundly committed to becoming conscious, they will not, cannot, give up until they know what it means. In the addiction is hidden the treasure—the knowledge of themselves—and they can take no other path toward it. It is their particular sacred journey, their Tao, their Way."

If I'd known during those years of therapy that addiction, according to Woodman, could be the holy road to God, it would hardly have mattered to me. God was the furthest thing from my mind as I secretly tore into another loaf of zucchini bread spread thickly with cream cheese. I didn't care about God or my menstrual flow. I just wanted out of the hell I was in.

Then, one day, two years into therapy, I arrived for my appointment eager to tell Linne about a special dream I'd had the night before. I was in unusually good spirits as I walked from the BART station to her house, because for once this dream was not some variation on the themes of collapsing houses, beached whales, being chased by menacing "bad guys," dark, murky pools, or drowning. I took my customary place on the burgundy cushion, lowered my eyes in reverie, and began to recount the dream.

I am at a mountain lodge resort, standing in the spacious outdoor entry hall. A man enters with an old and dear friend I haven't seen since college. I am delighted to see her and am struck by the elegant older man she is with. The man's thick white hair is neatly styled and trimmed, and he has a fine full mustache. He wears a handsomely tailored three-piece suit, soft and cream-colored. He reminds me of Hal Holbrook.

I paused to explain to Linne that Hal Holbrook is the actor whose fame for impersonating Mark Twain is worldwide. He had once performed at my boarding school, and I'd found him exquisitely and memorably handsome. Then I went on.

For a short silent time, the three of us stand and gaze out over the mountains, my college friend in the middle. Then, as if on cue, I turn to look at the man, and he at me. I know instantly I am in love with him, and that he loves me. My friend is forgotten as we come together, embracing with intense passion and fervor. I am startled to realize I am falling, and that I long to fall, to surrender myself to this stranger. Nothing else matters to me but my desire to merge completely with this man. I fall backward, float downward, reveling in waves of orgasm, although I feel no physical penetration. When it begins to rain, an umbrella is immediately raised over us.

Later, I carry my sleeping bag to the dormitory where I am to spend the night. All the bunks are taken. Then, from a bed in the corner, cast in shadows, a man calls to me: "Here, you can sleep with me." I see that it is "Hal Holbrook." I go directly to his bed, without pause, without fear.

Next morning we drive down the mountain together in my sports car. He tells me all the things he has to do. I am oddly relaxed and at peace, even though I sense I won't again see this man whom I love so mightily. I let him out at the chosen street corner, and we say goodbye as though we are old friends.

As I brought back the scene at the mountain lodge, I was immediately engulfed in the same intensity and passion and love of the previous night, yet I had no more understanding of its significance than when I had dreamed it. As I emerged from the semi-hypnotic state in which I'd been reliving the dream, Linne asked, "Who do you think that man was?" Something in her tone, and in the penetrating way she looked at me, gave me the impression that *she* knew, even if I didn't.

I hesitated, still puzzling over the identity of this man. Then, that very distant childhood image began to emerge, and I began, "He reminds me a little of what God looked like to me when I was six...." As the words left my mouth and the sentence trailed off into silence, I knew with absolute certainty that the man was God and that I had met, embraced and loved God. Even more unbelievable, He had embraced and loved *me*.

I was stunned. God. Suddenly God. Not an *idea* of God but God coming into me, filling up my entire being. God beckoning to me. God loving me. Me loving God. Me surrendering to my own passion and love for God. It was way beyond anything I could even remotely comprehend. It was astonishing how the unexpected and bizarre wolfing down of a plate of scrambled eggs had led to my inner searching for the cause of my terrible food addiction, and that that search had led me, through a dream, to contact with God.

The profound manifestation of God in my dream sparked in me the resolute and fervent desire to find God in my waking life. My sacred journey, as I would later call it, had seemed to be about finding myself, and now it was also about finding God. At the time they seemed to be two different tasks. It would be many years before I would pick up a copy of Thomas Merton's *New Seeds of Contemplation* and read the description of the path I'd found myself on. He writes: "Ultimately the only way I can be myself is to become identified with Him in Whom is hidden the reason and fulfillment of my existence. Therefore, there is only one problem on which all my existence, my peace and my happiness depend: to discover myself in discovering God. If I find Him, I will find myself, and if I find my true self I will find Him."

It would be ten years after that plate of scrambled eggs—a journey that would be puzzling, agonizing, and ecstatic—before I would find what Thomas Merton had so well defined. If I had known what it would take, maybe I would have just chosen to be an anorexic bicyclist until I met my end. But once I set foot on the path of discovering myself and God, there was no turning back. I would do whatever I had to do, and face whatever I had to face.

Out there on a California road, that meant continuing on a 1,500-mile solo bike trip and finding the courage to go on despite beer-bellied rapists at the side of the road. At the end of that first day, I pulled down an unpaved side street into a seedy trailer park outside Williams to camp for the night. I put up my bright blue tent on barren ground and hauled in all my packs. If I could have fit Sunny inside I would have. I'd named my custom-made bike "Sunny" because his frame was painted a cheerful light yellow, like a sunny day. His handlebars were wrapped in bright blue cloth tape. We'd ridden together for a couple of years, and he was a true companion. I lay him down on his side directly in front of the tent and gave him a pat of gratitude.

I zipped up the tent flap and lay back, holding close my other companion, a little stuffed dog named Puppy Jr. His predecessor, Puppy Sr., was at home on my bed. Having been with me since I was a baby, he was no longer in shape for the adventure that lay before us. Puppy Jr. was the size of a small eggplant, blonde fur, dark brown ears, a wry smile on his face. His "home" for the journey was my front pack, and I hugged him gratefully. Clearly he had been responsible for keeping my purse from falling out on the road!

As I lay on my sleeping bag, recuperating and reflecting on the day, a barely audible male voice broke into my reverie: "Lady want some pussy?" *Oh my God.* My body seized up again with disgust and fear. For a few long moments I lay there paralyzed. Not until that morning had I ever encountered this kind of ugly aggression. I'd made it through one encounter, but now what? I had to do something. Putting on a very bored tone of voice, I said, "I'm not interested." Then, after a few minutes of not hearing a sound outside, I crawled out of the tent and went to the manager's office to complain. Not a word after that.

It took me a long while to fall asleep. I had met what Jungian psychologists call "Threshold Guardians"—that which challenges us as we set forth on a quest—and my fledgling warrior had risen to the occasion. I'd known I would have to face many challenges on the trip, but I was not expecting to confront my worst fear *twice* on the first day! It was a test, and I was coming to quick and sobering terms with the nature of my journey. The questions on the test were: *Can you handle what lies ahead? How badly do you want to bike to the Tetons? And how badly do you want to find God?* I had passed one test. And I knew I really wanted to ride to the Tetons. And I wanted very very very badly to find God.

2
SEEDS OF INSPIRATION

As soon as I woke in the morning, images and fears of the previous day flooded my mind. My vulnerability as a solo woman cyclist was no longer just a possibility but a sobering reality. What would *this* day bring? Still inside the relative safety of my tent, I did some stretches and circled my arms vigorously to ease the tension in my body. To keep from replaying frightening images and thoughts, I concentrated on my route ahead.

I was bound for Chico, California, sixty miles north, where I would stay the night with a longtime friend, Gerry. From there I could take backcountry roads all the way to Portland, where I would again see friends. *How safe am I going to be on these remote rural roads?* After that, I knew no one along the route. I'd be entirely on my own. In my mind I could see myself riding east along the Columbia River that borders Oregon and Washington. Cutting across the narrow, northern part of Idaho would get me to Missoula, Montana. From there I would at last head south into Wyoming to reach my final destination, the Grand Tetons. *I can do this. I'll be there in about a month.* I saw myself cycling—safely—through the increasingly warm spring days of May.

With a deep breath, I crawled out of the tent and purposefully focused on packing my panniers and loading up Sunny. As I shoved off on the gravel road that led to the highway, I silently prayed for a more peaceful day.

The route to Chico was taking me through rolling fields plowed and mostly still barren, save for a blush of bright green sprouts like the new growth of beard on an adolescent boy's face. It was relatively easy riding through peaceful farmland and still air. The thought of getting to Gerry's house—and somewhere safe for the night—buoyed my spirits and took the edge off my heightened sense of vulnerability.

I'd first met Gerry when my husband and I were building our house. He'd shown up looking for a job and ended up staying on for several months, patient and meticulous in everything he did. In fact, Gerry had a lot to do with my own long distance bicycling adventures. The last time we'd seen each other was several years before, just after he got back from bicycling solo from San Francisco to Boston. The very idea of Gerry cycling alone across America was unbelievable to me. I'd always thought you had to be a Super Athlete for such an undertaking, and Gerry seemed more geek than jock. When I saw that he'd successfully completed his long

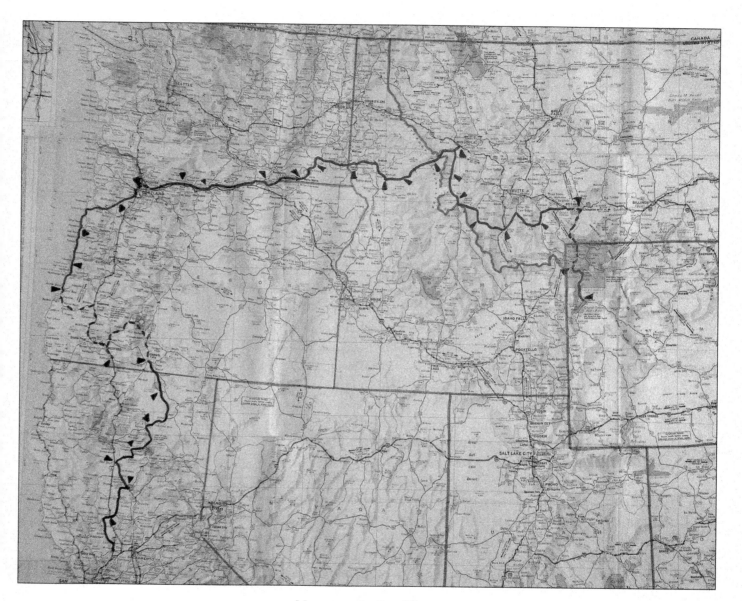

My route to the Grand Tetons

journey, my mind had begun spinning with fantasies and dreams. *If* Gerry *can do it, so can I.* I may not have been able to vault over anything higher than a gopher hole, but I could definitely ride a bike. Soon I found myself telling a few friends, "Someday I'm going to bicycle across America." I was surprised by my own conviction.

Then one March afternoon in 1978, I was lying on the couch in the kitchen reading a bicycling newsletter when my eyes fell upon a classified ad: "Cycling Companions Wanted." That dream was suddenly set into motion. I couldn't believe what I was reading. A woman my age, twenty-nine, was looking for another woman to cycle across the country with. For a moment I wasn't sure that I hadn't put the ad in the paper myself. I began to run through a long list of pros and cons; it took me all of thirty seconds to decide to call the name and number in the ad.

"Carol?" I hoped she wouldn't hear the tremor in my voice. "I saw your ad, and I'm interested in talking more about your plans."

Two days later we met for lunch in a San Francisco café. The night before I'd dreamt of twins, so it didn't surprise me to find we were remarkably alike. That weekend we took our first ride together through the rural area near my house. Since we were both quite sure we would get along, we began making preparations for a May 1 departure from my home in Alamo, California, bound for Washington, DC. Thankfully, my husband was fully supportive of this journey, even though it meant he was left with all the care of house and property and animals for two months. The trip was one of those "wild divine inspirations," although at that time I wouldn't have thought of it that way. I was just following an idea Gerry's trip had already planted in my mind.

For many of my close friends and family this plan had come as quite a shock. There had been little in my personal history up to that point to encourage adventure or risk-taking. No one expected much for my future besides a quiet, safe life—perhaps a New Age version of Debutante/Country Club/Junior League/Do Gooder. But ride a bike across the whole country?!

We five Mudd children had been born into a prominent, wealthy Los Angeles family and raised to do what was conservative and conventional. My parents kept a low profile in the community, not wanting to attract any attention from the media out of fear of my sister or me being kidnapped. My mother's earliest stories to us were not of brave pioneering women like Narcissa Whitman or Amelia Earhart. Rather, she told us household horror stories, like how the maid, answering the front door for the plumber, would be bound and gagged by the disguised villain, the child grabbed and carried off; then the ransom note and threats would follow.

I don't know whether these stories were made-up or true, but she got her point across. The Mudd children were wary and mistrustful. We weren't supposed to talk with strangers, and were absolutely never to *dream* of accepting an ice cream from some nice man. We were not allowed to ride our bikes four blocks through The Alley (a narrow sidewalk between upscale walled houses) to the shopping center, let alone camp out in our own backyard. In the thirteen years I lived in Los Angeles, I never once rode a city bus and was permitted to be in only a few "respectable" parts of town. My general conclusion was that the world was a threatening and scary place; that people, unless they were in the same social register, were not trustworthy at best; and that I always had to expect that my worst nightmares would come true.

I must have had a longing—so deep I was unaware of it—to break out of this paranoid prison, a longing to feel self-confident and secure in the world instead of fearful, to feel powerful instead of incompetent. That longing part of me leapt at the cross-America bike trip with untempered enthusiasm, and even a sense of urgency. Something vital was at stake. I had to go. I needed to prove my mother wrong. I needed to see if I was, or could become, something more than a debutante. I needed to follow that dream of a long-distance bike journey that Gerry had first awakened in me.

Now here I was, six years after that cross-country journey with Carol, on my own solo cycling trip, and about to see Gerry, the very person whose own courageous trip had first inspired me. As I pedaled past farmhouses and pastures full of horses, I reflected on my decision. The idea for the trip had come to me five months earlier. I was cycling through a foggy morning on one of the country roads near my home. Having recently left behind the burdensome tasks of managing my restaurant, I was enjoying a new sense of freedom. But along with relief I was also feeling that uncertainty about what I would do next in my life. The restaurant had been just one more of the things I'd built my life around that had fallen apart in the last three years. As I pedaled into the chilly mist, suddenly the crazy idea of making a solo bike trip to Wyoming burst into me like fireworks. I love Wyoming, but in particular I love the Grand Teton Mountains around Jackson Hole. Ever since I'd gone to camp there in my early teens, they had been a profoundly sacred place to me. The idea of seeing them again lit up my mind and heart with exhilaration—and panic. I felt a simultaneous "O boy!" for the thrill of the adventure, and an "Uh-oh!" of fear for the challenge I could imagine ahead of me if I decided to go.

It was a wild scheme but not so far-fetched that I couldn't imagine doing it. After all, I had bicycled clear across the United States. But that had been with a friend. A solo bike trip all the way to the Tetons was a different matter. I had once read a respected artist saying something like: *Wild inspirations are gifts from God. If the idea fits the person to whom it is given, it should be taken on and expressed; otherwise such inspirations may not come again.* I'd followed such inspirations—such gifts from God—several times in the past. They'd always come with a sense of deep knowing in my heart, a quality of solidity and rightness I could count on.

Five zany and very fast miles later, I'd arrived in town at my favorite bookstore. Breathing hard and feeling giddy all over, I grinned at my friends who owned the store and babbled something about going to Wyoming by bike. A few minutes later I left with a road map of the Western United States This inspiration from God had grabbed me so hard, I'd barely paused to second-guess it.

The last wild inspiration from God that I'd followed had set in motion a project that had been both my fulfillment and my undoing. One Saturday morning in October 1976, my husband and I were lazing around in bed, talking about whatever came to mind. Our topics at the time often related to our concerns for the planet and how to bring people into harmony with the earth. The entire previous year, ever since Tory had sent me *Diet for a Small Planet,* I had read voraciously, educating myself about the link between personal diet and planetary health. That had led to questioning the political and philosophical structure of my country, and the entire industrialized world. The answers had turned my world upside down.

Barry Commoner's *The Closing Circle* revealed how all life is connected in a closed circle, and how this system cannot be interrupted without damaging consequences. I studied and evaluated the modern method of growing food in this country: agribusiness vs. small farming, chemical vs. organic farming, and monoculture vs. diversity. Paul Ehrlich's *End Of Affluence* and other books showed me how inequitably wealth was distributed in this country and the world. The worlds my father and grandfather functioned in—my world—began to crumble as I saw the inequities and destruction created by economic and political systems designed without regard for the true costs of our actions.

I became a "devotee" of Gandhi's path of non-violence and civil disobedience. Ivan Illich's book, *Medical Nemesis,* educated me about how healers other than western allopathic doctors and hospitals treat disease and illness. I learned how other cultures and people were living in cooperation rather than in competition with nature and each other. E.F. Schumacher's *Small is Beautiful* showed me the importance of human-scale, local economies, and ways of supporting our modern lifestyle that are more energy-efficient and less wasteful: conservation, recycling, appropriate technology, alternative energy sources, local economies, and "voluntary simplicity." I was a convert to Eleanor Roosevelt's motto, "Use it up. Wear it out. Make it do. Do without."

Inspired and determined, I'd set out to make some radical changes in my life. *Mother Earth News* was the hot new magazine on my coffee table. I enlisted my husband and, as much as we could, we'd turned our new home into a homestead. We cut our electrical and gasoline energy use by half. I rode my bicycle about

2,000 miles a year on errands. Knowing how wasteful a meat-based diet was, I completely altered our eating habits, and my husband and I were soon full vegetarians. I put up food all summer long, ground my own grain, and hadn't bought a commercial loaf of bread for two years. We made soap and candles and tofu, and planted a garden. Our basement wall was lined with shelves of glass jars full of our own produce and the efforts of our new craft. It had been a tremendously satisfying period of my life. In our small corner of the world we had evolved a lifestyle that seemed ideal for the health of both people and the planet.

That Saturday morning as we lay talking in bed, all those seeds that had flowered inside us and in our lives suddenly exploded beyond the boundaries of our own little paradise. A vision, like a balloon lifting off in front of us, occurred to both of us simultaneously. We sat up in bed, our animated thoughts tumbling over one another.

"We could have a restaurant and grow lots of the food in an organic garden right on the property. People could walk out into the garden and actually *see* where their salad and tomatoes and all those fresh herbs came from, and all *kinds* of vegetables!"

"It would be a passive and active solar design building. People could actually see how this sort of energy works in real life."

"Yeah, and we could offer educational programs that would teach people how to retrofit their own homes with solar, and how to raise organic produce."

"*And* the restaurant business could *support* the educational part of the project."

My husband and I talked nonstop the entire day and into the evening. Every single planet-saving concept I'd studied for several years would be merged and developed into one coherent form. All the practices I was convinced could bring people into harmony and in balance with the earth and with each other suddenly came together as if they were ingredients in a big stew pot that had been simmering in the back of my mind for several years. I was bubbling over with excitement. I'd recently read those insightful words about wild inspirations, and I knew that this was a gift from God that we could not let pass by.

I wasn't a very good gardener, and it wasn't that I had ever dreamed of being a restaurant owner. (Who in their right mind would dream of that!) We didn't even know about Alice Waters and her renowned Berkeley restaurant, Chez Panisse, which had been founded in 1971. That forerunner of the movement to serve fresh, organic foods in American restaurants was only twenty miles away. As our own idea evolved and developed over the next five years, we frequently went to dine there for inspiration and counsel. Our own mission statement would be to "enlighten and delight our community."

Five years from its conception Mudd's Restaurant and Crow Canyon Gardens opened for dinner on

August 12, 1982. I would be the manager of that restaurant—a role that wouldn't last as long as I wanted or expected. In the end, the project would be the undoing of the paradise I'd created with my husband and launch me on this mysterious journey I was on.

Mudd's Restaurant and Gardens

I arrived at Gerry's home by mid-afternoon, I lugged Sunny up onto the porch and collapsed into a chair, relieved to have had the peaceful day on the road I'd prayed for. It would be a little while before Gerry got home from work. Fruit trees were in bloom in the orchards across the road. I savored the smells of the wild rambling roses hugging the porch railing, and the pungent smoke from the neighbor's burning yard debris. The whine of insects filling the air on this warm Chico day lulled me into a reverie.

Images of bicycling across Kansas with Carol rose in my mind. Kansas had been absolutely beautiful, peaceful, and welcoming. As we were pedaling through endless acres of lush, very green wheat fields, I'd felt suddenly caught up in the story of the *Wizard of Oz*. In the distance a shiny, silver grain elevator rose majestically in the misty early morning sky, like the castle in the Emerald City. I felt like Dorothy on the Yellow

Brick Road on her way to see the Wizard, the one who she and her companions believed could grant their fondest wish. At the time I didn't know what *I* would ask for, and years later I would learn that one of the interpretations of Frank L. Baum's renowned story is that it is an allegory of the spiritual journey to wholeness, to an inner home. Little did I know then that I was on that very journey. But basking in the afternoon warmth on Gerry's porch, I now knew that on that magical Kansas road, I had set foot—and wheels—on the road to God.

Before I left on this trip, I'd pasted a couple of my favorite quotes on the back cover of the journal I was taking with me. One of them was from Charles de Gaulle: "We may go to the moon but that's not very far. The greatest distance we have yet to cover still lies within us." I had hundreds of miles ahead of me, but I could not have known how far the inner miles would take me. I could not have known that the farther I traveled in outer miles, the more intense the inner process of self-discovery would be, and the more intense my longing for God would become. Distance traveled would increase and intensify in both directions.

3
PREPARATIONS

When Gerry arrived home, I eagerly showed him how well I'd prepared for this trip. I wanted to acknowledge his influence as my first long distance cycling "guru." Before I'd left on my cross country trip with Carol, he had given me an all-nighter course in bicycling mechanics. So I was especially proud to show him Sunny's "trued" wheels, all the spokes completely straight from the hubs to the rims. He admired Sunny's new paint job and sparkly clean components. He wanted to see all my gear and how I'd put it together. The bright blue panniers, filled with tools, clothes and toiletries packed in plastic bags, had an extra quart water bottle strapped on top with a bungee cord. The front handlebar bag held my purse, maps, and Puppy, Jr. With just the essentials for me and the tools for Sunny, my thirty pound load, Gerry agreed, was about average for bicycle touring. He thought I'd done a great job of putting everything together.

I felt too shy to tell him about all my inner preparations and my spiritual motivation for this journey. I didn't know anything about his beliefs, and I didn't want to get either of us into an awkward conversation. But I did at least show him the cover of the journal I'd created to take with me on the trip.

The Teton Traveler's Guide **and Puppy Jr.**

Pasted on the pale burgundy background was a photograph of the Grand Teton Range. Below that was my title for this journal—*The Teton Traveler's Guide*. On the back cover was a photo of Mt. Everest with the Charles de Gaulle quote and another saying: "Life is hard by the yard; but by the inch, life's a cinch!" I knew he'd appreciate the two pages inside that I'd entitled "Coming Home Alive," so I also showed him these strategies for defending myself against an attacker, like how to break a neck hold, and a list of a man's most vulnerable body parts. I didn't bother telling him about the opportunity I'd nearly had my first day out to try these strategies.

The Teton Traveler's Guide was a six-by-nine spiral-bound notebook, about an inch thick, and filled with lined pages, pockets for keeping mementos, and blank pages for drawing. I'd meant it to be both a diary and a source of inspiration. I'd copied into it some of my favorite quotes and pasted in a number of inspiring photographs. Many of the Psalms and Proverbs I'd included were about trusting God to give me strength and protection in times of trouble. I copied out the last verse of Robert Frost's poem, "The Road Not Taken," because I knew I was on an untraveled path and hoped it would "make all the difference." And from Magellan, the daring, seafaring explorer, "I determined to experience...and to go."

I knew I wanted to focus on what was positive, to keep limiting thoughts or experiences at bay. So from the Indian guru, Swami Vivekananda, I included: "The best guide in life is strength...discard everything that weakens you, have nothing to do with it." But I also needed to remind myself to have a good time, that even though my life had been very hard since I left my home and marriage, there was still the prospect of uplifting energy and fun out there. So I included a quote from one of my favorite authors, Annie Dillard: "Be a victim of the swelling of heart. You'll climb trees. You won't be able to sleep, or need to, for the joy of it." And because I knew that now was the time, if ever there was one, to muster my greatest inner resources, I included a quote that would be one of the underlying themes of my journey. It came from one of the first books my therapist Linne had recommended to me, *The Nature of Personal Reality*, by Jane Roberts: "You must begin to trust yourself sometime. I suggest you do it now."

Could I handle the challenges that I knew were ahead? On my cross-America bike trip with Carol, fifty-nine out of the sixty days it took to cover 3,500 miles, I'd awakened to a chorus of voices inside me chanting, "You can't! You can't! You can't!" But every evening I could chant back at them, "I did it! I did it! I did it!" I *could* make long, hard miles; I *could* fix flat tires and basic mechanical problems; I *could* keep my wits about me in bad traffic and dangerous, gusting winds; I *could* handle scary personal situations. Contrary to what my culture, my socio-economic class and my mother had been telling me, I had discovered on that trip that I could do things I'd never imagined were possible. But the "I Can't Ensemble" still sang a familiar refrain in my mind, and I'd wanted to be ready for them, armed with the inspiring words and images of my "allies."

The Teton Traveler's Guide also included the verses of the song "The Impossible Dream" from the play Man of La Mancha. This was the theme song in the depths of my heart: "To dream the impossible dream... to reach the unreachable star; this is my quest...." And I'd pasted in the images of two spiritual leaders. Paramahansa Yogananda was an Indian master whose book, Autobiography of a Yogi, had become one of the most important ones given to me by Paul, who during the course of our relationship was my spiritual guide in so many ways. Yogananda reveals some universal spiritual principles that made sense to me: lovingkindness, compassion, acceptance, doing no harm. He talks about finding meaning and purpose in one's life, and the importance of being tested. He describes the practices of prayer and meditation to bring the spiritual seeker to the realization of the divine within, which he calls God-realization and Self-realization. These were challenging concepts for me to embrace. The divine *within*? The teachings intrigued me, but I couldn't help but continue to believe that God was a vast being somewhere "out there," not within *me* at least.

The other image in my journal was of Jesus, or Christ, as I preferred to call Him. For some reason, I didn't even like to say or hear the name "Jesus," and I'd never had the kind of personal relationship with Him people talked about. But Yogananda regarded Christ as a great teacher, and I'd come to realize that I didn't really know who He was and what He meant—beyond the story of being called the Son of God, born in a manger, dying on a cross and being resurrected. But who was He to me, or I to Him? Under the small image I'd pasted in my journal were printed the words: "I am the way, the truth and the life." Something about this felt important.

Little did I know at the time what role Christ would play in my life. I was just going along with what felt right in the moment. So when another equally mystifying connection with Christ came up, I just let it unfold. Six days before my departure, I'd been rambling through the Old Town area of Danville, near my home. Wandering into an antique store, I came upon a cluster of silk ribbons gathered into a little bouquet. The thin shiny streamers, each about six inches long, were all of different colors—lavender, gold, lime green, pink, orange, red, yellow. Strangely delighted by this cheerful bouquet, I bought it. At home I laid it out with all the other gear I was assembling to pack.

As I sat on the bed contemplating the growing collection of things that felt essential, I picked up the special orange silk rose that my dear friend Maxine had given me. Maxine—always aglow with a big smile and bright spirit—was a former neighbor and pastor of the local Church of Religious Science. Thinking the little ribbon bouquet seemed to match the rose, I picked it up and idly ran my fingers through the streamers, putting the rose in the center of the ribbons. I was startled to see that I had unintentionally assembled them into what looked to me like a bridal bouquet.

At that moment, somewhere inside me, the words arose: "I am going to the Tetons as Christ's bride." It was the kind of simple, declarative statement you would hear from the TV weatherman saying, "It's going to be sunny tomorrow." I was stunned and puzzled. Where did that come from? This had the same quality of conviction and rightness that I associated with ideas I considered as coming from God, but this was the first time such an idea had been delivered in specific words. This proclamation was so out-of-the-blue that I felt almost like a foreign entity had been implanted in me in secret and was now delivering cryptic messages.

Even as I sat there dumbfounded with a bridal bouquet in my hands, I also accepted that this was just another part of the mysterious journey I was on, not much different than starting a search for God based on a dream I'd had. So I tied the rose and ribbons together into a bridal bouquet just as calmly and matter-of-factly as I had packed a baggie with spare parts, tire irons and tube patches for Sunny.

Maybe the bridal bouquet and the mysterious message about Christ were little tests of my acceptance and willingness to just move forward into the Unknown. They certainly shook up my sense of who I was, of who was setting out on this journey. Obviously I was not someone who had it all figured out and knew what I was doing. Was I somehow a bride of Christ? What in the world did that mean? But they were small compared to a more radical shaking up I'd already gone through, one which I only later knew was an essential part of my preparation for the journey.

Three weeks before my departure date, a reporter from a local paper contacted me. I will call her Brenda Starr, after the name of an old comic strip journalist. Starr had heard about my solo trip and thought it would make a good personal interest story. My previous bike trip with Carol had touched and inspired many people we knew and had met on the road, especially women, and we'd realized that our journey hadn't been for us alone. My trip to the Tetons likewise felt like something to be shared. But I was wary about a newspaper interview. From years of contact with the press—while working at my congressman's office and at the restaurant—I knew that truth and accuracy were not necessarily guiding lights in the newspaper business. And I dreaded personal exposure because it usually meant being judged as "a rich person," as if I was some odd creature at the zoo, or like I was carrying around a sandwich board with a dollar sign painted on it.

After much consideration, I agreed to talk with Starr. While I didn't feel comfortable saying in public that my bike trip was a spiritual journey, I hoped the story might speak for itself and inspire others. I told Brenda Starr how the idea had come to me while on a bike ride in December in the nearby hills, and how my cross-country bike trip, which had been so important to my self-discovery, was a source of strength and inspiration for this one. She wanted to know how many miles I'd be traveling, where I was going, how many days on the road, did I know anyone along the way, why I had chosen the Tetons as my destination, where I would stop for the night, how I felt about traveling alone. It seemed like a pretty innocuous interview. Although I don't remember doing so, I must have given her a copy of *Across America on the Yellow Brick Road,* the book I'd written recounting Carol's and my journey, because she called a week later, after reading the book, and wanted to talk with Carol and with my former employer, the congressman. She wanted photographs taken for the article as well. She was very excited about the whole story, more than at our initial interview. This pleased me but also made me somehow uneasy.

Brenda Starr wanted the photos done at the restaurant. While I was sitting on the patio waiting for the photographer, I overheard a conversation at a table nearby. "Yeah, that Mudd woman is loaded," one of the parties was saying. I was shocked. They were talking about me as though they had just seen my financial statement. Suddenly all the distress I'd struggled with, about being an heir to wealth, flooded over me—the shame, embarrassment, confusion, fear, and guilt. I'd always tried to be private and quiet about my money. It was true that I had exposed myself to a small degree in *Yellow Brick Road,* because my upbringing had been so much a part of my emotional struggles on that first bike trip. And of course it obviously had cost a small fortune to buy the property for the restaurant, build it, and create the garden and educational center. Only to my former husband and myself had I acknowledged that I chose the name of the restaurant to be Mudd's (rather than "Gibi's Truck Stop," my second choice) to pay positive tribute to my grandparents who had made such a project possible.

By the time the photographer finally arrived from the newspaper, I was feeling sick to my stomach, realizing how exposed my life was and how much more it was going to be when the article came out. He took my picture as I feigned a debutante smile and fought back tears.

Two days later Brenda Starr called me. "Have you seen the article? It just came out." Something in her voice sounded a little less than excited. "No, not yet." I said. She hastily went on to tell me she had given the article to her copy editor, who had prepared the piece for printing and had put together the headlines. "I had nothing to do with that," she added. I thanked her for calling and drove down to the market to buy the paper.

The article and a seven-by-ten photograph were on the front page of the second section, with the full article finishing on an interior page. The headline read: "Disabled Heiress Tests Her Limits in Bike Journeys." I seized up. I wanted to disappear. I couldn't move for a few minutes. Then I tossed the unread article face down on the passenger seat and drove home, feeling confused, scared and empty. I put the newspaper in a drawer, and tried to carry on with the many preparations for the trip still before me.

"Disabled Heiress." The headline kept circling around in my mind. How could she call my very slight limp and poor eyesight a disability? I had struggled for years to get out from under the mantle of being an unwell, physically inept person, and had certainly proved to myself, if not to everyone, that I was physically as capable as anyone else. Now to that sandwich board with the huge dollar sign on it, were added the words "Disabled Heiress," and it all flashed in bright neon. Is that what I was?

Four days after the article appeared, I decided I had to read it so it would no longer have power over me. I pulled it out of the drawer and read passively, unemotionally. Brenda had clearly done some digging to find out more about my "prominent wealthy LA family." She noted that my grandfather "had made millions in copper mining." I cringed as I read this, remembering my first visit to one of those copper mines.

My grandfather and his business partners had developed the mines after reading in ancient books that Cyprus was rich in copper. They were adventurers, explorers and entrepreneurs and set off to see if this was true. It was, and they proceeded to build a company around extracting and marketing that resource. My father inherited that venturesome spirit. He was willing to take risks. It was he who took us girls out to the breakers in the Pacific to duck "the big ones." It was he who wanted us to swim out too far from the Hawaiian shore to play with the porpoises. It was he who loved to travel, to explore new places, try new things, and took us with him when he could. I attributed all of my adventurous impulses and willingness to take risks to him. I was grateful for my father's bold spirit, which balanced my mother's fear and life-suppressing energy, but this Mudd pioneering nature hit a sour note for me when I finally saw some of how it was manifest in Cyprus.

I was sixteen years old when I went underground into one of those copper mines. It was with great pride that my father had taken "his girls"—my mother, Tory and me—halfway around the world to see this treasure. We put on white topcoats, white hard hats, and protective glasses, and were led into the bowels of the earth, into the mine that was the core and foundation of my family's business and fortune. As we dutifully toured the operation, Dad was dignified, confident and proud. I was terrified, embarrassed and ashamed.

We descended by elevator into the subterranean levels of the mine. Walking, stumbling, stooping with ducked heads, we made our way through the hot, dripping, dark corridors and tunnels, supposedly admiring the advanced technology of a modern-day mining venture. The miners—mostly Turkish—stared at us. Their dark faces, smeared with grit and grime, dripped with sweat. The bright white of their teeth and their eyes—red from the heat and irritation—sparkled in the dark. They seemed to be glowering at us with anger and hatred, and I passed through those tunnels in fear and pain, my stomach and heart clenched.

At last it was over, and we were escorted out to view the above-ground part of the mine. The open pit was a gigantic hole in the earth. Dug out in concentric circles, it was bigger than a football stadium. Dump trucks, looking like little toys from our vantage point on the rim, made their way upward with loads of earth to be scoured for iron ore. It was an awesome and awful sight.

The tunnels and the open pit, the hatred and the pain, buried themselves deep inside me. I carried them as the shameful and hidden foundation of my fortune. It was years before I realized the magnitude and effect of that experience. Brenda Starr's article had opened up that hole inside me that was greater than any open pit mine.

Although shaken by reading it, I carried on with my normal daily activities. I took my usual bike rides, went to a bike repair clinic, met at Mudd's with my business partner, wrote letters, cooked meals. But that headline kept repeating over and over in my mind like a mantra or a song you can't stop humming. Every pedal turn, it was there—*Disabled Heiress, Disabled Heiress, Disabled Heiress*. I began to notice a slight pain in my tailbone, but I assumed it was just another of the many passing glitches that had come up in the four months since I'd decided to make the solo bike trip.

Soon, however, when I was on my bike saddle, it felt like I was sitting on a little sharp rock. I continued biking, and within a couple of days that little rock at the base of my spine had turned into an arrowhead of jagged glass. Any pressure on my tailbone was intensely painful, but I was determined to keep in shape. So one day when I had a lunch date with Maxine, I rode the twelve miles to our meeting place, mostly standing up on my pedals. After we talked for a while, I confessed that I was worried about having such a terrible time with my tailbone. Then I pulled out the newspaper article. I hadn't shown it to anyone. A few friends who'd seen it had called to offer their support and condolences, but I hadn't wanted to talk with them about it. Yet I needed to tell someone how deeply upset I was, and I knew I could confide in Maxine.

She was shocked by what she read. Then she casually asked me when my tailbone had started hurting. I tried to think. "It's been about a week. Yes, a week. Every day getting a little worse." I stared at her, suddenly understanding the implication of her question. "Do you think it's possible that my painful tailbone is connected to my reading the article?"

Shortly afterwards we hugged and said our goodbyes, and I began my painful journey home. As *Disabled Heiress* began its automatic roll through my mind, I realized I had become exactly what that headline had proclaimed me to be. There was nothing I could do about the heiress part, but I was *not* going to accept "disabled."

The beauty of being on a bike in heavy traffic is that no one can hear you. So as I coasted down a short stretch on Pleasant Hill Road, I started to reflect out loud about the situation. As I rounded the turn onto Olympic Boulevard, headed for the steep climb over to Alamo, I let thoughts and feelings leave my mouth uncensored. I stopped being rational and thoughtful and nice about the whole episode. I started to let fly whatever came up. The volume increased. The language got graphic and crude and unladylike. By the time I reached the bottom of Hillgrade Avenue, rage had taken over.

"No! I am not fucking disabled! Where do you get off writing that kind of shit? Have you ever seen a disabled person bike up Hillgrade Avenue? Have you ever seen a disabled person ride across the fucking country? Where do you get permission to lie about people and come on to me so goodie-goodie and interested in me and so trustworthy? You have no fucking idea why I am going on this trip or any idea about who I am. My inheritance is none of your Goddamned business! And you have no right to put my private affairs in your fucking paper. And then blame it on your copy editor. Bitch!"

This eruption went on for four miles at full volume. Flames and molten lava were spewing out of my mouth in an uncontrollable stream. I sped down the grade into Alamo, oblivious to the pain in my tailbone. The furies had been unleashed from my depths. I couldn't have stopped them if I'd wanted to. I turned south onto tree-lined, suburban Danville Boulevard, still screaming at the top of my lungs.

"You have no idea what I'm about or who I am. You came up with something your copy editor loves. A little local dirt, some gossip, something juicy for your readers that will make them buy your paper. Well, Miss Brenda Fucking Starr, you haven't a clue about who I am. You haven't a clue about my life and what matters to me or what I do or think. Nothing! You know nothing! Not a Goddamned thing! I am neither disabled nor heiress. *I Am*!"

When those last two words left my mouth, I was instantly shut up, as though a great hand had been clamped over my mouth. I was stunned into silence. My breath caught mid-stream in my throat. My heart stopped its rhythmic cadence and everything went very very still. I couldn't believe what I had said. Or what had said me. I knew that this *I Am* came from a very deep place in myself, and even though I only vaguely remembered reading about "*I Am*" and its connection to God, I now knew that I had uttered, or rather screamed, that the divine was *in me*. Not God without, but God *within*. The realization was as startling and life changing as God coming into me in my dream five years earlier. This had to be the Self-realization, the God-realization that Paramahansa Yogananda described as "the knowing—in body, mind and soul—that we are one with the omnipresence of God."

In that moment the title of a book that had both mystified and intrigued me came to mind—*Neither This Nor That I Am.* Suddenly I understood exactly what it meant; I was not a rich person, not a divorced woman, not a woman who had cycled across America, not an author, not the owner of Mudd's, and definitely not a "disabled heiress." At the core of my being, I was neither "this" nor "that." Just the divine essence, *I Am.*

Years later I came across a book by John Carroll, *The Existential Jesus*, in which the author says "...the struggle to *be* takes place in the darkness. *I Am* is buried deep within. It is shrouded in oblivion. Yet it is given. Every man coming into the world has his share of the all-creative presence." The *I Am* buried deep within me had broken through to the surface. It was just a taste, a beginning, but it was a first step in knowing who I truly was.

Equally surprising was that I had come to *I Am* by walking through the door of an emotion that was probably the most forbidden and scary to me. Rage. I had by-passed my self-censorship and manners. The struggle had taken place "in the darkness." I had exploded down to the core of my being. And to my amazement I had found God there—a piece of God in me. In that moment of recognition, it was like the clouds had parted and I suddenly saw the sun. I didn't utter or scream another word for several miles. I was stunned into complete silence.

On my way through town, I pedaled past that same antique store where I'd found the bridal bouquet. Something in the window caught my eye, and I had another of those feelings of being compelled to do something. Maybe acknowledging these impulses was part of my preparation as well. I now trusted and followed them without question. I pulled over and gazed through the window. There was a brass candleholder, about two feet tall. The short broad candle at its base had a slender rod rising above it, holding a lacey brass butterfly. I knew at once it was for me. It was my trophy for finding God within me through the darkness I'd been in due to the newspaper article. It was to acknowledge my triumph in seeing beyond my superficial, limited, and often painful identities to the divine core of my being.

The butterfly was already a powerful symbol for me. Because of the phases of a butterfly's life, it has been likened to spiritual evolution. The caterpillar represents earthly life, the chrysalis or cocoon can be seen as the tomb the caterpillar dies into, and the butterfly is resurrection into new life, into a new understanding of our divine and human nature. During our intense and transformative romantic relationship, Paul and I had often given each other gifts of butterflies—a tiny gold pendant which I still wore around my neck, a butterfly-shaped tile, chimes with dangling butterflies. These symbols reminded us that we were in a time of great change in our lives.

I went immediately into the store and bought the candlestick, strapped it onto Sunny's rear rack, and rode home victorious, having turned the poison of the newspaper article into gold.

That night I lit the candle and burned the newspaper article in the fireplace. Of course it would be nice if that had been the end of the disabling tailbone and the banishing of the negative inner voices. But unfortunately, like the classic journey of the seeker, the understanding that had burst from my depths in that moment of awakening dissipated like mist. I didn't wake up the next morning saying to myself, "Okay, I've found God. End of journey." Instead my whole being proceeded to become a battleground for the struggle between dark forces and light, between panic and faith. Even though that *I Am* experience had been a momentary knowing of God within me, I went right back to feeling I was separate from the God I longed for and that I had to search for Him, in particular through my impending bike trip. I kept the candle burning day and night. When my tailbone hurt, I would think, "I won't be able to go on my trip, and I won't find God." That would send me to the refrigerator to binge helplessly. Then I would hear in my mind the words from the Bible that I remembered from high school: "By your faith you have been healed," or "O ye of little faith," and I would feel encouraged to proceed with my preparations for the journey. But then again the refrain from inner dark forces would begin chanting, *I can't I can't. Disabled Heiress.*

Of course my mother called on the phone to tell me how risky my trip was and that she didn't want me to go. The battle between the forces that threatened to stop me and the forces that wanted me to go on raged even more fiercely. But two days after *I Am*, two days after my butterfly candle had first been lit, my tailbone definitely began feeling better, and I'd managed to slow down the force of the food addiction. I was winning, gratefully feeling my personal victory over old identities I was hanging onto. I had seen that at my core I was simply a divine being. That glimpse fueled in me the longing to find and know God not as a momentary experience but as a daily living presence. With my tailbone healing, my determination returned. I was going to do that—somehow—by bicycling to the Tetons.

I wanted to *live* God, to *feel* God, whatever that meant. Would marrying Christ be the way to that? I knew nuns considered their vocation to be a marriage to Christ, but I didn't feel called to join a convent. I did, however, finish my preparations by getting my hair cut very short. The feeling I had was that I was making myself beautiful for God. I was also inspired by *Yentl*, one of my favorite movies, in which the main character disguises herself as a boy so she can escape from a limited, homebound woman's role and pursue a religious education open only to men. Like me, Yentl was pursuing God. Although I learned my first day on the road that the disguise didn't fool anyone, cutting my hair before leaving had made me feel as if I was dedicating myself to a sacred journey.

I received a surprise package from my mother four days before my scheduled departure. Immediately wary, I sat down to open the small box. I happened to be reading *People of the Lie* at the time, a book by M. Scott Peck, author of one of my favorite books, *The Road Less Traveled.* In his case studies and analyses he accurately described my experience of my own mother. It seemed to me that her affection was contingent on my behaving in a certain way. The many times when she'd tell me how special I was and how she loved me, an odd, uneasy feeling would grip my chest. She was saying things I wanted to hear, she *seemed* to be warm and loving, but somehow her words were coming across as cold and critical. I wanted to believe her and I desperately wanted her to love me just the way I was. This left me feeling deeply confused and guilty, because I was *supposed* to love my mother; I *wanted* to love her. But not only did I not feel genuine love, but I also felt that she was trying to instill in me a sense of fear and limitation, to kill my spirit.

When I lifted the lid on her gift, my heart began to flutter like a trapped bird. Inside was an I.D. "dog tag" necklace, and a little white hankie with tiny red hearts all over it.

I jumped up off the couch as if I'd been bitten by a rattlesnake. I snatched up the dog tags and took them all the way out to the trashcan by the road. I stuffed the hankie into my collection of things already in the car to take to the Goodwill. No way was I going to wear dog tags as though I were waiting for the mortician, and no way was I going to carry the little red hearts which were supposed to be an expression of love but felt instead like poison. As I walked back to the house empty-handed, it felt like another triumphant moment of following my inner impulses and freeing myself from past limitations in order to move on.

That evening at Gerry's house renewed my confidence as we exchanged stories and he gave me solo touring advice. We decided it would be fun to ride together for a day and a half; he was delighted at the opportunity to do a short bike tour. He loaded up his own bike with a few supplies, and the next morning we set out. On our way out of town he took me to see the glass factory where he worked. In the showroom of exquisitely crafted glass vases, paperweights, dishware, lamps and jewelry, I found a silver ring set with a glass ornament the size of a shirt button. In the center of a circle of tiny flowers was a bird in flight. To my eye it was an eagle, and I thought instantly of a quote I'd put in my *Guide*, "They who wait for the Lord shall renew their strength; they shall mount up with wings like eagles; they shall run and not be weary; they shall walk and not faint." Maybe partly hoping they would also *bicycle* and not grow weary, I bought the ring and immediately put it on. At the time it was like a St. Christopher good luck charm for travelers. Later on in the trip, as I thought more about going "as Christ's bride," I began to think it was more like an engagement ring. My preparations were complete. I was ready and on my way.

4
FALLING IN LOVE

It was hard to say goodbye to Gerry. I enjoyed his company and it was comforting to travel with a companion. Being with him put off the inevitable—embarking on the solo trip I'd set out to do. Standing at the edge of a KOA Campground near Mt. Lassen in northern California, I watched Gerry's back recede as he set out on the road back to his home in Chico. I dug through my rear pannier to find the pack of American Spirits I'd purchased on a whim before leaving, and I lit up the first cigarette I'd had in years. "Now the real journey begins," I thought, with both trepidation and excitement—and a touch of resignation. As I crawled into my tent that night, only one thing was on my mind: *Can I handle being alone, with only Sunny and Puppy Jr. for company?*

In the morning I woke with the same question: *Can I make it all the way to the Tetons—alone?* But by the time I was headed north on California State Route 289 I was facing a different and more immediate challenge. *Never mind about the Tetons. Just get up this grade. Get out of this cold, awful crosswind.* I was headed toward the town of Nubieber, nineteen miles away and what I hoped would be breakfast in a warm café. Thin gray clouds covered the entire sky, letting in a little light but no warmth. A cold wind was penetrating the layers of clothes I'd put on. I had prepared for spring, not this blast of what felt like winter.

I pedaled along the quiet, two lane road through open high desert country, slowly gaining 1,000 feet in elevation. Distant snow-tipped mountains undulated along the horizon to my right. Sometimes the land was barren except for scattered tall pines, sometimes it was covered with thickets of low shrubs in every shade of spring green. The sweet aroma of sage filled the air. As I neared Nubieber, the open meadows became increasingly crisscrossed with ranch fences and dotted with farm buildings. Occasionally, a brilliant pink-blossomed fruit tree would dazzle the overcast day.

The warm café of my dreams appeared on the deserted main street of Nubieber. It had taken me two hours to cover the nineteen miles. *Jeez, that's not even ten miles per hour. I ought to make better time than that!* Feeling grim, I sat down in a booth next to a window. Maybe I was hoping I'd see the sun break through the clouds.

"Wow, it is sure cold out there," I said to the waitress as she took my order.

"Honey," she answered, "we *never* have such cold weather at this time of year."

"Just my luck to hit a cold snap," I muttered to myself as I huddled over a plate of hash browns and a chili-cheese omelet, hoping the wispy steam would warm my body. It was depressing to look out the window. Even more discouraging than the low-hanging gray clouds was that the flag in the parking lot was being whipped horizontal by the wind. It was pointing due south; I was headed due north. The outside thermometer on the café wall read thirty-five degrees, which meant about twenty degrees with the wind chill. When Carol and I had left on our trip on the first of May, we'd had great cycling weather for two months, so I'd figured spring would be an ideal time for this trip. Not this year. People all along my route would comment about the unusually harsh weather.

Drinking endless cups of hot tea, as if that might fortify me against the cold, I gazed out into the empty grayness. It looked to me like a picture of my current life. Everything that had meant something to me was gone—my husband, my home and animals, the restaurant. Even though I'd see Paul again, something about "us" was not working out either, though I deeply hoped for it to.

I was still married when I met Paul three years ago, before this bicycle adventure had even occurred to me. Paul was one of the host of vendors, builders, contractors and consultants who were preparing Mudd's for its Grand Opening. I was mightily attracted to him, but I'd never had an affair during the thirteen years of my marriage. It had crossed my mind only once, and I'd resisted because I didn't want to break my commitment to my marriage. My husband and I were best friends and effortlessly compatible in many areas of our lives. We had been shaped and woven together over the years, especially during the turbulent, exciting, hopeful and transformative years of the Hippies and Flower Children, the Beatles, the Vietnam War, the Kennedy/King assassinations. We had cultivated together a steady relationship based on shared adventures, projects, friends, travel, and work experiences. We had managed to get through some difficult personal struggles intact. But I had not fallen in love with my husband; I had grown in love with him. Like other committed partners, we had issues to work out, but it had never occurred to me to seek a new love relationship.

Nothing could have prepared me—least of all the foot-high stack of love comic books I'd devoured as a teenager—for the life-shattering experience of falling in love with Paul. Whenever I was working at the restaurant and he was around, I could not take my eyes off him. While I was attracted to him physically, and appreciated his integrity and careful work, what really struck me was his whole way of being—the way he moved with such grace and ease, the way his eyes seemed to glow with light, the way he looked at me with such a radiant gaze.

Shortly after the opening of the restaurant, a celebration party had been held to toast the new venture. Paul and I found ourselves dancing closer than might be the norm for business associates. I tried but I couldn't contain how I felt. As we ended a slow dance, I said to him, "You're one of the finest people I've ever met." It seemed like a pretty innocuous thing to say to someone I admired greatly, but it was clear to both of us that I had exposed something deep in my heart, to myself and to him. Once this feeling was revealed, it was as though I'd pulled a single orange out of the bottom tier of a tall stack at a fruit stand. Everything came tumbling down, rolling every which way. There was no way I could pick up the pieces and put them back again.

I was at a total and terrible loss as to what to do. I hadn't communicated again with Paul, so I felt completely alone and helpless to understand and deal with my inner turmoil. I felt like I'd been dropped from an airplane without a parachute into a foreign country without any provisions or knowledge of the language, culture, terrain, or location. I didn't know what was happening to me except that overwhelming emotions were exploding within me, and I had to fight like a banshee to keep them under some control.

Not knowing what else to do, I turned to God. One night when I was working as maitre d' during the dinner service at the restaurant, I scrawled a hasty note on a scrap of paper: *Dear God, I am in trouble. I have fallen in love. What do I do? Can you help me? What must I do to help myself?* I hadn't spoken to, or even thought much about God for the past two and a half years, not since that "Hal Holbrook" dream I'd had in which I felt so overwhelmed and deeply connected to God. The task of bringing Crow Canyon Gardens and Mudd's Restaurant into being had been all consuming. Turning to God as I wrote that note reminded me of the deep desire the dream had awakened in me—to find God in my waking life. Could it be that what I experienced in Paul—something so profoundly sacred—and the depth of what I was feeling with him was part of fulfilling that desire?

Even though my good marriage and the new business screamed for me to disengage, I fell forward and plunged ahead in spite of every attempt I made to stop my fall. I was caught in the grip of a humungous, indefinable, invisible force. I had never lived in such intense pain, or in such wonder and joy. I desperately needed to find out about the light that I saw radiating from Paul's eyes, from his being. He was hardly a man to me. He was *a* god, if not *the* God. The way I saw it, Paul was Light; Light was God; Paul was God.

A few days after writing that first note, I desperately wrote to God again: *Dear God, I believe you have revealed yourself to me through this man. I don't know why this is, or whether I can be so certain of that belief. But I see such an abundance of love in him that I don't see any other explanation. Light radiates from his eyes, from his whole being. I believe I would die for him. Am I crazy? My whole body aches. Yet if he is you, then I should be very happy and very blessed that he is here, and am grateful for your presence in him.*

I had never seen such light, or goodness or love, and I wanted to be close to that essence. I wanted to be close to him and what he had. I wanted it like a fix for an addict. I needed more of it. I was in love with Love. I was swept up in the flow of Love: pure, holy, beautiful, continuous, expanding, overpowering, uncontrollable, all-encompassing, passing beyond any world I knew into a realm where I felt guided and loved by God, and totally surrendered to Him. Never before had I felt such huge and expansive love to exist in me, or in the world. The thought of doing without it was unbearable.

But it was also unbearable to think of what I was doing to my marriage, of the hurt this was causing my husband, even though he didn't yet know of the situation. Was it right to hurt and destroy so much to get what I wanted? I abhorred the thought and made many futile attempts to stop the course I was on in order to maintain my marriage. With all my will power I tried to turn my heart away from Paul and focus on my marriage. But the agony of my longing, my aching for this love, this man, was overwhelming. I was utterly taken by the ecstasy of discovering something I recognized as truly of God in my waking life, and of feeling the depths and heights of love I never knew existed. I couldn't stop myself. I felt like I was a nuclear reactor headed for a meltdown.

After a month the inner turmoil I felt by pretending at home that there was nothing amiss finally drove me to tell my husband what was happening to me. It was a Saturday morning, not unlike that relaxed morning when we had "received" the idea of Mudd's Restaurant and Crow Canyon Gardens. I said I'd fallen in love and didn't know what to do. I felt utterly undone and confused. I told him that this wasn't the thrill of an affair but that my relationship with Paul "had something to do with God." He believed me, but this was only a weak painkiller for the deep hurt he felt. "How can I compete with God?" he asked.

He couldn't. Nor could I. We tried to stay together while I "pursued God" in this other relationship, but after a tense and tearful month and a half, we realized this was an emotional impossibility. I moved out of my house and into a condominium next to the interstate freeway. I left it all, everything I loved in my life: my husband, my dear animal family, my handmade home, the beautiful ridgelands where I rode my horses and ran with the dogs. We had worked so hard to create not just a beautiful place to live but also a solid place in our relationship. My agonizing move—it seemed the only option—was devastating to all this. I left in search of I knew not exactly what; I just knew it was something I was missing and that I had to have.

Years later I would read the work of Jungian psychologist Robert Johnson and understand something of what had been happening to me. In his book *WE*, Johnson writes: "The suffering of romance is ultimately no different than the suffering of mysticism and religion: It is the pain shared by all mortals who would give birth to the divine world within their own lives, within this physical life and its finite limits." I had set out on an unknown path to "give birth to the divine world" within my own life and found myself traveling a centuries-old path. I was also struck by a quote Johnson includes from Denis de Rougemont, author of *Love in the Western World*: "Why is it that we delight most of all in some tale of impossible love? Because we long for the *branding*; because we long to grow *aware* of what is on fire inside us." Yes, something in me was deeply longing for the unbearable fire I was in, longing to be branded by the searing flames of God's power and love.

Something else Robert Johnson said helped me understand more of what was going on in me at that time. He points out that our Western culture is so closed to the life of the Spirit that the only gap in our armor through which spiritual life can emerge is through the door of romantic love. In the act of falling in love and projecting our own divinity onto the beloved, we reawaken our spiritual life. The beloved radiates Light and Love. It is the beloved who is worshiped and adored as a god, who embodies the divine qualities that inspire reverence and desire to serve. I felt like I was reading about myself.

In reading Robert Johnson's retelling of the myth of Tristan and Iseult in *WE*, I came to understand how love and intense attraction can be completely connected with the divine—and also perhaps why my love for Paul had so much trouble translating into a daily partnership. In that twelfth century story of romance and tragedy, the Knight Tristan and the Lady Iseult are engaged in what was known as "courtly love," a practice in which the lovers' attraction for each other was directed toward their spiritual awakening. In this practice, sexual union was completely prohibited, so that the fire of their love could fuel their spiritual transformation. But the Knight and Lady mistakenly drink a love potion and fall hopelessly, passionately in love. They forsake loyalty and devotion to wife, husband and king in order to be together, even unto death.

If my "Tristan" and I had been knights and ladies of the twelfth century, guided by the practice of courtly love, I might have said to him, "Beloved Paul, you have shown me that God is within me, as I am in Him. I did not recognize this until we met and I saw the divinity in you." He would have said to me, "Dearest Ginia, your being is proof of pure light and love made manifest. I see the Holy Spirit within you." We would have acknowledged with deep gratitude, reverence and humility that God was at the heart of our union, and that we had found God in each other and in ourselves. We would have awakened to our own divine essence. If we had been those courtly lovers of old, we might then have said, "With this new awareness, let us return to our former lives, expressing God's love in all that we do." Then Paul and I would have gone our separate ways. Because we would not have been physically intimate with each other, I would have been able to return to my husband, bringing my new awareness of God into my marriage.

But we were not those courtly lovers. We drank the love potion, and my deep desire to find God that had been reawakened by Paul became completely interwoven with human desire for this beloved. That call to know God in my daily life remained as deeply genuine as my love for Paul, and romantic and divine love blended and merged until there was no difference between them in my mind and heart. I know now that the love Paul and I shared had indeed "something to do with God." As psychologist and philosopher Dr. Jean Houston describes it, "The breadth and depth of human loving both gives us the sense of what human-divine loving is about and instills in us the preparation for spiritual union."

What had been in the past just words and nice spiritual ideas—reverence, adoration, worship, devotion, surrender—became throbbing, vital feelings in my whole being. My entire way of seeing and being in the world was turned upside down. What I wrote, what I spoke, what I read, what I listened to were now all new. What left my mouth and pen had a new softness and eloquence, and there were new words in my internal dictionary. Letters I wrote to Paul were lyrical, poetic, graceful. I read them over and over, not believing I had written them.

Paul and I talked about spiritual life, about God, and about knowing and doing God's will. He introduced me to many books: *The Way of the Pilgrim; Mister God, This is Anna;* and the one that had opened me to Christ, *Autobiography of a Yogi.* I plunged into two huge tomes called *The Philokalia,* texts written between the fourth and fifteenth century by spiritual masters of the orthodox Christian tradition, simply because Paul had read them. I listened to the music he did, and instead of The Doors and The Beatles I now steeped myself in the haunting electric guitar of Pat Matheny, and found myself discovering the ethereal and "spiritual" music of musicians such as Kitaro.

The more time I spent with Paul the more aware I became of my expanding capacity for love. The love in me that had once filled a thimble could now fill a swimming pool. This was revealed to me in unexpected circumstances. On one occasion we were staying at a little beach bungalow for a weekend when Paul was suddenly struck with severe abdominal pain. We assumed it was the fish we had eaten the night before, that it would pass and wasn't an emergency, but we were both scared by the intensity of his pain. Clutching his stomach and moaning, Paul rolled onto the double bed in the tiny bedroom. I watched, helpless.

Not knowing what else to do for him, I sat on the floor at the foot of the bed, as though keeping vigil. My heart broke open with love for him and compassion for the pain he was feeling. I awakened to feelings I did not expect or fully understand, but I savored the new dimension of love for another being that filled my heart. I didn't know I had it in me to love so much. It felt as though a rose bud had opened within me, and I was filled with the fragrance of devotion, caring, and compassion. I sat in that open space of love for the entire length of the day it took Paul to recover.

On another occasion I suddenly felt compelled to tell him that I would be honored to have his child. Before our time together I'd never felt I had enough love within myself to be a good parent. Now I could actually imagine myself being a loving, nurturing mother. It was as though I had given birth to a new reality within me. I didn't see it at the time, but I had truly found something of God in my waking life, and it was not in Paul; it was *within me.*

Our time together, which for several months after I left my husband and my home was limited to weekends, often felt like being on an acid trip in heaven. We lived in a magical and mysterious world where our bodies were messengers and vehicles of the Spirit, spilling over with passion, wonder and joy. When our bodies and hearts joined, the exquisite high was not only in the physical pleasure but even more in how our boundaries disappeared, our spirits merged, and we became one. Years later I would read the exact description of my experience written by a thirteenth century woman mystic, Hadewyck of Antwerp. She says, "God, my dear child, will teach you who He is by making you know the ineffable bliss of lovers who enter each other and are so completely absorbed in each other that they are no longer able to distinguish their individual selves but live the total fruitfulness of their love mouth to mouth, heart upon heart, body within body and soul within soul, while a gentle divine nature suffuses them entirely."

In contrast to those weekends of bliss, my daily life was taking a different turn. About a month after moving into my own place by the freeway, I crashed into the rocks of my new reality. I missed my husband, our easy communication, our comfortable routines, our emotional and intellectual camaraderie. I couldn't bear to go back to the house we'd built and shared to visit the animals—we all missed each other so much. I felt suddenly "homeless" and homesick. At some point, with unspeakable sadness, I realized I would not be going back. My life had been inexorably altered. I would never be the same again. It had all changed so fast. In the thup of a heartbeat I'd been flung out of my old world into a new universe. A world that had guarantees and forevers and certainty and stability had suddenly disappeared. Only the moment existed, one moment following another, day after day. Not until I was on my own and in great emotional pain did I find what it meant to live day-to-day, moment-by-moment. My life was now chaos. I felt I was floundering in floodwaters instead of resting safely on dry land. Would I ever find solid ground again? Why was something so good—my love for Paul—be so bad? My faith in the world and myself was shattered.

I succumbed to huge forces of sadness and rage. At the same time that I grieved, I flailed myself for having "an affair," for hurting and leaving my husband, for being so crazy and out of control. I berated myself for being selfish and spoiled and immature. I had gone after what I wanted like a hungry wolf after a rabbit. I felt myself to be the worst person in the world.

Yet every weekend I re-entered that divine mystery of love with Paul. The contrast between the two states inside me was totally disorienting. Out of desperation I retreated for two brief days to the peaceful town of Mendocino on the northern California coast to sort things out. I hoped that with some time away I'd figure everything out, get my life all fixed up and tidy. But instead of regenerating on the beach, or looking out over the rugged cliffs at the vast Pacific, I sat miserably in my lovely cottage immersed in two books. Og Mandino's *The Greatest Miracle in the World* was written for people whose lives are in the gutter. Since I still clung to a perfect image of myself as in-control and master of my universe, above the emotional upsets and upheavals suffered by "ordinary people," it was totally humiliating to resort to pop psychology to get out of the miserable state I was in. I fumed. *I shouldn't need this! I am too intelligent for this!* But I kept reading, amazed at how much sense it made to me.

The other book was Kahlil Gibran's *The Prophet.* Dissolved in tears, I read the Prophet's words on Love, and every line was piercing truth for me. They spoke of my passion for Paul, for Love, for God. Just as the Prophet says, Love beckoned and I followed. Love spoke and I believed. And I was crowned and crucified by Love. Like corn, I was threshed, sifted, ground and kneaded, and given to Love's sacred fire to become sacred bread for God's sacred feast.

Amazingly, as I read I realized that in the suffering of love was exquisite joy! For all the wounding and pain and anguish, I found that I *longed* to be God's sacred bread! It gave me joy to be threshed and kneaded by the hand of God, which is what I was sure was happening to me. I believed that through Paul, God was touching me in my waking life. God had beckoned, and I'd surrendered and followed. My deepest longing was being fulfilled. The tears I wept that weekend, over and over, rose from that great pain and great joy. I left Mendocino more confused and humbled than ever.

All this had happened two years before I set out on the solo bike trip that had taken me to this gloomy day in Nubieber. I ordered more tea and cupped my hands tightly around the pot as though the physical heat could help me hold onto the beautiful times with Paul. I couldn't bring myself to get on the road yet, and the warmth of the café lulled me into further reverie as I dawdled over the last of my breakfast.

5

ALONE

After seven months of living by myself, the obvious next step was for Paul to come live with me. My husband and I had informed the restaurant management staff that we'd separated, but I had told only a few close friends about Paul. When he moved in, we rejoiced and celebrated our new beginning, and in the privacy of our life together, we brought one another deep joy and deep love. I was supremely happy, and easily envisioned being together for the rest of our lives.

But amidst the joy I slowly began realizing we had very different styles of making our way in the world, especially in our ways of communicating and working out our differences. Because his deep caring, kindness and support of me was so nurturing, I struggled to overlook what wasn't working for me in our relationship. But during the course of my marriage, I had gotten used to talking my way through difficulties. Sometimes that included expressing strong emotions. That had worked for my husband and me, and over time communication had become an effortless game of evenly matched tennis. Sometimes the games were intense and hard-fought, but we'd come out of them as closer friends, and with a sense of connection, to ourselves and each other.

With Paul it was different. When a difficult issue came up that I felt I needed to talk through, he listened but didn't respond in the way I was used to, or wanted. I'd send the ball into his court, expecting it to be returned as part of the game. So often it wasn't. I'd feel stranded emotionally, which only made me feel more upset. If I pressed him for a response, he would say something like, "Love, I'm not sure what you want me to say." Talking just wasn't the way Paul made his way through problems between us. He embodied and expressed love, but I was finding that wasn't enough for me in our relationship.

The same thing would happen when he seemed to be struggling with something inside himself. I kept wishing he would share whatever was troubling him. I knew that for me talking with a friend could at least bring more understanding to a problem, if not a solution. I wanted to be that friend for him. When he seemed under a cloud and not opening up to me about it, I felt distant and isolated from him. If only we talked we could be connected again. But that just wasn't his way. In the face of his silence, I would go down as well. Just as I so totally felt his love and light, I also sank into his darkness. My own energy would drain into gloom, and I couldn't find my way out until he emerged. This scared me, because even if I was feeling good in my own life, I didn't know how to stay up when he was down.

The longer we were together the more my emotional enmeshment and our different communication styles frustrated me. It felt like a black blob the size of a boulder had emerged in the center of our divine bubble. During our first summer together, I stumbled over this dark mass more and more frequently. While I never ceased to see Paul's radiant, pure goodness and light—his divinity—it became increasingly clear that day-to-day living was not working well.

We even went for a couple of counseling sessions to see if we could improve our communication skills. Above all else, I wanted us to work out a life together. I could not understand why God, who had seemingly ordained our union, was allowing this obstacle to come between us. Why couldn't God dissolve this blob!? I thought Love could move mountains! After months of frustration at constantly running into the same obstacle between us, I knew I had to accept that we were not compatible as day-to-day partners. It was heartbreaking for me to admit that free-flowing communication was such a basic need for me in close relationship that, without it, I would actually choose to end my connection with this man I adored.

One evening I knew I had to finally face this grim reality with him. It could wait no longer. I decided to bring it up as we sat together at dinner. I could hardly eat. This was the moment I had been dreading. "Paul, " I began, "I don't know how I can say this. I love you beyond anything I can imagine. But I just don't see how we can work out a life together when I can't talk to you openly. So many times when I share something with you and need a response, you can't talk to me. I can't do it like this any longer."

He didn't say a word, just looked at me in utter disbelief. We both sat frozen, looking at each other; the silence seemed to last forever. I don't remember what either of us said after that, except that we agreed separation was what had to happen because we both knew how dissatisfied I was, and that I didn't see another option. I felt like we would both be compromising our integrity, our basic temperaments and natures, to try to accommodate each other's style.

Exactly a year to the day after I had moved out of my former home and life—December 6—Paul left our home and the Bay Area. I might just as well have wrapped myself in barbed wire for the pain of watching my beloved drive off in his little red station wagon loaded with all his possessions. I was sure I'd never see him again. Despite the pain, I felt there was no other way. Gibran's Prophet's words on love—"as it is for your growth, so it is for your pruning"—were of no consolation whatsoever. I was drowning in an ocean of grief. Wave after wave of immense sadness poured through me. What had I done? Was wanting an uplifting, dynamic, and open communication with my beloved worth this drowning sorrow?

My grief was compounded by unparalleled, unimaginable loneliness. For the first time in my life I was truly alone—an empty bed, no intimate relationship, and a hollow, silent house that echoed mercilessly with each footstep taken. Every dish set down on the kitchen tile counter sounded as loud as cymbals crashing together. I had given up my home and marriage with high hopes for a deep, lasting relationship with Paul, and now it was over.

I brought two cats home for company, Alfalfa and Buckwheat. Within days they both disappeared. Napoleon, a two year old Bassett Hound, came home with me on trial, but he didn't like being hugged. What good was that for healing a broken heart? I tearfully sent him back to his foster mom.

In the empty darkness of my heart, I wondered if there was any point in giving myself to *anything* if it could be taken away. Was there any thing of the world which would bring lasting happiness or security? The negative answer was obvious to me. Paul's departure left me feeling that everything on earth was meaningless, pointless and of no value. The worst part of the darkness was that I had initiated my own fall.

No, the worst part was that Paul had been my link to God, and because the human relationship with him hadn't worked out, it felt like I'd given up the divine relationship he opened me to. Paul revealed God to me. When he was in my life, I could *feel* God. I could *see* God. By myself I didn't have that. Paul was the link in a chain that connected me to God. Without his presence the chain was broken. Without God I had nothing and was nobody.

I hated feeling so needy and vulnerable. I had, after all, bicycled across the whole fucking United States. I could do anything, right? I didn't want to ask for anybody's help, and least of all God's help. I felt like a rag doll, or a dog bone, in God's mouth, chewed on, tossed around, and violently shaken back and forth. I hated God for making me so weak and needy. Yet on one hand as I was raging at God for making me a rag doll, on the other, I *wanted* to be the rag doll in God's mouth.

My whole being was burning with an intense yearning for the God I thought I was losing, a roaring fire of longing and craving that made my food addiction look like a flickering match. But while I had eventually learned to manage my food craving, I could not manage my longing for God. *I had to find God.* After all, it was God in Paul, God *as* Paul, that had led me to give up everything to be with him.

But who or what was the God I was searching for? I was obviously not looking for the Hal Holbrook of my dream, or the Rip van Winkle-Uncle Sam of my childhood. Those images had been important and revealing representations but not what I was looking for. Was this also true of Paul? In retrospect I can almost hear God saying to me, "What you see and feel in this man is a clue. Here I am, but it's not what you think. This is only part of the picture. There is more. You have to keep looking." In my dream years before, God had planted a seed of Himself in me, as though He were calling me to Himself. He'd given me a taste of His sweetness, His passion, His trustworthiness, His love for me, and my love for Him. I'd been looking to live in that love. But how? Confused and in pain I sank deeper into a heart-sickening interior darkness.

It took a few days for my need for help to overcome my pride and anger. Embarrassed and humiliated, I began to pray out loud to God. Distraught, desperate and angry, I prayed for consolation, prayed to be eased from the agony of loss, prayed that He would help me get my life back together. Even though the pain didn't cease, it was a relief to acknowledge my helplessness. I prayed out loud and played recordings of devotional music to soothe my heart. I would have died of humiliation if anybody had heard me, but I needn't have worried—I was most definitely alone.

Within a few days after Paul left, we were talking on the phone again and making plans about how to spend Christmas together. I clearly wasn't yet ready or able to find God on my own, and I definitely wasn't ready to give up Paul and the link to God he represented. He was longing to be with me as well. I felt confused and uncertain—but relieved to be connected again with my human beloved.

I began flying to Southern California every other weekend to see Paul. During the two weeks of separation between, we wrote each other countless letters, talked on the phone, and then came together like magnets when we were finally reunited. Our joy in coming together was explosive. Each time I walked off the airplane and down the jet way, I thought I would literally burst with happiness and love at seeing him. The black mass that continued to constrict certain types of communication got relegated to some distant corner of my mind. There was no point in trying to bridge the communication gap with such short periods of time together. We simply wanted to be in each other's presence.

My deeply romantic relationship with Paul continued to open me to my spiritual life. On one of our rendezvous, we were sitting in a lovely garden by a little pool. I suddenly felt washed over by a feeling of infinite time. No time, really, just existence going on and on forever from one infinite end of the universe to the other. I knew that the two of us existed forever, that we lived and would be together beyond death, that death did not matter to us. The boundaries of time and space completely disappeared. I had heard about eternity, but now I was experiencing it. I knew this was a taste of being in the presence of God—where there was no time, no space, no form, and infinite love.

Another time during one of our visits, I discovered my soul, the soul that still so deeply longed for God. Paul and I were walking up the beach toward our car. I was behind a few feet when I suddenly became aware of a new being inside me. If I had been pregnant, I would have known it was the fetus showing itself to me with some subtle movement. But this was not a possible explanation for me. So then what? I knew instantly this force was my soul. The internal movement was like a tiger waking up after a long, long sleep.

For the first time in my life, I could feel I *had* a soul, or *was* a soul. This shocked me into a state of absolute awe. I held my breath. I moved carefully, afraid that if I stumbled she would disappear or become frightened and leave me. I knew that my soul was connected with God. Just as *I Am* had arisen from my depths, this was another hint of God within me.

I had to catch the 6:45 flight to Oakland on Monday mornings back to what had become for me a battlefield at Mudd's Restaurant and Gardens, back to my empty house and being alone. Severing myself from my beloved Paul drove a knife into my heart. It was sheer agony to walk back through the door of the jet way and have him disappear from view. Yet I continued every other weekend to fly like a moth to the flame of our love, and I continued to get singed and fly home again to emptiness. Years later Robert Johnson's words in *WE* would again offer perspective on my painful journey: "Suffering is the inevitable path that must be trod on the way to consciousness, the inevitable price for the transformation we seek.... This, then, is why we suffer, and this is why, unconsciously, we even seek to suffer." But I didn't know I was choosing suffering in order to transform. I only knew I couldn't forego my connection to Paul, no matter how difficult it was.

We desperately wanted "us" to work, in the earthly realm as well as in the divine one, so off and on we tried living together, for several months at a time. During one of these attempts, I committed wholeheartedly to working on myself to see what I could change to accommodate Paul's way of being without compromising my essential needs. I wanted to learn how to be happy *in spite of* outer conditions, rather than *if only* something would change. As a guide I used *The Handbook to Higher Consciousness* by Ken Keyes. The premise of the book is that if we upgrade our "addictions" to "preferences," outer circumstances won't as readily rattle our peace of mind. Keyes defines "addictions" as desires, attachments, demands, expectations, emotional programming. He says there are models of how we think life should treat us and what we believe we *have* to have in order to be happy. So by noticing when we are upset, uptight, or in pain, we can identify and then reframe our addictions.

Keyes's focus on "addictions" made me squirm, as if he had seen me scarf down a second bran muffin when I clearly wasn't hungry. But while my food addiction had diminished to a significant degree, I could see that I was deeply addicted to wanting Paul to be a certain way. It was hard to reframe this as a preference, yet at times I actually did succeed in feeling more tolerance and equanimity around our discordant way of communicating.

Something else Keyes says was important for me in trying to undo old patterns and develop "higher consciousness." He writes, "You have every right to feel exactly as you feel. If others are bothered, that's their problem." Knowing what exactly I felt was still a challenge in itself, but with great determination I worked to know and honor my feelings. Still, expressing to Paul a feeling other than joy and love would most often be met with a puzzling and frustrating silence. Since I had no idea what he felt about what I'd expressed, knowing my own feelings didn't go far in solving our communication problems.

My own work with a therapist had been so helpful for uncovering and resolving past hurts that I felt hopeful when Paul went to see a counselor. I hoped that one day we would be lying safely in each other's arms and he would haltingly tell me the story of a terrible trauma of his past that had so wounded him that he'd been unable to speak of it. An inner dam would burst and his tears, and fears, would break through the floodgates he'd erected to protect himself. The flood of released emotions would wash away his guardedness, the black obstacle between us, and we would live happily ever after. But several sessions didn't yield any new insights or release of energy. I tried writing letters to him if I had some important and deep feelings to share, hoping a letter would be less threatening, or put less pressure on him. "Dearest Paul, you seem so low. Tell me how you are feeling. Is there anything I can do? When you don't respond I feel abandoned." He would write back love letters apologizing for upsetting me and repeating that he wasn't holding back but didn't know what more to say or do, and my emotions and feelings would be left withering like forgotten flowers. When I told a friend how frustrated I felt, she suggested I "fall out of love" with Paul so we could break up and I could get on with my life. But Paul's life felt as important to me as my own, and I could hardly imagine breaking up, even though part of me longed to. Very slowly I was realizing I couldn't "fix" Paul or make him happy in the way I wanted him to be. And I was having a hard enough time "fixing" myself.

By the time I was ready to leave for the Tetons, we'd been together, off-and-on, for a little more than two years, and our relationship still wasn't clear in my mind, and I saw little promise for change in our future. One day I told him that at some point we would have to *completely* separate. He was deeply saddened and hurt and I felt unbearably guilty. But since neither of us was yet ready to let go, we'd made those plans to meet in Jackson Hole when I arrived at the Tetons, and to drive back to California together. At least I finally knew that finding God was something I would have to do on my own.

I reluctantly finished my Nubieber Café omelet and tea, urged myself up from the table, and paid the cashier. I went outside and pulled more clothes from Sunny's rear panniers, then returned to the little sheltered entryway to add layers, bringing the number up to five. Carol had given me bright blue rain booties, and even though it wasn't raining, I pulled them on over my shoes for warmth while grimly considering what lay ahead. It would take me two days to reach the next real habitation, Klamath Falls, Oregon, about 138 miles north. For most of that route I would be on a small county road—only a thin, gray unnumbered line on my map. There would be no warm motels and hot baths to look forward to along that route. At the end of the day, I would be camping out in this miserable and unnerving cold.

The weather was so bleak and the way so uncertain that a foreboding sense came over me. The idea of heading into a long stretch of uninhabited territory felt like entering a deserted wilderness where anything could happen. Would I ever see anyone I knew again? I knew it was an irrational thought, but it was convincing nonetheless. I reached for the pay phone in the entryway and called a friend. Kerry was sympathetic about my situation and gave me encouragement to keep going. It was comforting to hear a familiar voice and to know that at least he knew where I was.

After hanging up, there was nothing else to do. I just had to get on the road. I pushed through the café door, swung my right leg over Sunny's saddle, and slipped my booties into the straps. The deserted main street of Nubieber was lined with dreary old brick buildings and storefronts not yet open; it was eight o'clock in the morning. At the stop sign I clenched my jaw and steeled myself as I turned north into the headwind.

6
WHO AM I?

At 4,000 feet the bare and rocky land I entered outside Nubieber was still trapped in winter's dreary grasp. No green shoots were emerging from the bare dirt, no blossoming trees brightened the landscape. Low sagebrush and scrawny junipers dotted the desert ground. The wind tore through the scattered pine trees as if it meant to strip them of all their needles. The rush of sound filled my head like static fuzz. My face felt like it was being sandblasted with gnat-sized ice needles.

Suddenly there she was—my mother, dominating my mind again, telling me I was too fragile, too incapable, living in a dangerous world that would defeat me. During her phone call a couple of months before my departure, she'd pointed out all the risks of solo bike travel that she thought I was being very naïve about. I'd dutifully listened and then said, with all the conviction I could muster, "I disagree and I'm going!" There. The "good daughter" had struck back. I'd wanted to hang up on her. I wanted to smack her across the face. Like Dorothy in *The Wizard of Oz,* I did feel like I had thrown a lethal bucket of water on the witch. Would she now shrivel up and leave me alone? I was shaking with fear and exhilaration as we politely finished our conversation. I had actually—really for the first time—stood up for myself against her. I was thirty-five years old, and I had finally taken a big step in the process of what psychologists call "individuation." I was me, and my mother was...well, someone else.

My mother was a lovely woman, medium height, small-boned and graceful. Her dark hair was coiffed each week with a subtle purple tint to hide the gray. She had an extensive wardrobe of understated, stylish and eye-catching outfits that she wore beautifully. She "dressed" every night for dinner, and met my father at the door when he returned from work. Her artist's eye for design and color created a home that could easily have been featured in *House Beautiful.* She was soft-spoken, kind, and exceptionally thoughtful of others. She was a lovely Victorian lady. I can't imagine anyone ever saying a bad thing about her.

But I did not love her. When I was about four years old, I started having dreams of a witch, and somehow I knew that witch was my mother. She would be smiling warmly at me and be scrutinizing me at the same time, seeming to critique my every move and word. I felt tense and apprehensive around my mother. Because I didn't trust the loving things she said to me, her endearments often felt like poison apples. I recoiled from her disingenuous sentiments.

Perhaps not surprisingly, her mother, my grandmother, was the same way. She acted as though she was glad to see us kids—which thankfully didn't happen very often—but I could tell it was as much a chore for her as it was for us. We always had to give her a kiss on the cheek. I would rather have snuggled up to the underbelly of a dead salamander than touch her face with my lips. I always cringed while giving her the obligatory peck.

Perhaps her own mother was what left my mother afraid of the outside world. It seemed to me she was afraid of life itself, and I felt her trying to snuff out the lively, energetic and happy qualities that emerged around her. I remember very clearly the moment when I decided that expressing joy was a no-no. My sister and I must have been about eight and ten. We lived in a two-story house with a wide carpeted staircase to the second floor. One evening after dinner Tory and I were "horsing around" downstairs in the main hallway, our parents lingering about us. Tory took off up the stairs, and I bolted after her. We were both on all fours, shrieking and laughing hysterically with glee. I don't recall whether my mother actually said anything, but suddenly it felt like a sopping wet blanket was thrown over us, stifling our fun and our joy. We proceeded up the stairs subdued, mannerly, as befitting our emotionless family. Joy, excitement, passion, warmth, happiness, fun, creativity—these were not for us.

By the time I was thirteen, I was the only child left at home, the others all off at boarding school or college. Without allies, I felt like I was in a leaky one-person submarine sinking in the Arctic Ocean, and there was no one to help me. I became more and more uptight, unsure of myself, more unwilling to express any but the most docile and pleasant sentiments. Inside I felt mostly fear, depression, stifled anger and loneliness. During that year I comforted myself by writing secret hate notes to my mother, which I kept locked away in a little red wooden treasure chest.

As I bent my head into the blasting wind outside Nubieber, I felt like I was coming up against this mother and reliving all the ways I'd had to fight against her to try to claim my life. As the icy headwind froze and battered me, I felt her oppressive force push against me, her cold hand squeeze my heart. The wind was so fierce that on a perfectly level road I was in my second lowest gear, one I normally would only have needed to climb a steep grade. I fought for every inch of progress until, frustrated and discouraged, I started shouting at the wind. "I hate you. I despise you. You're always trying to keep me down." The emotions and feelings I'd stuffed all those years exploded from me. I unleashed my own "furious truth," the way my sister had years before. "Fuck you, mom. I will *not* keep my voice down, *Mommy Dear*! You're always trying to stomp out my life. Can't you see it isn't going to happen? So fuck off! Get out of my face!" The rage alternated with sobs so wrenching that I could barely keep pedaling. At last I pulled over to the side of the lonely highway and, doubled over my handlebars, convulsed with sobbing.

By the time I set out again, I felt drained and empty. It was a brutal ride, but by late afternoon, I'd met my goal—sixty-five miles, halfway to Klamath Falls. Except for the emotional meltdown, the only other time I'd stopped that day was to stretch out my shoulders, which were painfully tight from trying to keep the cold from penetrating my body. A little before 5:00 p.m., I pulled off the highway and walked Sunny about fifty yards into what I hoped would be a hidden spot in a cluster of pines. My hands were numb, and it took forever to get the tent up. By the time I crawled into my sleeping bag, I felt like I'd been mummified in ice. I probably had a touch of hypothermia, because even curled into my arctic-grade down sleeping bag with clothes piled on top, I couldn't get warm. I huddled into myself, hoping my blue tent was invisible from the road. I was counting on a passage from Psalm 91, which I'd copied into my *Teton Traveler's Guide* to protect me. In it, God assured me that "no evil shall be allowed to befall you, no plague come near your tent." I prayed that the God who'd sent me on this journey would get me safely through the night.

Blue tent in pines

Twelve hours later I emerged. Ice covered the tent, and I struggled with stiff fingers to pack up. I set out, thankful that at least the sky was a clear blue. But as the sun came up so did the wind, and within an hour scattered white clouds began to form. Soon an oppressive gray blanket once again lay over everything, making the gaunt forest on either side of the road look dark and unwelcoming. Despite energetic pedaling, I couldn't get warm, and it scared me that I could barely shift gears because the muscles in my hands were so stiff with cold and my fingers so numb. As the piercing, sharp pain between my shoulders started again, I resumed the tirade against the icy headwinds…and against my mother. Not many miles into the day I broke down once more with rage and sobbing.

At the time I didn't know what was happening to me. But years later I would read something that put a lot of the pieces of my life together. In *The Pregnant Virgin*, Marion Woodman writes: "Once she discovers what her mother never introduced her to—the deep, rich love of being alive—her life becomes her possession. She is then free to shape her own life." On that freezing cold, lonely road, I was struggling mightily to do just that. I knew that this solo bike journey was a statement to everyone—especially myself—that I was an independent, capable adult claiming my own life. I was separating myself from my mother, breaking the bonds that restrained me, and valiantly trying to claim my own identity.

I'd gone through a similar process with my husband several years before, when I was beginning to "find myself." One of the first questions Linne had asked me in therapy was "How is your marriage?" To my great surprise, I discovered that I felt totally inferior to my husband, and that even though I was married I was blindly oriented toward attracting and securing the appreciation of the male sex. In retrospect, however, that makes sense since I had been born into a generation and a family where guys were gods, and that included my three older brothers and my father. They were the stars of the show. Men ruled, and as a woman I existed for and in relation to them. Tory and I, along with our mother, were clearly our men's supporting cast.

I'd passed directly from that family scene into my freshman year in college and a boyfriend who was a senior. After living together for a year, we married. I was four days' shy of my twentieth birthday. He had interesting and important friends, among them the son of a politician in Texas and a prince from India. I was rather in awe of him. Not long after we married he was admitted to law school where, with his strong intellectual abilities, he excelled. From there he was hired by one of the best law firms in San Francisco and continued to stand out among his peers. He was athletic and fearless. Once I watched as he did a beautiful dive from a bridge thirty feet above the Middle Fork of the Salmon River. He was equally at ease and confident in social gatherings. I, on the other hand, was a wallflower—shy and ill at ease with people. I'd always been more comfortable with my animals or alone. In therapy I discovered that I measured myself about an inch tall next to my outgoing, confident, capable husband.

After a couple of months on my therapy cushion, I ventured out alone to a major event for the first time in my life—a two-week community organizing course at the Midwest Academy in Chicago. My year of reading had left me passionate about the changes we as a culture had to make in order to keep from destroying the earth, the human race included. I wanted training in how to communicate this to others. I hadn't known, as I boarded the train for the Windy City, that for me the course would be about much more than community organizing.

Up until those two weeks in Chicago, I had been my husband's wife and companion. At the Midwest Academy, I was on my own. I had no lawyer to back me up intellectually; no confident, witty, engaging man to fill in for my social awkwardness. It was the first time I had to relate to the world as an independent person, unattached to my family or my husband. I began to take on a shape of my own, to see myself as an individual entity. I caught a glimpse of what it meant to be me—what *I* thought, how *I* felt, how *I* made decisions, what *I* liked to do when I got up in the morning. It was like watching the development of a Polaroid self-portrait— the image begins to emerge, cloudy at first, then sharper and more defined until *Presto!* the picture becomes clear. I loved what I saw.

Those two weeks didn't free me from the food addiction I still battled, but they gave me a taste of something I wanted besides food. I'd seen that I could not only stand by and for myself, but I had totally enjoyed my solo performance. I'd made friends. I'd had intelligent and personal discussions with relative strangers. I'd had something to offer other participants. It was as if I had introduced myself to me for the first time.

After that trip I began asking a lot of questions: Who would I be if I were not married to and identified with my husband? How much did I do because I loved him, and how much because I didn't want to lose him and the support and protection I received from being married? Was I allowing myself to feel inferior so I wouldn't have to be alone in the world? Shortly after my return I took a big step toward independence by telling my husband that I wanted our burgeoning idea of Mudd's Restaurant to be "*my* baby." I wanted to take the lead in making conceptual, design and operational decisions. He was gracious about stepping into the background and supporting me in my work, perhaps glad to see me blossoming as a person.

I also began to question not just my relationship to men but *everything* about my internal world: What were *my* values? *My* opinions? What did I feel in any given situation? What were my wants and needs? Was I even *entitled* to have any wants or needs? What was my place in the world? What was my place in myself? What did I want to *do* with my life? What were my talents and skills (if any)? What did I want to become?

Who was I? The questions were as terrifying to me as the food addiction that tried to stuff them down. I knew with everything inside me that it was time for me to find out who I was, claim and shape my own life. I hadn't yet read Thomas Merton's insight about the dual process of finding yourself and finding God—I was not yet consciously searching for Him; I had not yet had the dream of God making love to me—but I was steadily being drawn in that direction.

As I emerged from the pine forest into more open land, the headwinds intensified. All around me dry, pale, barren hills were crisscrossed with rusty barbed wire fences and crooked, rotting wooden fence posts. If I'd seen whole skeletons of cows on the ground, I would not have been surprised. This borderland between California and Oregon was as bleak and dismal a landscape as I'd ever been in, and it seemed endless. Stroke by stroke, I fought my way through the oppressive forces inside and out.

The poverty and emptiness I was biking through whipped up another headwind inside me, one that felt deeply humiliating and defeating. I knew from a very early age that something was "not right" about my circumstances compared to how most other people lived. When other kids were riding their bikes home after school, I was occasionally picked up in a Rolls Royce driven by a black chauffeur, a prim grandmother sitting in the backseat with a white French poodle on her lap. I remember wanting to shrink into the sidewalk. While my parents did not live in a showy place like Bel Air or Beverly Hills, I knew that very few people in that vast city of Los Angeles lived in a large house overlooking a golf course. Most people didn't have French Impressionist art hanging on the walls, or plenty of help to keep the antique furniture dusted everyday.

When I was seventeen, my father took me on a trip to India. We hired a car and driver to take us to see some rural villages. As my father leaned out the window taking in the exotic people and scenery, I watched the hatred in the glaring eyes of the young boys who followed, some asking for coins, others banging angrily on the car. I wanted to crawl under the seat. I was embarrassed for my father and his lack of sensitivity, and ashamed for our wealth and the gross unfairness it represented.

When I received an inheritance at the age of twenty-one, my guilt was compounded exponentially. Most people think that inheriting money would be the best thing that could ever happen to a person—not having to work for a living, being able to buy what you need or want, traveling where your heart desires, living in a place that suits your fancy, having a vacation home, being able to help a friend in need, funding causes you care about. Those are indeed extraordinary benefits of being gifted with an inheritance, and I deeply appreciate being a beneficiary of my family's good fortune. But for me there was a dark and intensely painful side to this gift.

I honestly would not wish an inheritance on my dearest friend. Not having to work for a living doesn't mean you don't have to work for your life. A trust fund does not provide meaning, purpose, fulfillment or happiness. It didn't protect me from haunting questions: *Why am I here? What work should I be doing?* Wealth doesn't protect you from hurt feelings or disappointments or broken hearts. Nor does it buy you trust. I never knew for sure if my friends liked me for myself or for my money. Much of the time I felt like I was wearing that big sandwich board with a huge, red dollar sign on it.

Not until I was in therapy, where I was prodded to delve into my past and allow buried feelings to emerge, did I discover just how pained I was about my situation. I fell through layer after layer of guilt, shame, and loneliness, like descending into an abandoned mine shaft. Sometimes I would go so deep into the pain I thought I would actually throw up my insides in gut-wrenching sobbing. Deep under the pain and guilt, I found anger. Nobody had asked me if I wanted to have a big wad of money dropped on me. Nobody taught me how to handle it, or prepared me for the psychological difficulties I would face because of it. These emotional purges released some of the repressed emotional energy but did not completely relieve me from torment. I would continue to face these emotional headwinds for years.

One memory stands out as a perfect example. Several years after my Teton trip, when I had learned fine press printing, I was displaying and selling my handmade cards and broadsides during a local studio tour. At the end of the day, I was talking with another woman artist about how the event had gone for each of us. "How were your sales?" she asked. And then as a sudden afterthought, she added, "Oh, I guess it doesn't matter to you...." Her voice trailed off, but the implication was clear that I didn't care about what I'd sold because I didn't need the money. She had no idea how much it meant to me that people admired and valued my hand-printed objects, and that I had *earned* my own money.

As my pedals cranked over on that cold and windy road, so did the questions in my mind. How could I ever atone for having what I did not earn? What did I have to do to deserve this inheritance, to have what so many others did not? Like many people of wealth, I would use my good fortune to serve society and the earth, but that didn't make me feel any more deserving of what I'd been given. And when I had more than enough, how could I possibly have the right to deserve or ask for anything more? How could I need anything when I had been given so much?

While I found that inheriting money was undermining to self-worth, paradoxically, having money made me feel I was superior to other people. After much contemplation on the subject, I concluded that the only way for rich people to assuage the terrible guilt they feel at the injustice and inequity of the haves and have-nots in the world is to believe and feel that they are better than other people, and hence *deserve* all this wealth. This was the only way I could explain the arrogance and superiority that often exudes from wealthy people. I know I felt it. Part of my life was in the dungeon of low self-esteem, and part of it was on a throne. My task was to crawl up out of my hole, and climb down from my pedestal in order to become unburdened, healed and free. I was caught somewhere between living a life of entitlement without feeling entitled to it, and allowing myself to accept the gift and enjoy the benefits it offered.

Meanwhile, as I fought my way north against the wind, I wondered if I would ever find answers to these tangled questions I was struggling with. I dragged my load through, up, and over the bleached, dry hills, tightening and releasing my shoulders as I tried to ease the constant sharp pain. By the time I arrived in Tulelake, California around noon, my body felt like it was wrapped in crushed ice. I stiffly climbed the wooden steps into the local café. While I brooded over many cups of hot tea, I calculated that it would take me a total of eight hours that day to reach Klamath Falls, still thirty-seven miles away.

I would end up averaging a mere seven miles per hour over the entire sixty miles. With a fully loaded bike I could normally go about twelve miles per hour, but the turmoil I was in and the external conditions were slowing me down to a virtual cyclist's crawl. I briefly considered hitchhiking just so I could end the day and get to some place warm. But after my experiences in California on my first day, I didn't want to risk an uncertain pick-up. The cold was at least the "known devil." But I felt so battered, so cold that I started thinking about another option. Quitting.

7
MY WILL OR THY WILL

I woke up the next morning in the cheesy motel I'd found on a back street of Klamath Falls. As I lay in bed, feeling too exhausted to move, I looked around the room. Everything was a shade of dull brown: pale beige stucco walls, dirt brown carpet, a shiny synthetic quilt bedspread in gold and brown paisley. Limp tan curtains covered the window. I supposed the glitter on the low beige ceiling was an attempt to brighten the place up. I ached all over, like I'd been thrown off a horse. Even the slightest move caught the stinging pinch between my shoulders. When I got up to pee, my leg muscles felt bruised.

I pulled aside the curtain to see what kind of day it would be. The same thin, cold, dreary layer of clouds covered the sky. I slumped gloomily back into the pillows and pulled the quilt up under my chin. Deep down I was still cold. *Why am I doing this?* The answer was almost automatic by this time. *God.* I felt He had given me the inspiration for this bike trip—more like an assignment—and it was part of my search for Him. But was this the way it was going to be? Did I have to continue through hell in order to find Him?

How would I feel if I just quit now? How would *He* feel? Bailing out was a hard thing to consider; I had quit so much. I had quit my marriage of thirteen years, and I was likewise unsuccessful in creating a lasting relationship with the man I had fallen in love with. And Mudd's Restaurant—I'd ended up quitting that too. I'd felt that God had given me the inspiration for Mudd's. If "wild ideas" were gifts from God, as that artist had said, then why should they be so hard? As I lay in bed trying to get warm, I found myself grappling with some of the same questions I'd faced with the restaurant.

When I took on the job of managing the restaurant part of the project, my business partner and good friend, Kerry, had stepped into directing the garden and educational side of the venture. Honoring my post-Chicago request my husband had substantially pulled back so I could make Mudd's more my own creative work. It took only a couple of months for my baby to enter its "terrible twos." I found myself burdened with crisis management. On one particularly memorable Friday, I arrived in the morning to find the answering machine garbling out of control. I spent the morning scrambling to answer the phone to take reservations. Then the hostess called in sick, and I jumped into my party-girl act. That day the customers were unusually full of demands and complaints about service and food; the frustrations carried to the whole staff, and I took the heat of it all. During lunch service, the main water line broke, which meant there was no way to clean up lunch or prep for 150 reserved dinners. All the while the coffee maker, as if wanting to take part in the turmoil, wouldn't stop making pot after pot of coffee. This was fortunately not the same Friday we were robbed. Some days were not this chaotic, but it seemed there was always some staffing or mechanical crisis I had to deal with.

Soon the relentless stress of my new, brilliant career as owner / manager of a restaurant complex began to take its toll on me. By the sixth month of this, I was slurring sentences and often didn't recognize familiar faces. My brain seemed fuzzy more often than not, and one day as I was talking to Kerry at lunch, I almost passed out. These symptoms culminated in my worst-ever case of herpes, with two-thirds of my lower lip covered by an ugly, thick, dark brown, lumpy and painful scab. I stood at the hostess desk, cringing as I greeted every diner with a half-hearted smile, deeply embarrassed and humiliated.

My lip was not the only part of me that was burning. In spiritual life the teachings often speak of the fire of purification, the process by which one is compelled to give up attachments to material things or personal identities, illusions, judgments, history, old patterns of behaviors and self-conceptions to attain enlightenment. Therapy five years before had started the process of self-investigation and opened the door to my spiritual journey, but the pace and intensity of Mudd's was turning up the heat.

One of my identities that was being sorely challenged was that old belief that I was a somewhat superior person and that life was supposed to be smooth sailing. Therefore I shouldn't suffer the humiliation of a physical disfigurement like herpes, especially not in public. And I certainly shouldn't have base emotional problems, such as embarrassment, disappointment, frustration, hurt feelings, and anger.

In addition, I also believed that because I was well-intentioned, I was above making mistakes or being criticized. This was radically unrealistic in a business in which nonstop decisions on the fly were being made round the clock. One of my worst mistakes—which still makes me wince—was firing two waitresses, one of whom happened to be the wife of my partner, and the other a good friend of the project. My floor manager had received criticism of their service and was very negative about their performance. I took her complaints to heart, and without talking to them or to my partner, I impulsively fired them. The justified criticism that came at me for this move went a long way to burning out my belief in my infallibility and perfection.

I'd also mistakenly believed that since our project was for the good of others and the planet, we'd have immunity from problems and difficulties. I thought everything should run smoothly. I think I even believed that God should not be allowing these crises to happen because we were doing good, and because this was *His* big idea.

To do God's will, to surrender to His will, had become an overriding concern in my life. But what was

God's will? And what was *my* will? My desire to be of service through the restaurant, garden and educational programs seemed at odds with the incessant day-to-day battering of my body and spirit. Did doing God's will mean abdicating my own responsibility for self-determination and even self-care? Could I say, "God wants me to be manager of my restaurant so I have no other choice but to go through this ordeal?" For me, God was still a huge external force that knew what was best for everyone. Did God and I both want the same thing?

I wanted to know what I wanted, and I wanted to know what God wanted, but every day all I could hear was what everyone else wanted. I listened to customer complaints; I listened to a litany of problems followed by thirty-five explanations and solutions; I listened to some of the staff who wanted to make structural changes to the restaurant and others who didn't; I listened to arguments for closing the restaurant on a holiday weekend because we were understaffed; I listened to my accountant sounding a financial alarm; I listened to an employee who wanted me to build a dog run so Fido could come to work; I listened to all the Mozart and Vivaldi I could stand.

I didn't realize at the time that one's particular nature and temperament need to be taken into account in choosing the kind of work one does. It was more my nature to be a hermit than a restaurant manager. For me to be in a hectic, people-intensive environment was like trying to fit a square peg into a round hole. I hadn't yet arrived at the point where I felt I could take my own inclinations just as God-given as the gift of a wild idea.

I told myself that if I only set my mind to it, we could make the place work in all the ways we'd envisioned. I could not, or would not, hear my own small inner voice—wordless inner promptings which began after the restaurant had scarcely been open a year—telling me to stop what I was doing. I continued to persevere with my tasks, ignoring the knots in my stomach, the exhaustion, the emptiness, the fuzziness, the reluctance to go to work. I often drove several miles past my exit just to delay my arrival. On top of daily crises, twelve months in, when we made a radical change of chefs and menus, our customer base rapidly declined. At one point we had so few customers that the staff parked in the public parking area so it would appear that we had at least a few diners. I was pouring in money like blood transfusions to keep us running. I was way out of my depth, but I was determined: *I'm going to make this place work, or die trying.*

One afternoon—it was the Spring Equinox, three months after Paul had left—I was home between shifts, and I'd gone upstairs for a short rest before getting dressed for dinner service. Without taking my clothes off, I eased myself under the warmth and safety of the pink comforter and sank into gloom. Music and prayer had only gone so far to ease my deepening depression. Between the desperate situation at Mudd's, the difficulty and uncertainty of my relationship with Paul, and my physical deterioration, I saw little that was positive in my present, or hopeful in my future. My heart felt hollow. My mind was dull as though coated and clogged with thick, black oil. I lay there, numb and empty, looking around at the apricot-colored walls that surrounded me. The little flame that had burned so steadily inside me, the candle of my spirit that kept me going, seemed very close to being snuffed out.

The few friends I'd confided in thought I was just going through a normal depression due to stress over the restaurant and my troubled relationship with Paul. They'd tried to cheer me up, saying I'd find new meaning for my life. I didn't believe them. They didn't know what they were talking about. I wanted them to take their Pollyanna cheerfulness away. This was something different, deeper, but I didn't know what. I felt not a flicker of care for anything.

As I lay there a creeping panic and anxiety seemed to radiate from the core of my being into every nook and cranny of the room. I felt like I was wrapped tight in seaweed and sinking. A cold, skeletal witch's claw rasped through my insides, scraping away everything that made my life rich and motivated me to get out of bed in the morning, scraping away meaning, purpose, love of nature, my dreams and visions, goals and aspirations, maybe even my desire for God. Without anything to guide or drive me, to inspire and comfort me, I now truly had nothing. No Paul, no God, no husband, no animals, no flame of spirit. Nothing. Nothing. *This is all there is—me and four apricot-colored walls.*

Suddenly I saw one of the walls open onto a three-dimensional place that was suffused with a gentle but bright, intense, purely white light. The place was filled with "people"—although they were more like spiritual entities —who were convivial, confident, full of joy. The energy of the gathering felt like a locker room after a winning ballgame. I wanted desperately to go there, to join them. I could leave my sorrow and loneliness and struggling business behind. I had no doubt that I could reach that place if I chose to. Right now I could exit the life I was trapped in and join in their happiness and freedom. Physical death would be far less terrifying than continuing on with what my life had become.

But as I lay there looking into that light-filled room, it also occurred to me that it would be a mistake to take my own life. I felt sure that ultimately I'd have to face the same problems in another lifetime. With that realization my depression and fear deepened. There was no way out. I pulled myself out of bed, dressed for work, pasted on my most convincing smile, and drove back to Mudd's for the evening shift.

I don't recall how, but in the midst of this inner darkness I happened to come across *The Courage To Be* by Paul Tillich, a theologian and Christian existential philosopher. Tillich did not try to talk me out of my anxiety or deny the state I was in. To the contrary, he *confirmed* it all! He got right down in the swamp bottom with me and said, "Yes, I see what you are seeing. You are perceiving correctly. It is everything you say it is. Here, let me tell you what I know about where you are."

I let Tillich take me mentally by the hand and lead me through the rooms of fear, emptiness, meaninglessness, anxiety, despair, and desire for non-existence. He explained to me the difference between fear and anxiety—that fear has an object which can be identified and confronted, or run away from. Anxiety, on the other hand, is a shapeless, objectless fear. There is no dragon you can identify, then slay or flee from. He was right. I couldn't say, "Oh, I'm afraid my restaurant will fail." Or, "I'm afraid I'll die if I'm alone for one more day." Anxiety leaves you mired in a dark, murky, slimy cesspool. You cannot identify a way out. "Anxiety," Tillich writes, "is the state in which a being is aware of its possible *nonbeing*." In this state everything that supports our daily life and gives it meaning is threatened; our very existence as a physical being is at stake. The anxiety created by our self-rejection and self-condemnation adds another threat to our existence, and we become acutely aware of non-existence. We arrive at the "boundary line" of life, and there we can turn either toward courage or toward despair. Courage, Tillich says, is the act of affirming our existence, or being, *in spite of* the power of nonbeing.

It was the "in spite of" that eventually lifted me out of the dense darkness. The "in spite of" said that this was not an either/or situation, not a black and white struggle where Nonbeing wore the black hat and Being wore the white, and only one would prevail. This was an *inclusive* situation in which both states were present in life—in *my* life—and would remain that way. My task was to allow the anxiety and despair to exist, and to go on with living *in spite of* them. I had to *accept* these threats—meaninglessness, the forces of nonbeing, despair—and keep going.

Accepting these forces seemed far more possible to me than overcoming them. Accepting, Tillich was telling me, meant having courage. I liked the idea of myself as courageous. I *wanted* to be courageous. *If I'm only being asked to accept these forces, I can do that. My enemies have now been identified and named.* So I set up a truce: On one side of the room within those four apricot-colored walls, I would place Life, Meaning, Self-affirmation, and Being; Death, Meaninglessness, Self-rejection, and Nonbeing on the other. Courage would stand boldly in the middle on solid ground. At that boundary line, I would accept being as well as non-being. Okay. What now?

For the next leap toward curing my dis-ease Tillich asked me to see that these opposing forces on either side of the room were—paradoxically—actually *dependent* on each other and interrelated. There could be no Being without Nonbeing; no "Yes" without "No." "Nonbeing," said Tillich, "drives Being out of seclusion." Nonbeing forces Being to reaffirm itself in dynamic action. I needed the "No" to have the "Yes," the dark to have the light. A deeper understanding of these opposing forces dawned on me. I was getting my first lesson about the meaning of non-duality—that ideas or beliefs or forces that appear to be separate and distinct are really part of one whole. I didn't know it at the time, but on my journey to God, I would be faced with this truth over and over.

But what did acceptance have to do with God? My desire to find Him seemed to be the only aspiration that had survived the darkness. Tillich now told me that the ultimate source of the courage to be is the "God above God." It was hard to fathom exactly what this meant, but when I read the phrase "God above God," my whole inner being swelled with desire to have that. This was what I was looking for. And I knew I'd know it when I found it.

Tillich had given me cause for hope even though I thought I had nothing. Tillich told me I could find God through despair, *in spite of* despair, maybe even *because of* despair. I didn't know what my next steps were, but I knew I was only—and absolutely—driven to the search. I might be searching till my death day for God, but if that's what I had to do, I would.

The determination to find God on my own is what had gotten me on the road to the Tetons. But now lying miserably in a dark Klamath Falls motel, this venture didn't seem to be going any better for me than Mudd's Restaurant. Should I quit this one too? In my mind a replay of the "quitting script" was unfolding, highlighting the same theme: God's will vs. mine.

At Mudd's it had become clear that neither the restaurant nor I could survive if we continued in the same way. Quitting had not been an option until quitting became a necessity. When I finally surrendered to the need to find someone to replace me, we hired a restaurant consultant to help us with this task and with making interim adjustments so that I would be less stressed while the search was on. He counseled me to take some personal time for myself. He also told me something that helped me not be so hard on myself. He said there are three kinds of people in the business world: founders, who are great at creating and bringing a venture into being; operations people, who excel in taking care of the zillion details—and crises—that go into managing a business; and development people, who skillfully build the business. I fell into the founder category; someone else was needed to step into the other roles. So we set our course to find a new manager, rebuild our business, and get me out of the restaurant side of the venture so I could develop the broader vision of our project. I was encouraged, but I still felt so used up I just wanted out altogether. Yet the question loomed: If I quit, would I be doing God's will or opposing it?

The pivotal moment of clarity about God's will vs. my will came while I was attending a business management seminar on a beautiful Saturday. I still considered this kind of training part of my responsibilities. I was trying to learn advanced procedures in sales accounting, and what was new and exciting in cash registers. I was fighting off the flu, which I could not let grab me because we were right in the middle of getting me out of the mess I was in as Mudd's manager. I was also feeling that the little flame of spirit that gave me energy for living was getting dimmer and dimmer. All I wanted to do was curl up in a ball and cry while someone held me.

As the seminar leader droned on, I started writing random thoughts in the margins of the course syllabus. *Is this what God wanted for me?* Immediately I felt a response rise up inside my mind. I didn't actually hear a voice, but it was as if God answered, "This isn't really what I had in mind when I produced with you the idea of Mudd's and Crow Canyon Gardens." As I sat with this voice in my mind, the thought arose that I might actually be offending and hurting God by being so near a complete meltdown. Knowing I was wasting a beautiful Saturday in this boring seminar, and sensing that I was offending God at the same time, I suddenly felt unbearably sad, and angry too, for allowing myself to get into such a low state.

As the room lights dimmed so the presenter could show slides, I went deeper into reflection. *Did God want what was good for me? Did He want me to be happy and enjoy myself?* Some seemed to believe that God was like a mean tyrant, a policeman or judge. I had never thought that God was a punishing God and at that moment I felt God regarding me with great compassion and kindness. It occurred to me that maybe I was just pushing myself so hard because I didn't think I deserved anything but slavish hard work to atone for my social privilege and inheritance.

Sitting in that dim room surrounded by people eagerly taking notes on the latest and greatest cash registers, something suddenly became clear to me. It would please God most if I were in good physical health, doing what I enjoyed, and tending to my own needs. *If neither God nor I want me to be on this edge of sanity and physical stability, then at least some aspect of me and some aspect of God are aligned.* This was big. It meant that *Thy* will and *my* will were possibly the same, or at least not at odds with one another. It meant I had to get really clear about what sort of person I was, what my nature was, what made me feel good, and what made me feel like a scalded chicken or a broken prizefighter. It meant I could believe that in spite of my good fortune, I still deserved to be good to myself. *I'm going to take better care of myself and enjoy my life, even if it kills me!*

After that day I'd made some practical changes and did more things I enjoyed. With regular bike rides, light reading and resting, my health and spirits improved over the course of the six months it took to find and train a new manager. I was immensely relieved to be able to leave Mudd's entirely in the hands of my partner and the new manager.

Now as I lay staring at another set of walls—bland and meaningless beige—I realized that my journey over the past two days had been a mirror of the time leading up to leaving Mudd's. I had pressed on then, no matter how miserable I was or how beat up my body felt, until I could go on no longer. And now here I was, surrounded by a bleak room and an even bleaker outside where I was supposed to get on a bicycle and ride sixty miles. Should I quit this too? But looking back, it occurred to me that maybe I hadn't exactly quit Mudd's; I had re-arranged my responsibilities and chosen a different path.

Even though both Mudd's and this solo journey were assignments from God, that didn't mean I had no choice in how to carry them out. Maybe such assignments were "set-ups," gifts that helped me find and accept myself as I was. Unlike managing a restaurant, which didn't suit me, long-distance bicycling was actually something I'd done successfully and was fitting to my nature. I enjoyed traveling by bike. The speed—assuming it was a normal kind of day rolling along at twelve miles per hour or more—is perfect to catch the smells, see the plants, the rocks, feel and hear the insects, and witness the subtle changes in terrain and weather in the course of a day's ride. Although sometimes long distance traveling by bike was tedious, stressful and too slow, the overall experience was unquestionably positive. And even that contrast was a good teaching about life.

Images began to roll through my mind as I lay quietly in bed. I could remember almost every road I biked with Carol on our journey to Washington, DC six years earlier. Some rides were exciting beyond my wildest imaginings: flying down the east side of the still-snowy Sierra and then coming up over a rise to behold the moonscape of Mono Lake; or passing a truck leaving the summit of Monarch Pass at the Continental Divide in Colorado because we were going so fast; or racing storm clouds to find shelter in Kansas because of a tornado warning. Some roads were outrageously beautiful: the route leading through Death Valley in the cool of a clear early morning in that surreal landscape; the road along the south rim of the Grand Canyon, which we had gotten to on our very own steam, in itself a marvel! And, I thought, as a smile broke through my glumness, there is *nothing* that compares to riding on a glass-smooth road with a warm strong wind at your back! I could still hear the sound of the wind rushing through the foot-high Kansas wheat, my pigtails blowing out *in front of* my face.

Even though there'd been hellish times along the way—extreme heat, intense traffic, breakdowns, exhaustion—heaven was there for the pedaling. In spite of the past two remarkably awful days on my way to Oregon, there would surely be those heavenly roads ahead, and I wanted to ride them. Deep down in myself I also wanted that victory of knowing I could do it. And overarching and embracing all other reasons was that call to fulfill my assignment from God.

Carol and me at the Grand Canyon

One of my favorite inspiring quotes that I'd written in my *Teton Traveler's Guide* came to mind. Ralph Waldo Emerson said: "What lies behind us and what lies before us are tiny matters compared to what lies within us." I had discovered so much about myself and the world, through Mudd's Restaurant, through my glorious and agonizing relationship with Paul, through the miles I'd already covered cycling. What else would I find inside me as I continued on this journey? No, I didn't want to quit. But as I'd learned through the restaurant, I needed to find a way to continue that would also allow me to enjoy myself, as I believed God wanted me to. The better care I took of myself, the more at peace I would feel, and certainly God must want that.

I stared blankly out the window at the gray day. My gaze turned to Sunny leaning against the wall. The bridal bouquet was still affixed to the front handlebar pack. The streamers were a little tangled but still bright. I got out of bed and ran my fingers through them. Yes, I wanted to continue. I would go on, but with more nurture and less torture. I would need to find ways to refresh myself to balance the inevitable hard parts. *So now what do I do?*

Contemplating this question, I dressed and stepped out into the day. The side street was quiet, the storefronts of faded wood and brick either boarded up or not yet open. The digital clock on the small bank read 8:00 a.m. and flashed the sobering temperature—thirty-two degrees. I walked across the street to a breakfast café, ordered a pancake and two poached eggs.

"I'm riding my bike to Portland," I told the waitress, trying to sound confident. "But these last couple of days have been unbearably cold." I must have had a dejected and pleading expression on my face, as though I were hoping she could warm things up for me, because she immediately replied:

"Oh, it would be much warmer on the coast." And then, as if God were inspiring a change of plans for me, she added, "You know, there's a rental car agency down the street. It opens at nine."

Something lit up inside me. The detour to the coast would take me west of my intended route, but...I had only a moment's flash of guilt that it would be "cheating" to take a car. I smiled broadly at the waitress and thanked her as I pulled out my map.

After breakfast I gathered all my gear and happily wheeled Sunny through the freezing air, down to the rental office. With great pleasure I loaded up a little white station wagon, turned the heat up high, and began a relaxed, warm, 138 mile drive northwest to Coos Bay on the Oregon coast.

8

TRUSTING

"What does a girl like you eat on a trip like this?"

"A lot!" I blurted out, feeling self-conscious and a bit giddy as I faced this unexpected attention from an attractive man. This was certainly the opposite of the man I'd fled from on my first day out. This one had a nice face and a gentle way about him. When he spoke to me, it felt genuine, playful, and not at all threatening.

It was 5:30 in the afternoon, and I was standing outside the local grocery store in one of the small towns that line the highway along the Columbia River Gorge. My time along the Oregon coast had been three days of beauty and relative warmth. After staying with friends in Portland for a few days, I'd arrived in Washington early this morning to begin the third week of my journey.

When I asked the clerk inside the grocery store if she could recommend a place to camp, she'd phoned the local police for suggestions. Evidently they said they wanted to welcome me in person. I was feeling in high spirits as Sunny and I waited for the police to arrive and tell us where we'd be camping that night. My spirit and body felt renewed, and I had a growing sense of confidence I could do this. I *am* doing this. *God and I are doing this.*

That's when an old beige jeep wagon had pulled into the parking space in front of me. That nice-looking, middle-aged guy had stepped out, given me and my loaded bike a curious look, and come over to ask me what I was doing. When I told him, he looked surprised and more than a little impressed. We'd chatted idly about routes, looked at my maps for a few minutes, and then he'd continued on into the store. I continued thinking about how well my new insights and understandings—about life, God, this journey—were working to make the trip more pleasant.

I'd left my friends in Portland that morning resolved to enjoy the journey as much as possible, and to be more at ease with whatever came along. I was determined to do more intentional wandering so as not to burn out on goal-oriented biking. I wanted to explore, to simply *be*, with eyes and ears wide open, like a child. I resolved not to look at the map so often—this journey was not about just getting from one place to the next in the least amount of time. At every moment I wanted to be aware of and feel connected to the road and all that was around me. I wanted to be out in the way of life at each given moment.

Realizing that God didn't want me to suffer had given me a new way of approaching my travels. It also meant taking better care of myself, maybe more in the way a loving mother cares for her child, or as God would take care of me as *His* child. So as not to be as much at the mercy of the wind, cold and rain, I'd purchased a dark blue pair of wool knee socks, a pair of warm-up leggings in brilliant purple, and my friend had donated her wool hat. Knowing I would still face cold weather, to give me courage and strength I'd bought a little book called *The Year Long Day* about a Norwegian man who spent a year alone in the Arctic. I hoped it would give me strength and courage to face less-than-Arctic cold weather.

My friends had driven me over the long bridge crossing the great Columbia River that forms the border between Oregon and Washington. They dropped me off on the two lane highway that passes through the beautiful Columbia River Gorge. Even in the drippy, misty morning rain I'd been excited to finally be alongside this mighty river flowing toward the Pacific. This highway was on the same trail Lewis & Clark had taken in their unsuccessful search for an all-water route from St. Louis, Missouri, to the Pacific Ocean. In August of 1804, President Thomas Jefferson had sent out the two captains and thirty explorers, hoping to open up trade between the Far East and the United States. Jefferson had instructed the two captains to keep extensive records of their observations and experiences. Historical markers based on those journals would inspire me at many points along my route over the next 600 miles.

Heading up the Columbia

As I toiled up and coasted down the hills overlooking the Columbia, I imagined the ragged and exhausted team of explorers in their canoes heading toward the completion of their historic 8,000 mile journey. I took inspiration from their efforts. Since I was traveling against the flow of the river, I thought also of the millions of salmon who struggle against the current, launching themselves up and over the many locks and dams on the Columbia so they can return to their birthplaces to spawn, and die.

Across the river on the Oregon side, a half mile away, I could see trucks roaring along the interstate. From a cyclist's point of view, I was on the right side—this Washington two lane road had a good two foot wide shoulder and little traffic. It was noticeably quiet as I wound through forests of pine, fir, maple and alder trees, all bright green with new spring growth. The Scotch broom was blooming bright yellow, and wild rhododendrons in red and purple filled the understory of the woods. Every leaf and needle dripped as the mist wrapped us all in a thin wet fog. Wooded mountains rose on either side of the gorge. Despite the cold and wet, I felt peaceful and content. I was proud of myself when I turned off the main road for a short time to explore the Bonneville Dam, fulfilling my resolve to slow down.

I'd stopped for tea in Stevenson at a cheerful café with a view across the gorge. From my window seat table, I watched grain barges drift slowly toward the Pacific, and huge container ships labor upstream from the major port of Astoria, Oregon. Small fishing boats and pleasure craft were scattered across the broad waterway.

After Stevenson I had about eighteen miles to go until my anticipated day's end. Riding at about the same elevation as the river, I caught a brisk tailwind out of the west. The ribbons of my bridal bouquet fluttered and streamed out in front of my pack, and when the sun managed to break through the gray, all the world glittered. It was icing on the cake, turning my inner peace into pure joy.

The low, strong growl of a big engine behind me broke into my serenity. I dropped to my low handlebars to be ready for the inevitable undertow of wind that accompanied the passing of a big truck. I checked my rear view mirror, a small dental mirror attached to my sunglasses. There was nothing on my left, yet the thunder of that engine was getting louder. I twisted around to double-check and, out of the corner of my eye to my great surprise and absolute delight, I saw a train advancing in my direction just a quarter mile behind. I hadn't noticed the railroad tracks hidden behind the guardrail just a few feet to my right. I *love* trains, and here was one I could almost touch! The road was throbbing. My heart was throbbing. As the huge engine loomed over my shoulder, I raised my left arm and made a repeated downward motion to inspire the engineer to blow his horn. I was beside myself with glee as the blare of the horn filled the air and he waved from the cab. I did my best to keep up with this great beast, and gradually was left behind with only my exhilaration.

The train was barely out of sight when I confronted something I'd never dealt with before as a cyclist. A tunnel loomed ahead. Not planning to do any night riding, I had no light or reflector on my bike, and there were no lights in the tunnel. How should I do this? Would cars entering behind me even see me? I thought I could make out a pale speck of light at the far end. I could see there was no sidewalk or shoulder. In spite of my trepidations I felt confident and ready to take it on as an exciting challenge rather than a dreaded passage.

I sucked in an enormous breath, as we did as kids in the car going through a tunnel, and prayed no cars would come. Then I was swallowed up in the darkness, deep inside the belly of the mountain. I pedaled as fast as I could, looking behind me, prepared to scrunch myself up tight to the rock wall if a car came. The light at the end grew brighter with each pedal turn. No cars yet. I burst out the other end with a huge gasp of relief and gratitude for my safe passage. The tunnel, I thought, was a useful lesson—for the rest of my journey, and for life. I had entered the unknown and gone forward with trust and determination.

As I waited on the curb for that promised patrol car, the man I'd talked with came back out of the store with a bag of groceries. I watched as he walked to the Jeep. He was forty-ish, medium build, muscular with a bit of a belly. Jeans, work boots, a light blue work shirt—casual, nice-looking. His thin black hair was combed back from a receding hairline. After he set his groceries in the car, he turned and walked back toward me.

"Would you like to have dinner with me?" he asked. "Nothing like a good meal to satisfy a big appetite." It was an appealing invitation, especially since my dinner was going to consist of some combination of bran muffins, banana fruitcake, cookies, dried fruit, and soy nuts that I had stuffed into my panniers that morning in Portland.

But much as I loved food, I wasn't about to jump too fast at a dinner invitation that might set me up for trouble. I was now in brand new territory and knew no one on the route east. Even though I was feeling more confident, I was totally dependent on God, and on my own judgment, to stay safe. I was learning to rely on my intuition, which more and more felt informed by God. I was learning to pay careful attention to its language, which most often came as a felt-sense in my heart and chest. Tightening or uneasiness meant "Beware!" Opening and relaxing indicated something positive and okay. *God, what do you think about my going out to dinner with this guy?* I didn't get a definite "No," and maybe I could feel a hint of opening, so I decided to go for it. After all, what could possibly happen in a public restaurant?

"Great," he said, pleased with my acceptance. "Where are you staying?"

"Someone mentioned a city park here, and I know from past experience those are usually good places to camp." With no cops yet in sight, I welcomed his directions to the local park. He said he'd pick me up there after I'd gotten set up.

As I coasted downhill to the park I thought about my evening with delight and anticipation. Food and company felt welcome at this point. When I got to the park, however, the glow I was feeling after my exciting day was somewhat tarnished by what I found there. It was adjacent to an abandoned lumberyard with a road dead-ending at the river. No houses or businesses around, and only one way out, gave me an uneasy, trapped feeling. I went ahead and set up my tent anyway, hid Sunny in the trees nearby, and sat down to wait for my "date."

As promised, Josh picked me up at six. I could see he'd gone home to shower and change out of dusty work clothes. He had a clean blue work shirt on, slacks, and loafers with no socks. I was surprised at how happy I felt to see him.

Before dinner he drove me around the valley to see the views of magical, magnificent Mt. Hood. Until Mt. Lassen a week earlier, I had never seen the great volcanoes. I was spellbound. Josh told me he had a trucking job at a local lumber company, and clearly he knew and loved the area. As he showed me the great mountain rising into the sky, brilliant with spring green and topped by a bright white peak, I felt like I'd fallen into a fairytale scene and I was the enchanted child.

We had dinner at a Chinese restaurant overlooking the river. Josh was curious about everything—where was I from, where was I going, how many miles a day did I ride, where did I stay at night. I enjoyed sharing my story with him, though I deliberately left out the part about how my trip was about finding God. For all I knew he might have felt about God the way my brothers did, which would be the end of a good dinner!

One of the first things Josh told me about himself was that he was an alcoholic and hadn't had a drink for twenty years. I had never met anyone who was involved with AA, and I was touched that he confided something so personal. It added to the sense of trust in him that I was feeling. As we continued talking, the comfort I felt with my new acquaintance increasingly highlighted the unease I was feeling about my park campsite. I finally decided to say something to Josh about it. I told him my concerns and asked if I could pitch my tent at his house for the night. He readily offered me his place—either a bed in a spare room or a tent site—and I gratefully accepted.

After dinner we picked up Sunny and my gear and loaded it into the back of the jeep. As we wound our way into the darkening hills above the Columbia, I began feeling a little nervous. No one knew where I was. This was many years before cell phones were invented, so I couldn't call a friend and say, "Hey, Pal, I'm on my way into the backcountry with this neat guy I've just met, and he's taking me to his house to spend the night. I'm somewhere across the Columbia from Mt. Hood. I just wanted you to know." Even if I'd had such a device, I don't think I would have used it. Maybe I was taking a risk, but I trusted my intuition. I was feeling open and relaxed. It was new for me to be living on such a fine edge—and I liked it. I leaned my head back against the headrest and watched the light fading on the river and the volcano, enjoying the warm car ride and the feeling of well-being.

But as the darkness descended further and we continued along lonely mountain roads, my mother's rule suddenly flashed through my mind like an alarm: "*Never* get in a car with a stranger!" *What am I doing? Maybe Mother was right. This is too risky. I'm entrusting myself to a man I've only met a few hours ago, and it's a little late to reconsider.* In the midst of battling with my mother's voice, I remembered the quote in my *Guide:* "You must begin to trust yourself sometime. I suggest you do it now." I took a deep inner breath. *Now's the time.* My body relaxed again as I pushed aside my mother's voice and settled on following my own intuition.

When we finally arrived at Josh's house, ten winding miles later, my fears dissolved as we were greeted by a black dog, a spotted dog, and a black cat, all tails waving and wagging with pleasure to see their beloved master home. It was a good sign, and I was all smiles and calm inside as I bent to greet the furry trio. It felt so good to leave my mother's fears farther and farther behind me.

Josh put a pot of water on to boil and then showed me around a house still under construction. "I'm the contractor and builder," he explained, "and as you see, I've got a little ways to go." We passed through the kitchen with an open stud wall to the living room and into the garage full of tools and boxes. "I figure it might take a while." His voice sounded resigned—maybe a little apologetic—but determined. Returning to the kitchen he brewed a pot of black coffee for himself, and some tea for me. We settled into what passed for a living room with its concrete floor and open stud walls. He relaxed into a well-used recliner; I curled into an old stuffed chair that looked like it had come from the thrift store. The dogs lay about on a couple of tattered rugs. The cat nestled into his lap.

We were both surprised at how easily we connected. I appreciated how carefully he listened to me, and we stayed up till midnight, talking like old friends. We both had suffered the nightmare of addiction, and we were relieved to share this with another person who understood the struggles so well. It was comforting to admit to each other how powerless we were in the face of our respective substances. We were both trying to let a Higher Power, God, direct us more in our lives. I was happy that I could now reveal to him that God inspired my trip, though I didn't say that this journey was also about trying to find Him.

Josh told me how his alcoholism had pretty much doomed his marriage. He had a grown daughter with whom he had a strained relationship. He still attended AA meetings. He had managed to get enough money together to buy the few acres we were sitting on, and he added to this house as he could. He'd lived in the region all his life, and worked at the same mill since he was a teenager. I got the feeling he was well-known and liked in this small, tightly knit community. He said he didn't do much socializing because he was either working at the mill or on his house.

I shared with him my own painful divorce story and how I had fallen in love with another man. I didn't say too much about Paul, only that I wasn't sure if we still were, or should be, a couple.

I was still so conflicted about Paul and who he was meant to be in my life. The contrast between our heavenly sexual and spiritual life and our day-to-day connection pulled me in two directions—between heaven and earth, spirit and matter, divinity and humanity. The realm of Light had so often felt higher and better than being stuck on earth, grappling with day-to-day issues. But by this time, I knew I wanted to be human and live on earth. I'd made that clear choice in that apricot-walled room, and now the task of reconciling the two apparently opposing realms lay before me.

Meanwhile, here I was in an incredibly beautiful place, having a fulfilling, personal conversation with a stranger. *This is the way it should be. Maybe this is heaven on earth.*

The long, easy evening with Josh removed my last reservations about him, and I made up the overly springy bed he'd offered across the concrete-floor hall from his bedroom.

"Goodnight, friend," he called after the lights were turned off.

"Goodnight," I replied, wide-awake.

I could scarcely sleep for the live, excited energy cooking within me, the butterflies, the wonder and gratitude that stirred my entire being. I was alone in a secluded house, with no neighbors in sight, with a strange man, and not a soul knew where I was. I had never felt so alive. I kept saying to myself, *God maketh my way perfect....*

I got up after a few hours' sleep and tiptoed out of the quiet house and into the countryside. I walked briskly in the cold dawn along a gravel road that wound among meadows and sleeping farms. I was in a state of incredible peace, and when I rounded a bend and walked into a view of Mt. Adams, another volcano in the Cascade Range, I thought I'd died and gone to heaven. The spectacle of this flat-topped pyramid mountain soaring 12,000 feet into the sky stunned me. Like Mt. Hood it wore a bright green base to its upper third, which was cloaked in brilliant snow. It loomed over the valley like a lord surveying his vast domain. The mountain seemed to exist in an entirely different world, and its power drew me into its magical realm. I couldn't imagine getting on Sunny and leaving this all behind today.

When I returned from my dreamy walk I told Josh that I had the idea of spending a couple of days with him.

"Would that be okay?" I asked hopefully. "I mean, I don't want to interfere with your plans." He beamed and said, "That sounds good to me." It was the Sunday of Memorial Day Weekend, a free day for Josh. After breakfast and tending the animals, we set off in his jeep for a tour of the region.

I was as thrilled by the views as I was thrilled by what was going on inside me. The sense of kinship, and oneness I felt with this man amazed me. My physical body was beginning to stir like a cat waking up from a nap. But Paul...even though I'd told him my deep sense that we were not meant to be together as a couple, I was still deeply bonded to him. Our sexual connection surpassed the physical; it had been a part of my spiritual awakening. Could I give myself now to another man? I also felt that the act of making love creates a mysterious bond between people, and I wanted to be very sure I would not regret such a connection with Josh. Yet I knew I needed and wanted to take further steps to let go of Paul. Opening up to Josh would be a huge leap in that direction. I knew I would be bonded to Paul all my life, but I did not want to be bound to him. I turned my attention back to the moment, trusting that the answers to these questions would be revealed, if I just continued trusting—myself, God, the enchanted world around me.

Sitting next to this kind and gentle man, I passed the next magical hours winding slowly along snaky roads through tiny villages in the forest, and driving idly along the great Columbia. I loved how spacious the region felt as we passed from dense forest into lush, green meadows, and then along the borders of newly planted crop fields, young vineyards, and brightly blooming orchards. Josh drove me all over Klickitat County—the name sounded like a train and I loved repeating it in my mind. Over the magnificent volcanoes of the Columbia River Valley, the Washington sky was a sparkling clear blue. It all looked a lot like heaven to me, and I sank into the peace and sense of enchantment I felt right where I was—on earth.

Josh and I stopped at an overlook and watched the wind surfers under colorful sails whizzing along the white-capped Columbia. My pleasure in his company and attraction to him had grown stronger as the day went by. As we stood side by side, lightly touching, enchanted by the view, I released myself in trust to this magical world. As if responding at once to the same call, we turned toward each other, and gently kissed.

9
THE BRIDGE

Filled with gratitude and love, I swung my leg over my bike and rolled into a warm, gentle day, headed east up the Columbia River. Mt. Hood looked over my right shoulder as I easily biked along the two lane road bordering the train tracks. The Columbia River was about a quarter mile to my right. Meadows and scattered pines sloped gently upward on my left. I pedaled along in a dreamy state of well-being.

I'd awakened that morning at 4:00 next to Josh's warm body. After our holiday weekend together, he said he felt ten years younger, and I was deeply happy being with him. While we knew we were not potential mates, we'd thoroughly enjoyed our sweet, very human connection. My peace of mind and heart affirmed the rightness of taking this inevitable step beyond Paul

In the early morning quiet, we'd driven down the mountain to the mill where Josh worked. The yard was bustling after the long weekend—guys in yellow hard hats and overalls were moving briskly about, trucks lined up, waiting to get out onto the road. We picked up his old Peterbilt and joined the line. I was beside myself with excitement as the massive truck roared out onto the highway and up into the National Forest. I felt filled with the earth-shaking power of this lumber truck, and thrilled that I was actually there, mounted on this thunderous, growling beast.

When we arrived at the logging site, I was relieved to know that Josh's lumber company engaged in selective logging so I didn't have to watch a patch of earth being scalped as a clear-cut. Josh introduced me to his crew, who were impressed—and not quite convinced—that I was bicycling to Wyoming. After a little guy-talk, some knowing smiles and playful elbows in the ribs, Josh began his work of artful log loading. He backed his long trailer into the clearing of felled logs, and then climbed into a control chair on the crane above the trailer. He picked up each log as though it were a fine pen and placed it carefully onto the trailer. When it was stacked high with logs, we'd headed back to the mill to unload. I'd felt even more appreciative of Josh as I watched him slow the truck to make sure the birds in the road made it across safely.

We'd bid a sweet goodbye on the road outside the mill. Letting go of being in such a beautiful place with such a wonderful person and his animal family was hard. Knowing it was the nature of my journey didn't make it any easier. But I felt very blessed to have been with such a good human being and to have seen the world through his eyes.

As I continued farther east I frequently looked over my right shoulder to gaze at Mt. Hood as the majestic volcano slowly receded in the distance. I had followed my intuition rather than my mother's fears. I had enjoyed myself, and it was not only okay, but I now knew I had the power to choose to make good things happen. I was learning how to free myself in so many ways. That included knowing that I didn't have to stay on any schedule, or make a certain number of miles per day. I only had to slow for birds.

I'd been so lost in my reflection that I'd scarcely noticed the weather. Within twenty miles of leaving Josh, the day had turned hot, *very* hot. I was suddenly in the treeless country of eastern Washington. Mt. Hood was barely visible now through the haze of heat and dust. I had not realized how protected I'd felt riding through the lush forests of northern Oregon and western Washington. This barren landscape made me feel very vulnerable and exposed. The little seeds of sadness I felt at leaving the magic of Josh and the volcanoes began to sprout along with little seeds of doubt about changing my relationship with Paul—and maybe to God. Suddenly they were growing into some kind of tangled vines inside me. My appetite for vigorous biking decreased, and yet I pedaled hard, as if to escape something. I started drinking large quantities of water. Sweat dried as quickly as it appeared on my skin. I could feel a rising sense of panic, a panic I had known once before.

It was on the ninth day of the bicycling journey across the U.S. Carol and I had left the cool of the Sierra and headed east toward Death Valley. We soon found out that our destination wasn't called "Furnace Creek" for nothing. When the road turned away from the mountains, it was like stepping from a refrigerator into a 400 degree oven. The land was devoid of any trees. Low, twiggy plants and sparse grasses dotted the rocky ground. The deserted road wound between low embankments and hills. Huge rocks gave way to vast expanses of dull, hot sand. The black asphalt steamed; the white center line glared; the sand and dirt on the roadside radiated heat like coils in a toaster oven; the sun glowered. A fierce headwind took all the heat and blasted it toward us like a wind tunnel.

"What is to give light must endure burning." There in this blazing, hot California desert, a quote from philosopher Victor Frankl had suddenly come to mind. I felt I was burning in hell. My heart was beating fast, my chest and throat were constricting, and I was pedaling furiously for no reason. It was a shock to realize how frightened I was of actually dying right then and there—collapsing and frying mid-stroke. I'd never met Death before, and I was terrified. If I pedaled fast enough maybe I could outrun it. I started to cry. I squinched my eyes nearly shut against the heat, tears, wind and the fear, but I knew that was a hopeless defense. Carol was quite far ahead of me and I felt very much alone on the road, like a single biscuit in a vast oven. I didn't want to lose track of her, but I had to stop—I couldn't cry and ride at the same time. In the roasting heat on the side of the road, sobs and fear shook me to the core.

After the tears and terror were mostly spent, I took stock. I was still alive, still breathing, still physically able to carry on. I had water. Perspiration was cooling my skin in spite of the heat. I could still use my mind. *I'm okay. Carol will come looking for me if I don't show up. I'll be okay. I can go on.* I had no control over Death's wishes for me, so I had to let go and surrender to whatever my fate was. As the panic subsided, I began to look at the desert around me. Now it looked different. I was able to see the delicate colors of the sand, the rich colors and intriguing shapes of the rocks, the alluring openness of the vast space, and the stillness. I stepped back into the pedals and moved slowly onwards into the blistering heat and headwind. Carol was not far ahead, waiting for me.

Now in eastern Washington, remembering that panic near Death Valley, I knew what I had to do. I slowed my cadence and my escalating emotions. I stopped frequently to look at and feel the hot, dusty earth around me, touching it instead of running from it. I stopped whenever I found a shade tree. I stopped at historical markers telling about the Lewis and Clark expedition. I stopped at roadside ditch creeks to splash water on my face and arms and neck. I settled my body and mind into the hot day's ride.

Although I grew more at ease with the outer landscape, the dry and bleak country in my heart remained. I missed Paul. I had taken a necessary step to let go of him, but it was hard and made me sad. I wanted so much for our relationship to work out, but clearly it wasn't. We'd tried over and over. Maybe the way I sank with him in his low times were too reminiscent of the life-suppressing effect my mother had on me. These periods triggered old fears and feelings of helplessness. When I was alone, I gained confidence in myself, my actions, my decisions. In our relationship I somehow wasn't able to hold onto that strength. The worst part was not talking about any of this. I had to let go. Being apart from him would be the only way for me to grow as I needed and wanted to. But the thought of breaking my ties to him was like ripping stuck tape off my heart.

As the day became hotter and the eastern Washington terrain grew bleaker, I sank into a dull hollowness. Riding slowly into the late afternoon, I felt alone and lonely, cut off from those I loved and cut off from the recent empowering sense of my ability to enjoy myself. I knew talking to God would help.

Please help me get me through this darkness. My loneliness was now making me worry about where I was going to spend the night. *Please help me find a safe place tonight.* And I continued pedaling and praying.

Both prayers were answered. By the end of the day I arrived at the big road sign announcing Marysville State Park. My relief at the promise of a safe place to camp was tempered by realizing that the road to the park dropped down 1,000 feet, which I would have to regain in the morning. Grumbling about that inevitability, I sped down the grade with only half the usual downhill rush.

The facilities were arranged on a wide, flat bed along the Columbia. I pitched my tent on a scruffy patch of grass amidst a sparse group of young trees. The area felt very calm, and it had two amenities that were just what I needed—a shower and a pay phone. I called Josh. "Honey," he said enthusiastically, "we've put up a map at the office and we're tracking your journey." He added I'd been helping him even without my knowing. I wasn't exactly sure what he meant, but hearing his upbeat voice and knowing I was still connected to him boosted my spirits.

The wind picked up before dawn, and by the time I was ready to leave at 6:00, it was gale-force. From where I was camped in the hollow at the river, I couldn't tell for sure which direction it was blowing. Of course I hoped it would be out of the west and give me a tailwind. I packed and hauled myself the 1,000 feet back up to the bluff. On the main road, I was hit by unpredictable and vicious gusts that whipped Sunny and me all over the road. On the exposed downgrade near John Day Dam, I had to stop several times, leaning thirty degrees into the wind just to stay upright. Sometimes Sunny and I just sat down by the road and waited until the blast let up a little and it was safe to proceed.

After about twenty more miles of wild turbulence, the chaotic gusts settled down to a consistent blast pushing me from behind. Alleluia! I blew into tiny Roosevelt, Washington, (population seventy-nine) at 10:30, having already covered thirty-two miles. Even though I was less rigid about calculating miles, I still had a daily plan, and this was half my usual goal for a day.

The café in Roosevelt was one of only a few simple wooden buildings on the left side of the road. We were inland from the Columbia about a half mile; the area was still desert-like with sparse vegetation of sage and twiggy shrubs. Over breakfast of two poached eggs, crustless toast, walnut pie a la mode, and the usual multiple pots of tea, I thought about how to approach the rest of the day. Umatilla, the next habitation, was fifty miles east. I'd be continuing along the Columbia until the Umatilla Bridge, which would take me over the wide river to the Oregon side. My route to Umatilla would be a flat and well-paved road for a smooth ride. Most of the traffic and trucks would all be on the interstate across the river. It seemed too far and too goal-oriented to aim to make those fifty miles, but outside as I straddled my bike, braced myself on the handlebars against the gale coming from behind me, my decision was easy.

I clocked the next twenty miles in one hour! I was barely pedaling, more like flying! It was amazing and exhilarating to be traveling at such a speed with a loaded bike. In that intense wind, it was actually safer and easier to be on the bike than on foot. When I paused to study my map, I barely managed to stay upright. I quickly decided to let the wind determine my day's ride.

After gobbling up another seven miles in twenty minutes I knew I would easily make it to Umatilla, so I decided to stop for a look around. Even though I could see the river through the trees and bushes lining the banks, I wanted to get a better view. I pulled over, climbed up a bank, and nestled into the sandy dirt, amongst the sage, tall grasses, wildflowers, and rocks. In the sudden peace of being out of the wind, I watched the white-capped Columbia, sand-colored and wide, flowing westward. In either direction the pinstriped road along my side of the riverbank stretched as far as the eye could see with only the rare car whizzing by. It was a dramatic scene: a great river, a mighty wind, an endless and vast view, and a train running through it. And I was there in the midst of it, having successfully managed the wild wind to bring my loaded bike so far so fast. I was filled with gratitude and joy. The sadness and emptiness of yesterday seemed to have blown away with the wind. In their place was a sense of power and celebration of life.

Back on Sunny, I continued to blow east as swiftly as if I'd raised a sail. It made me think of the movie *Chariots of Fire*, in which the hero, running fast along a beach, says he can feel God's pleasure when he runs. I was feeling God's pleasure, not only in my swift cycling but also in my joy of being just where I was.

Seven miles before Umatilla, I stopped again; I was in no hurry now for the day to end. Dirt blowing off the new-plowed fields that lined the river here filled the air with dust. I lay Sunny down and climbed a low bank to the edge of one of the fields. The grass I was nested in blew and gusted with each snort of the wind. Each head of grain, each blade of oat and wheat was alive, shaking and nodding and tossing red and gold heads around me. I started laughing. They seemed so happy. *I* was so happy. "It's a new day!" I exclaimed joyfully to the grass. "Yipee! Come get me!" I yelled to the wind. I turned my face full into the blast of its force, savoring its power, opening myself up to it, absorbing it through my pores, nostrils, and mouth.

Feeling ready to take on anything, I climbed aboard Sunny again and set sail for Umatilla. After a few miles the road took a sharp turn, and suddenly my helpful tailwind was a ferocious crosswind. I had to struggle to keep from being blown into the center of the road. When an 18-wheeler came roaring by—the only truck all day—I hugged the edge of the road but the force of the wind combined with the suction of the huge rig's speed and mass nearly pulled me under the wheels. Roaring past, it left my heart beating hard as I anxiously pedaled on. Oh, I was such a tiny object, utterly exposed to huge forces outside me!

When the mile-long bridge over the Columbia into Umatilla came into sight, I slowed and approached cautiously to check out what lay ahead. The road led directly onto the span, with only a narrow half-sidewalk crossing the bridge on my side. Across the two lane road, the sidewalk on the other side was normal width. I looked at the river below tossing with frothy waves. The air was thick with churned dust. The few trees I could see among some buildings on the opposite shore were bent low by the force of the wind. I decided I'd be safer crossing that long span in such a wind if I had a little extra sidewalk width separating me from the traffic. When there was a break in the swiftly moving cars and trucks, I wheeled my bike as fast as I could across the road and walked along the edge until I could hoist Sunny up onto the sidewalk.

Once I was on the bridge, the wind was even more intense, but I still felt confident about my chosen route. The traffic on my side was moving in the opposite direction, northward, and the big trucks rushing by scarcely two feet away created such turbulence that, between the force of the wind and those erratic gusts of suction, I thought Sunny was bound to go down, either under the green pipe guardrails between me and the river or into the road.

As I pushed onward, Sunny grew heavier in the open crosswind, wobbling so badly that I could move only a couple of feet before a gust would slam me into the green pipes. They were the only things separating me from the river fifty feet below. My left hip and arm began aching from continually banging into them. The wind would hold me there fast until either the velocity decreased a little or I could renew my strength. I was astonished that the force of the wind could pin me, like a heavyweight wrestler, against the bridge railing. The streamers on my bridal bouquet were blowing horizontally east. The din of the wind and traffic was filling my head like the static on a radio with the volume turned full up. I felt as vulnerable as a balloon on a car speeding down the road at sixty miles per hour, which I later learned was the wind speed that afternoon.

As I continued onwards though, I realized I was actually enjoying myself in an odd way. I was on a cyclist's version of a high seas adventure—roiling, white-capped water all around me, the howling wind pinning me to the railing of the ship's bow, glinting waves of steel trucks and cars washing over the deck. When a couple of drivers slowed down to offer me help, I waved them off. I wanted to go on. I wanted to meet the challenge of reaching the far side. And I was awed and captivated by this stunning force. I wanted to stay in the presence of what I felt was a taste of the all-powerful force of God.

But by the time I reached the halfway point on the bridge, the wind was so relentless and fierce that I was totally nailed to the green pipe rails and unable to move. A red pickup slowed down as he came toward me, and a young man inside yelled through the open passenger window, "Do you need help?" Holding onto Sunny for dear life, I shouted back, "Yes! Help!" and nodded emphatically. With a circular wave of his arm, he indicated he'd turn around and come back. I began to unload Sunny so we could easily throw everything into the back of his truck. But as I started to set my packs down onto the sidewalk, I realized that I had to hold on to each one to keep it from blowing under the railing into the Columbia. Then the red pickup was back; it stopped across from me in the southbound lane. The young man jumped out of the truck and began waving his arms above his head to halt the northbound traffic. He ran over, grabbed my bike, I grabbed my gear, and we dashed across the road, heaving everything into the bed of the truck and jumping safely inside the cab, all in less than a minute. "Where do you want to go?" he asked, stepping on the gas and waving to the stopped traffic in thanks. "Someplace nice," I panted, exhausted and scarcely able to think.

My "savior" delivered me to a luxurious motel with golf course, Laundromat, and room service, and bid me a polite goodbye. As I checked in I realized how lucky I was. He could have taken me *anywhere*. I shuddered to think about what *could* have happened. I ordered a glass of wine and some buffalo wings from room service, sat down in a comfy chair, and watched the wind raging outside the sliding glass door of my room. My arms felt weak, and I was banged up, but my spirits were soaring. I had met far more than my match. I had set across the bridge feeling strong in my own power, and wanting to test it. I'd gotten as far as I could on my own steam before yelling for help. I had not played the role of the "damsel in distress" that my mother, my background, my culture might have expected of me. I wasn't powerless. And when I needed help, it had come, and I'd accepted—God had sent a safe person who'd kindly delivered me to this lovely refuge.

As I sat, feeling with equal pleasure my sore muscles and the warm glow of the wine in my body, I thanked God over and over. I had experienced the power of a great natural force to the depths of my being.

My determination and will to succeed had shown themselves, but so had a good dose of common sense and humility. I felt so alive. Whatever tests and difficult circumstances I might encounter in the days and weeks and miles ahead, I now had more trust in my intuition, more confidence that I could handle Sunny in tricky and unusual situations, and more of a sense of balance and resilience.

Sunny and the Columbia

It was cool and sunny when I set out the next day. White lamb clouds dotted the wide-open blue sky. Sandstone cliffs loomed high to my right. This quiet highway along the river was lined with waving sage, grasses and wildflowers. A steady tailwind was blowing, but nothing like the gale of the day before. After twenty miles the river turned north, and the road continued east. I was sorry to leave the Columbia; it had been an animating and powerful companion. Before we parted, I stopped, parked Sunny against a guardrail, and went down to sit on its banks for a last visit.

As I gazed out over the water, thoughts and images from my past eight years of searching drifted through my mind. The path to find my way out of the food addiction had led me to look more deeply and carefully into everything. First I had looked at what was around me: how the United States was run politically and economically; what the culture was teaching me as a woman and how our society was based on "every man for himself" competition; what the negative human impact was on the health of our planet, and how our choices could effect change. Then I had begun to look within myself—at my family, my beliefs and expectations, my patterns, my interior wounds. With therapy and my own self-investigation, I had understood and resolved some troubling issues, but I had still felt a lack of something essential in my life. Even before my dream of God stirred the sense of a deeper search, I knew something was missing. I didn't know exactly what I was looking for or what "personal growth" was all about, but I knew the stakes were extremely high, and I had to do the digging to find this "something," or die.

I remembered the moment when the understanding really struck me that I couldn't fill the empty space inside or my deepest desire with "something" I could buy or acquire, with an object I could hold or drive or wear or look at. All my life I'd had the best of material things, and I did appreciate fine objects, things well-made with craft and beauty. When I married, my husband and I lived more modestly than my family had, but I always had nice clothes, some beautiful jewelry, and we had some fine art, good tools, and nice cars. Because I had studied and played piano all my life, we had gotten an upright, which I played for some years before wanting to advance to a baby grand. When the six-foot, shining ebony-black Baldwin was moved into the house, I felt I'd reached some sort of pinnacle, because for my level of ability and ambition it was the perfect piano. I was thrilled and satisfied with this beautiful instrument. But one day, not long after it came, I realized that the Baldwin was not "It." That piano would not bring me peace or happiness or fill the illusive need inside that I was already feeling. It was not going to fill a void or bring deep lasting satisfaction.

While gazing at the Columbia, I thought with considerable anger and sadness about how our culture leads us to cling to the hope and promise that our profound inner needs will be filled by how we look and smell, what we eat and drink, what we drive, where we live, how much money, information, and skill we have.

That disappointing realization of the piano not being It had compelled me to keep searching to fill that vague but haunting need inside me. It was disturbing that even though I had more than enough material possessions to use and enjoy, I still felt somehow poor. I could not define what my hunger was for, but at that pivotal moment I had known for sure that "stuff" would not satisfy it, and soon after I would be learning that neither could the hole inside be filled with food.

I had eventually come to know beyond a shadow of a doubt that it was God I was looking for, that God was It. As I followed my heart in search of Him, I'd gotten completely caught up in an unfolding mystery that was exciting, and scary. I had no idea where I would be led, what was around the next bend, or what God would ask of me. Nor did I know if I would find Him. But I did see that the more I discovered about myself, the closer I felt to God and to a deep source of inner strength and wisdom that I'd seen could carry me through emotional turmoil and physical challenges.

The sense of my own power—*and* powerlessness—that I had felt the previous day on the Umatilla Bridge had carried me deeper into myself. I was still amazed that I felt equally good about these two opposite states and how they seemed to merge into a harmonious whole. And the past three days had shown me that I could trust myself. My loving connection with Josh had proven it. I could also trust God. I knew He was guiding me, leading me, protecting me. I could count numerous times in the last 1,100 miles over the three weeks on the road when I could have been injured or killed or emotionally traumatized, but I hadn't been. In fact, the opposite was true.

I felt overwhelmed with gratitude and saturated with beauty and goodness, inside and out. Like a balloon released from some deep and mysterious place, the words arose within me: *How beautiful is Thy Name!* This spontaneous, resounding praise for God burst forth—from my soul that was full of gratitude for the things I had discovered in myself over the past years, for the great adventure of the last few days, and for the gifts I was receiving from God. *Praise the Lord!* I was creating my life and seeing things from a deep, more authentic place in myself, a place I felt was intimately connected to my soul—or perhaps *was* my soul. As I sat on the Columbia's bank, I thought back to when I first awakened to my soul, or it awakened in me. That day I was walking behind Paul at the beach. I'd felt my soul was closely connected to the divine, perhaps the place where God lived in a human being. As time and miles passed, I'd become more convinced of this. Now my soul was not only awake, it was active and participating in my daily life, bringing me a new awareness of myself and of God.

With a final farewell, I left the Columbia behind and started the climb into the agricultural region around Walla Walla, Washington. All was beautifully green, with acres of green wheat and green peas and more green wheat stretching to the green horizon. As I cycled up and down long, gentle grades, I enjoyed imagining myself living in one of the tidy farmhouses, though I knew it was not my kind of country—too tame, domesticated, and orderly.

When I eventually climbed out of the lowlands to the crest of the valley, there in the far distance were the tips of the mountains of Idaho and Montana. My spirit reached out to them, as though I were reaching for the most delectable peach on the very top branch of a tree, or for a star I might actually grasp. I *love* mountains. They are wild, rugged, and unpopulated. Mountain weather is often rough and wild, with thunder, lightning, hailstorms, and high winds. Reaching the top of a mountain can be hard, exhausting work, but the rewards are immeasurable. There I can see infinitely. I can fly with the hawks and eagles, seeing everything. On top of high mountains, my feet are on the ground, but my head and my spirit are in the stars. In those places where people go to pray, to contemplate, to be inspired, one might meet God Himself.

My heart raced as I continued on toward that little speck of snowy starlight on the far horizon. The mountains were calling to me as much as I was calling to them. "I'm coming," I whispered, and pedaled faster.

10
THE WILL TO LIVE

The last three days, after the struggle and triumph of the Umatilla Bridge, had been 147 miles of relatively easy riding through the farm country and rolling Blue Mountains of eastern Washington. At sunset on Day 26 I pedaled easily into Clarkston, Idaho, named after Captain William Clark of the Lewis and Clark expedition. This town, where the Clearwater River flows into the Snake River, marked a significant turning point for that "Corps of Discovery." After a year and a half and over a thousand miles of paddling upstream, walking, scrambling and portaging heavy boats overland, they would at last travel downstream on the Snake to the Columbia and finally to the Pacific Ocean.

Reaching this point must have marked a triumph for them in yet another way—they had survived the Bitterroot Mountains. One of the men in the expedition had written in his journal that they were "the most terrible mountains I ever beheld." Frequently lost in snow and freezing temperatures, the party had to eat some of their own horses to keep from starving. Was I too heading toward a big challenge? Kamiah—sixty-six miles away and my destination for the following night—would be my last stop before entering the Bitterroots. Maybe my easy-going days were about to end, again. But I didn't want to think about it. I pedaled onward, past Clarkston, and arrived—not surprisingly—at Lewiston, named after Captain Meriwether Lewis. The biggest challenge I faced there was a noisy night at the Pony Soldier Motel, where the local Little League team was celebrating a victory.

The next day a cold drizzle settled in as I pedaled "upstream" along the Clearwater. Water dripped off my bright yellow rain hat, blew into my face, and proceeded on down onto my yellow rain jacket. In a futile attempt to stay warm, I hunched over the handlebars and pedaled as vigorously as I could. Route 12 was a narrow two lane road with no shoulder, and it was the only way through this part of Idaho. On my left, mist shrouded the river, and I could barely make out the wooded bank on its far side, fifty yards away. The westbound lane ran smack up against a three foot high concrete barrier. Beyond that a short steep bank dropped down to the gray river below. On my side, a shallow ditch about two feet wide separated Sunny and me from the base of the steeply rising mountain. Clearly this road had barely been squeezed into the only available passage between the river and the mountain—suitable maybe for horses and mules but hardly for a two lane highway, let alone one that was the major route for 18-wheeler wheat trucks hauling grain across Idaho from Montana to Washington.

My first encounter with these beasts had been a few days earlier as I left Walla Walla. The two lane road there had been wide with a good shoulder on both sides. I'd been daydreaming about the mountains ahead when I saw two wheat trucks were headed my way, side by side, completely filling the road as one tried to pass the other. I'd pulled Sunny as far as I could onto the wide, gravelly shoulder. Only a couple of feet away, the trucks roared past me, going about sixty miles an hour, pulling and sucking on Sunny and me as though we were nothing more than another bunch of spindly grass at the side of the road. I'd been left quivering in their wake inside and outside.

This part of Route 12 had been relatively quiet with no trucks at all. I had just three miles to go before Kamiah, Idaho, and a chance to get out of the rain. I was trusting that God would find a nice place for us to stay. I was so near the end of my day that it didn't bother me much when I saw a westbound, navy blue wheat truck growling toward me. It was about 200 yards—two football fields—away. I'd been riding about a foot into my lane to avoid slipping into the roadside ditch. As long as that 18-wheeler and I stayed in our respective lanes, everything would be okay. But I dropped to my low handlebar position just in case I had to hit my brakes.

Just then, a light blue pickup truck in a bid to pass pulled out from behind the wheat truck and into my lane. My breath froze. *Shit! Does he see me?* I kept pedaling. *He can't miss seeing my bright yellow rain gear!* Two seconds later the pickup abruptly fell back behind the wheat truck. I let my breath out in a silent prayer of thanks.

But before I could draw in another breath, another wheat truck suddenly pulled out from behind the pickup, bearing down to pass both the pickup *and* the first wheat truck, which was now about 100 yards away. I could scarcely believe what I was seeing, and what it meant. It was too late now for No. 2 Wheat Truck to retreat or to stop before he hit me. I'd already learned on my bike trip with Carol that 18-wheelers require a minimum of a quarter mile to stop. The die was cast. A whole universe of consequences had been set in motion, like a great boulder pushed over the edge of a cliff. In this scene there were three great boulders, and I was at the base of the cliff watching them coming toward me.

My bowels shifted and my chest constricted. My stomach birthed a tangle of snakes. Everything turned icy cold, and I found myself wondering what it would be like to get hit by forty tons of steel. I pictured a bug splattered on a windshield. In that instant I felt the familiar monumental conflict inside me—the urge to give up, to not try, to abandon all hope. All those years of therapy and inner work to get the upper hand over dark forces seemed to have drained out of me. That lifelong pattern of not fighting back felt like a tidal wave rising within. And within that wave was a desire to let my life go altogether, to check out of the struggles of life, to be relieved of any further great effort or pain or disappointment.

Like survivors in a small life raft tossing on that monster wave, the smaller and weaker forces urging me to survive, to live and carry on, struggled to be heard. It was a replay of my first day on the road, as I had glided toward a dangerous end. It was David vs. Goliath unfolding within me as the three trucks and I all moved inexorably toward each other. By the time No. 2 Navy Blue and the first wheat truck were parallel, about fifty feet away from me, there was little in my mind at all.

And then, in an empty moment, as though moved by an invisible force, I turned Sunny hard right and dove toward the ditch. We rammed into the dirt cliffside, Sunny's front wheel cocked at a ninety degree angle. Straddling the bike, I draped my body over the handlebars and front wheel, pressed as close to the muddy wall as I could, and squinched my eyes closed hard. I suspected that part of my rear wheel still had to be on the pavement, but there was nowhere else to go. I was either going to be hit or not. I held my breath, waiting for the blast to Sunny's rear end and to my own body. Then I felt the wind and the roar and the shaking ground as though a freight train were on top of me. The air whirled with water, dirt and road grit. I felt like I was ducking directly under that tidal wave as it broke and crashed around me. I couldn't breathe. The turbulence lasted however long it takes a seventy-foot-long 18-wheeler to pass a huddled-up, petrified person in a roadside ditch, but it felt like forever. When "forever" ended, I peered behind me at the road. The three trucks were in chaos fifty feet beyond me, swerving and spewing watery gravel as they jockeyed to get back into the lane where they belonged. I don't know who ended up first in line.

Every part of me was shaking as I dismounted, straightened Sunny out and laid him down in the muddy ditch, and wobbled across the road. I sat on the concrete barrier facing the river below. Except for the soft noise of the flowing water and falling rain, the world around me was utterly quiet and still. No cars or trucks sloshed by. It was as if everything was holding its breath. I sat in the light rain, staring at the river, trying to come to terms with what had just happened. If I'd been heading westbound and the trucks eastbound, I would have been smashed into this concrete barrier, thrown over it and into the river, carried downstream back toward Lewiston.

It was terrifying to realize how close I'd come to dying, and perhaps even more frightening to see how close I'd come to *letting* myself die, even *wanting* to die. Yet my life had been spared. Had I chosen Life, or had Life chosen me? Had I consciously decided to try to avoid death, or had God put a hand on my front wheel and turned it at the last moment? The longer I sat with these questions the wetter and colder and more immobile I became. It was as though the full dose and force of fear I'd experienced, in the last thirty...ten... four seconds before the moment of anticipated impact, was still paralyzing any movement. Finally I forced myself to get up and walk back across the road. I inspected Sunny for damage. He looked awful—spattered with mud and grime, and everything soaking wet—but the gears and brakes still worked. I managed to mount and continued slowly on toward Kamiah.

The remaining three miles felt more like thirty. I stumbled into the first motel I saw. After checking in I went straight across the street to a convenience store and bought a beer. I don't like beer. I don't like the smell. I don't much like the taste or the fizz, and I don't like the picture beer brings up for me—macho guys hanging around together, with half-drunk six packs littered among them, making sexist jokes and smelling of beer belches. But this Coors Lite was oddly satisfying, and it finally stopped the inner shaking. I didn't have the energy to leave my room to look for dinner. I didn't even have the desire to sit outside for an evening smoke to let some of the tension and fear and adrenalin dissipate in a wispy plume. I wanted only to stay in the safety of my nest. I snacked on trail mix and went to bed feeling mentally and emotionally numb.

"Hope you have a nice trip," the breakfast waitress called to a local as he headed out to his pickup truck. It was seven o'clock at the local café. I was feeling depressed and worried about the route ahead. The image of three trucks bearing down on me was still haunting and unnerving.

"I hope to, as long as the trucks don't run me off the road," he called back to her. God, I thought, if *he's* scared of the trucks and he's in a pickup, how bad is this for *me!*

"Remember," she added with an encouraging smile, "rain is liquid sunshine."

I looked out the café window at the "liquid sunshine" pouring down. A couple of wheat trucks sloshed by, lumbering slowly through the speed zone like lazy bears, then turning into raging bulls as they hit the open highway. I gloomily mulled over my strategy for riding through the upcoming Selway-Bitterroot Wilderness. From Kamiah to Missoula, Montana, the next major goal of my journey was 124 miles of true wilderness—a mass of solid, pale green on the map with only one habitation, Lowell, thirty-one miles up the road. Too short for a day's ride.

Lolo Pass, on the border of Idaho and Montana, was three-quarters of the way to Missoula. It was 4,000 feet higher than where I sat in the café like a brooding hen not wanting to leave her nest. Lewis & Clark had arrived not far from this very area where I was now having breakfast, and their journals report the experience of their starving group going over Lolo Pass in the fall of 1805. The following spring, as they were returning to the east, they had to wait six weeks in this area for snow to melt. Was the rain outside turning to snow on the pass? I poured another cup of tea to consider that. I didn't want to ride in the cold rain, but I wasn't going to get to the Tetons by sitting around wondering how to navigate this daunting wilderness passage. *Just go, Gib!* I pulled on a wool glove over my cold right hand, the one that was always the coldest because of poor circulation, and a baggie over that, and urged my own little Corps of Discovery—Sunny, Puppy Jr., and me—out of the warm nest of the café and into the wet day, to share the road with wheat trucks.

Thirty-one drenching miles beyond Kamiah, through the gray curtain of water pouring from the sky I made out a neon sign flashing a quarter mile up the road.

Three Rivers Motel!...Three Rivers Motel!...Three Rivers Motel!

The brilliant magenta letters were beautiful against the gray backdrop.

It's too soon to stop. I really should make more miles!

The sign was getting closer.

Just then a wheat truck roared past, drenching me as it tore up the road, and driving all "shoulds" from my mind. I made a fast right turn onto the road that led across the bridge over the Lochsa River to Three Rivers Motel. *A good night's rest is the best thing to do before heading up to Lolo Pass.* I knew a dubious justification when I heard it, but the need to get off the highway and out of the rain prevailed. As I crunched down the muddy, gravel driveway to the cluster of log buildings, I was more than a little surprised to see two bike travelers, as wet and somber as I was, sitting under the dripping eaves of the office.

Karen and Paul, a twenty-something brother-sister team from Baker, Oregon, had been on the road a week and were feeling uncertain about their next move. Once I'd registered in the office, I invited them to come and hang out rather than get back on the road in this rain. As I opened the door of Cabin No. 8 and felt the warmth greeting me my mood and spirits rebounded. The simple wood furniture and two springy queens covered with red bedspreads looked as inviting as home. There was even a little kitchenette. I felt deeply grateful for my good fortune and pleased with myself for choosing to get off the road, even if I'd only covered thirty-one miles for the day. When I offered my guests the second bed for the night, Paul said he felt that staying in a cozy motel was "cheating," but they proceeded to unpack without much hesitation. I too felt only a twinge of guilt as I settled into the warmth and protection of the room.

We passed the afternoon telling our stories and swapping cycling tales. I read parts of *The Teton Traveler's Guide* to them, choosing from among the quotes I'd written those I felt might be especially meaningful or encouraging to them. For myself, the last two verses of Walt Whitman's poem, "Passage to India," about seafaring explorers, were poignantly appropriate after my traumatic encounter with the wheat trucks: "For we are bound where mariner has not yet dared to go / and we will risk the ship, ourselves and all." I realized I *was* prepared to risk it all to find God. And while there was danger in my journey, I, like Whitman, had faith in God's protective presence. "O my brave soul! O, daring joy, but safe! / Are they not all the seas of God? O, farther, farther, farther sail!"

At 6:00 the next morning I peered out the window of our cozy cabin. Rainy gray skies. A low mist was hovering just above road level. I consulted briefly with Sunny and Puppy, and we unanimously voted not to sail farther that day. What better spot to hole-up than a snug cabin? Karen and Paul wanted to push on though and, after mutual wishes for a good journey, they left in the rain. It had been a fortuitous meeting. Being with them had lifted my spirits and distracted me from thinking too much about how dangerous it was to be a lone cyclist sharing the road with wheat trucks. And their admiration for my bold adventure had helped me regain some confidence in my journey.

By mid-morning the sun broke through, but I resisted the temptation to put in some dry miles and settled down for a day committed to rest and recuperation. I was proud of myself for stepping off my goal-oriented fast track, and for my willingness to pamper myself a little bit. I knew it was something I needed to learn how to do on this bike journey, and beyond. My big activity for the day was going back and forth from the front stoop of my cabin to the bathroom—ten feet at most. Most of the time I prostrated myself to the sun when it was out and baked my bones against the earth as though I were in an electric blanket sandwich. My body reveled in the warmth, and I loved looking at my bare arms—they were lightly tanned, the veins bold under their skin shield and the muscles well toned. I brought Puppy out on the stoop to get some fresh air and sun as well. Stashed as he usually was in my front pack all day, he too was pleased to see the sun. I cleaned Sunny from wheel spokes to gear cogs until he gleamed. I played a little Mumblypeg with my Swiss Army knife, twirling the little knife off parts of my hand, aiming the knifepoint for a clean dive into the earth. And I listened to the music of the Lochsa River rushing past just a few yards in front of me.

The Lochsa was narrow, about half the size of the Clearwater. On the other side nasty wheat trucks were growling up and down the slight grade on Route 12. I was grateful for the distance between us, and the fact that I didn't have to think about my safety or survival for a whole day. The trucks whizzing by without their great trailers—tractors they're called—looked silly without a load. They could go faster with less weight, but without the trailer they looked to me liked they'd dropped their trousers and were scooting along the road bare-assed. Off and on I read a few more pages of *One Man's Arctic* and sympathized with Ivar, who was reckoning with deadly polar bears. "As close to death as I had ever come," he said about one encounter. *You and me both, Ivar! Only my polar bears have eighteen wheels, massive hard blue bodies, and growling engines.* The day slipped simply by as the sun inched its way across the sky, brushed over the roof of the cabin, peeked in and out of clouds, and finally settled slowly down over the cliff just fifty yards in front of me.

I was glad I had taken the day off. It was good to pause and breathe easily, to savor the moment. But I could see that taking a break also had its downside; I could feel an unmistakable reluctance to leave the safety of my haven and get back on the road. But I was dressed and ready to roll when I walked into the office the next morning to check out.

The receptionist handed me a message. Karen and Paul had phoned. The lodge sixty miles up the road—the good stopping place for the night that we'd talked about—had been closed by the local health department the day before. They'd had to ride all the way over Lolo Pass in the moonlight, arriving at Lolo Hot Springs at 10:30. *Now* what should I do? Lolo Hot Springs was eighty-four miles away. The rain was light but steady. What kind of mileage could I make traveling through that on an upgrade?

I left the Three Rivers Motel determined to reach the Hot Springs before the end of the day. As I steamed up Route 12, I began extending my goal. Somehow I had misread my map and thought that Missoula was only fourteen miles beyond Lolo Hot Springs instead of thirty-four. *Maybe I'll try to reach Missoula for the night.* After a few miles of pushing for this goal, the tightness in my chest and jaw began to reveal how uptight I was becoming. How quickly I had forgotten that what mattered most was not getting to my destination as soon as possible, and how contrary this goal-oriented pressure was to my resolve of slowing down. I did *not* want to kill myself, and I *did* want to enjoy going over Lolo Pass. As I cycled through the rain, I reflected on previous summit triumphs and eagerly anticipated the ones ahead.

Cycling over a mountain pass is always a time for a great celebration. First there's the relief of ending the physical exertion. Then there's the pride of accomplishing the ascent of several thousand feet to reach the route's summit. The expansive view is another great reward. And maybe best of all, there's the anticipation of the inevitable and thrilling downhill run.

My favorite and most memorable mountain high was on my bike trip with Carol as we flew downhill from the 11,312 foot summit of Monarch Pass on the Continental Divide. Carol and I had posed for pictures with our loaded bikes in front of the elevation sign just before plummeting down the mountain. We look like we'd just conquered Mt. Everest. Adding ecstasy to exuberance, we passed a medium-sized truck on the way down, because he was going too slowly for us! My pigtails were streaming out horizontally behind me, my eyes were streaming tears, and wind filled my open mouth. (Fortunately it was too early for bug season.) I shrieked and yelled with glee and excitement. The truck driver gawked at us in amazement as we and our loaded bicycles careened, flew, soared, tore, sped, catapulted, cascaded down the mountain.

Now I was on my way to the first of three passes in the Bitterroot Mountains. I was looking forward to these exultant celebrations, three exuberant "Hurrahs" and "Ta Dah's" as I rolled up and over the crown of each upcoming pass. First on the route would be Lolo Pass at 5,233 feet; then, two days ride south from

Missoula would come Lost Trail Pass at 6,995 feet, followed shortly after by Chief Joseph Pass at 7,241 feet. At that point I'd be almost to my goal, the Grand Tetons. I loved imagining the incredible views that would surely be in store for me.

Anticipating these eventual celebrations, I relaxed into not knowing or caring how far I would get today or where I would spend the night. Having again made it through my lifelong habit of pushing too hard, I began to look around me. I noticed the knobby texture and the slight upgrade of the road, smelled the fragrance of the wet pines, listened to the rushing Lochsa River. Despite the rain, I felt utterly glad to be on that road, excited and happy. *There will probably be no other time in my life when I will be here...here...here...this mile...this foot...this inch, biking on my way to Lolo Pass, Idaho.*

Carol and me at Monarch Pass

11

BITTER MILES

"You're by *yourself?*"

A sweet grandmother traveling to Lewiston with her family was incredulous. We were all at a rest stop across from the Lochsa River, halfway to Lolo Pass.

"How brave you are, and what with all the crazy people in the world."

I could hear the echo of my mother's voice, and I immediately commended myself for all the progress I'd made in proving the goodness of people and life as I cycled toward the Tetons.

"Honestly, the world isn't as fearful a place as we think it is," I said, trying to reassure her that most people were very kind to me. I didn't get into the business of wheat trucks or any of the other scary situations I'd been in. Most people *had* been very helpful and kind, and that had certainly been true for Carol and me as well. As if to prove the point, my well-meaning grandmother insisted that I drink more V-8 juice and packaged up a large quantity of molasses cookies for my journey. After she was helped into the front seat of the little camper, we smiled warmly at each other as we waved goodbye and headed in our separate directions.

As I continued climbing up the grade and through the woods above the Lochsa, I noticed a twinge of pain in the muscles over my left knee, but I figured it would work itself out and didn't pay too much attention. The rain came and went in spurts, but the sunless day stayed chilly. I could still hear the roar of the river far below as I continued upward. By mid-afternoon that twinge had grown into a significant pain whenever I pressed too hard on the pedals, impossible to avoid as the grade steepened. My body had been holding up remarkably well overall, so I felt annoyed, disappointed, and a little worried. *What if my body gives out on me? What if it won't get me to the Tetons?* I pushed those scary speculations from my mind. Lolo Pass was only eleven miles away, but the steepest part of the climb was yet to come. I longed to reach the Hot Springs and a warm place for the night, but I had to be honest with myself—this knee could not see me over the pass. Not heeding the warning would have consequences. I reluctantly began to look for a place to camp in mid-afternoon.

A small grove of tall, tall trees and bushy undergrowth near the road looked promising, and not far inside them I spotted a little clearing big enough for my tent. It looked to me just like the place where my film hero Yentl spent her first night alone in a vast wilderness one moonless night. I thought about her as I huddled over my little hurricane candle lamp just inside the open flap of my tent, hoping that any vehicles on the road would be going too fast to notice an odd speck of blue in the trees. I'd had Yentl's prayer engraved on the lamp: "May the light of this flickering candle illuminate the night the way your spirit illuminates my soul." Under the circumstances I didn't want my night to be lit up at all, so every time I heard a car approach, I blew out my candle and held my breath. I wanted to write in my journal, but my hand was too cold. I wanted to sit outside for a smoke and relax, but it was too cold for that too. I curled into my sleeping bag with all my clothes on and slept sporadically through the night.

The following morning, June 7, came dripping in at 6:00. Light, steady "liquid sunshine" continued to fall as I headed up toward Lolo Pass. It was not a difficult grade, but the pain in my left leg was screaming. With each pedal stroke, the muscle sheath on top of my thigh—the quadriceps—yelled as though it had been doused with gas and then ignited. To keep myself going, I counted off each of the mile markers—170...171...172...173...174. As I pulled myself over the crown of the pass, I managed only to whisper a depressed, half-hearted "Ta Dah," and that merely for formality's sake. The view was completely obliterated by thick, soggy clouds. The only thing I could see clearly was a big green sign announcing my location: "Entering Montana." I didn't much care at that point whether I'd crossed over a state line or a clothesline.

The Lolo Hot Springs Resort & Café was only four miles down from the Pass, but it took two and a half hours to reach it. I coasted when the grade was steep enough, then had to depend on each excruciating pedal stroke to move me forward. By the time I arrived, I felt penetrated by cold. Five cups of hot tea barely took the chill from my hands, and there remained a deep cold in my body's core that only a steaming hot bath, or a roaring fire, or a summer day in Death Valley could warm. Even a little sun breaking through the oppressive gray sky would have helped warm my body and lift my spirits, but there was not one ray to be seen. That the hot springs themselves might have been open for a soak didn't even occur to me. I'd only come eleven miles that day, and I'd already taken a break at the Three Rivers Motel. *If only I could have made it here yesterday! I could have spent the night. I could have gotten warm.*

My urge to keep going though was stronger than my need for bodily comfort. After all, this trip was not a vacation. This was not a cycling holiday catered by Club Med. Nor was it an adventure trip like an African safari, as my dad imagined it to be. My trip to the Tetons was more like those arduous and long pilgrimages taken by millions of spiritual seekers to places such as Santiago de Compostela in Spain, Lourdes in France, Chimayo in New Mexico, and Mecca, in search of healing, or vision, or forgiveness, or fulfillment of a deep longing.

I drank as much hot tea as my bladder could stand, curling around the little hot ceramic pot and its steam as if it were a promise of relief from what I'd just gone through and what lay ahead, then that overwhelming and urgent need to reach my destination, which somehow meant finding God, moved me out of my seat in the warm café and back onto the road again. Like a pilgrim of old, I would override my physical pain. I would follow God's will, and my will, to find Him.

I tied on my rain hat, slipped into my rain jacket, and walked my bike out of the gravel parking lot and back onto the wet road. Along with a deep tiredness, tears welled up inside me. *Why do I feel like crying? What's wrong?* Looking back I can see I was feeling utterly at the mercy of God's will, and my determination to find Him. I was feeling sorry for my body, which was paying a high price for those huge forces driving me. And I was feeling sorry for myself. *Why is it all so hard!?*

My right leg, my "good" leg, felt leaden as I hoisted it up and over the saddle. The route ahead would be flat or a slight downgrade. I could manage the thirty-four miles to Missoula. I *had* to reach Missoula—I couldn't stand another night outside. With the first push on the left pedal, a sharp pain shot through my thigh, and it didn't diminish as I pressed on. Was I damaging my leg? An even worse thought was that I might not even make it to Missoula. *And what if I don't make it to the Tetons? Will that mean I won't find God, or that I don't deserve to find God, or that God will abandon me?* As I moved along at a snail's pace, the panic inside me intensified. I had to get a grip. I coasted onto the wide shoulder of the highway and stopped. I straddled my bike, not daring to dismount for fear I would not want to get back on. The air was still, and gray, and drizzly. The pinewoods had given way to more open meadows with scattered aspens and elms. I urged myself to inner stillness. *Shhhh. It's okay. It's going to be okay. Just take it slow. Let the right leg do most of the work. Don't freak out.* I would have to fight for every mile to Missoula. I thought of how Lewis and Clark had fought for every mile to reach their destination. Here was my version of their saga. I looked down the slick road toward Missoula. *I'm the best little scrapper I know. I can make it.* I shoved off and scrapped slowly onward.

On the outskirts of Missoula, I pulled into the first sheltered place I could stop—a large gas station with four rows of pumps and a convenience store. The rain was still coming down steadily, making the day so dark that cars had headlights on even though it was only five o'clock. Grateful to be undercover, I dismounted by one of the gas pumps. I could hardly walk on my left leg so I eased myself down next to one of them, not caring that I was breathing in more gas fumes than air. The main road heading east looked like it went into the main area of town. I could make out a traffic light and figured it would be a likely place to find a motel. I climbed back onto Sunny and inched my way with slow moving traffic along several blocks of two and three story brick buildings, stores, and shops, and turned into the first motel I saw.

It was *the* most impersonal, dull, inhumane motel of my trip. It made the beige room in Klamath Falls look like the Ritz. My room was barely big enough for one bed, a cheap little dresser, and a chair. The curtains and the concrete block walls matched the gray sky. I felt like I was in a dog kennel, but I didn't much care at that point. Needing an encouraging friend, I called Josh. "Keep on trucking, sweetheart." His voice sounded so good to me, and I had no energy left to censor myself. "I love you," I told him before I signed off. It cheered and warmed me to hear him return the sentiment. I went to bed feeling grateful that God had helped me find such a dear and supportive friend on my journey.

I knew I had no choice but to heal my leg before going on, and Missoula turned out to be a wonderland of delights. I daily limped the few blocks from the kennel—which I was too tired to bother moving from—to a coffeehouse called Butterfly Herbs, full of beautiful cards, uplifting music, New Age trinkets, and great cappuccinos. Next door was the Little Professor, a warm, intimate, dark-wooded bookstore with comfy chairs for browsing colorful and alluring books. At the huge main post office nearby, I could mail my postcards and have friendly conversations with other customers. Last but not least among Missoula's offerings was the local Laundromat, which had bulk soap so I didn't have to buy a little box that I'd only have to throw away later...and chocolate chip cookies to eat while I washed my clothes.

Several times a day I applied Absorbene, Jr. to my left thigh and knee. The label on the bottle said that it was for overexertion and chilling. *Junior got that right!* I tried to be lighthearted, but the injury was a sobering reality. I took hot baths in the tiny tub in my room, walked slowly, and napped. It was a physical impossibility to ride anywhere. I had no idea how long it would take before I could go on.

On my second day there I was idly looking over the bulletin board at Butterfly Herbs when a flier caught my eye. "Mountain Visions: Guided Vision Quests." There was a picture on it of high mountains and a quote from a shaman: "All true wisdom is only to be found far from the dwellings of man, out in the great solitude." My heart seized up for an instant when I read that. *What is it about this image of being more deeply alone that grips me so?* I wanted what the mountains and the wilderness were promising. The paved roads I was biking on ran *through* the wilderness but were not *in* and *of* the wilderness. At that moment I knew I wanted more. I wanted *in*..

As quickly as my leg would allow, I hustled back to my kennel, phone number of Mountain Visions in hand. John Thorne answered the phone himself and was open, friendly and helpful in explaining more about his program. I could feel my enthusiasm for the adventure increasing. I didn't know how this idea would fit into my objective of reaching the Tetons, but I had to explore the energy that was arising in me at the thought of being alone in the wilderness. *Is that where I will find God?* John lived in Hamilton, a town that happened to be directly on my route south. I probably shouldn't have been surprised by this serendipity; something about this entire journey seemed to be orchestrated beyond my understanding. We planned to meet as soon as my leg was healed. I would learn then more about the process of a vision quest and how to prepare for it, and we would choose the dates—some time after I'd completed my journey to the Tetons.

After I got off the phone, a perplexing issue came to mind. What about the arrangements Paul and I had made to meet in Jackson Hole and drive home together? The farther on my journey I traveled, the less enthusiastic I'd become about the idea. I loved my independence, discovering my style, my preferences, my nature, who I was. The thought of being with another person felt claustrophobic.

Knowing I had to tell him about this change of plans made my chest tighten around a nervous heart. I was reluctant to disappoint him. But it was more than that. Even though with Josh I'd taken a big step toward establishing my independence, I loved Paul deeply. I still carried that hope for a lasting union. And despite the challenges of our relationship, he had been my touchstone and link to God. Maybe he still was. I was on this journey desperate to find God on my own, but what if I couldn't? I didn't know it at the time, but I feared that if I were to lose Paul completely, I might lose my tenuous connection to God altogether.

I picked up the phone and called. "I miss you," he said. His voice seemed to have little energy, and as I felt my own energy sinking to meet his, my chest clenched up tighter. But I still didn't have the courage to say, "Paul, I'm not sure I want to go home together." So I told him a little about the Vision Quest and finished the conversation saying, "Well, I'll call again in a few days and maybe we can figure out then what to do. I love you." I got off the phone and sank into the usual confusion I felt over Paul—my deep love for him and my hopes for our future crashing up against my simultaneous distress at how difficult it was for us to create a workable relationship. Little did I know then that this conflict inside me would persist for several more years.

"Do you know anything about a Vision Quest?" John asked. I was sitting at a round oak table with John and his wife Gayla in their little kitchen in Hamilton. They'd welcomed me warmly and put on the kettle for tea.

"Not much."

"Well, it's a traditional rite of passage in many Native American cultures. The idea is that you go into the wilderness for three days, without food, and seek a vision, an understanding of where you are in your life, and where you are headed."

Three days without food was daunting, but might be worth it to understand my life and where I was headed. And maybe to find God.

"Do you have a sense of what you are marking at this time of change in your life? Is it a severance? A threshold? Is it a renewal or a new beginning?"

The first thing that came to mind was that I wanted to know God's will. I wanted to see God's plan for me. I told John I wanted to let go of the pain of the past three years—my failed marriage, my failed tenure at Mudd's, my problematic relationship with Paul. I wanted to come to terms with the changes, the losses, the failures, and let go of the pain. I didn't want to pick up the old pieces of a life that had fallen apart. I wanted to start anew.

John nodded in understanding. "You might also think about creating a ritual," he said, "and about gathering some objects that will mark this time of passage and help you move on."

"If I had a Mudd's t-shirt with me, I could burn that," I laughed weakly.

The three of us made a plan: After I'd completed my journey to the Tetons, I would return to Montana for a Vision Quest right there in the Bitterroot Wilderness. This definitely meant I would be driving home on my own, and I loved that idea. Ever since that depressing phone conversation with Paul, I'd found myself imagining a solo drive home, retracing the route of my bicycle journey. Now all I had to do was screw up my courage to tell him.

"I'm sorry, Paul," I began that evening on the phone. "I know it would be really a good trip to drive home together," I said, not really feeling that way, "but I need to do this." I knew he understood I was on a spiritual journey and that I had to follow my heart and do what I was called to do.

He was stoic and, not surprisingly, didn't say too much. "We'll still have several days to spend together in Jackson Hole," I said, trying to sound encouraging and upbeat about being together. In truth I was feeling enormous relief that after our brief rendezvous, I would be a solo traveler again. I felt bad disappointing him—I knew how much he'd been looking forward to our being together again. And I was immensely grateful for and touched by his quiet support of my choices.

Leaving Hamilton, I was quickly reminded that I was still in the Bitterroot Mountains. I struggled upward toward Lost Trail Pass, gaining 3,500 feet in the drenching rain. It was forty-seven degrees. "I have been as wet and as cold in every part as I ever was in my life," wrote Captain Clark as he made his way through what he called the "Valley of Troubles," here in these very mountains. By the time I'd dragged myself the forty-two miles to the Lost Trail Hot Springs Resort, twelve miles before the pass, I was utterly exhausted, my legs were stiff, my head was buzzing and aching.

Leaving Hamilton

After I wiped Sunny down, I found the bar at the lodge for my now regular Coors Lite beer and a smoke. Frank Sinatra's melancholy and moody songs only added to my low spirits. I'd been traveling for thirty-seven days, mostly through what seemed like never-ending rain and cold. I felt deflated and depressed. I did not want to be defeated by the weather, but I didn't know how much more I could take. *How much harder does it have to get before I am really ready to quit? How badly do I want to do what God has asked me to do? How badly do I want to find God?* That night, cuddling Puppy, I cried myself to sleep.

The next morning offered no relief from cold, rain and depression. Even Puppy looked dejected as we peered into the wet, early morning gloom. "God is our only hope," I said, clutching him and starting to cry again. He was being so brave. "Don't worry, we'll make it, Puppy. God will help us." Sunny stood by, stoic and patient and willing as he always was. He would go anywhere with me. Even back out into the rain.

As I ground my way along the wet road toward the summit of Lost Trail Pass, I tried to encourage myself by keeping the Tibetan Buddhist chant *Om Mane Padme Hum* cranking over in my mind in time with my pedal strokes. I had no idea what it meant or where I'd heard it, but I hoped there was some kind of spiritual power in it that could keep me going. Intermittently I cried or let out some anguished expletive, cursing just to release my misery. My runny nose and the tears from my eyes joined the rainwater running down my face. I didn't even notice when I arrived at the top of the pass. My head down, the water running off my hat, I just kept the pedals turning over. *One more Bitterroot pass to go.*

12

THE BIG HOLE

A hundred yards before reaching Chief Joseph Pass, I ran into a construction zone. The wretchedness of pushing upward in the relentless rain was compounded now by gaping holes in the road, loose gravel and debris, and wooden roadblocks. A lone construction worker called out as I struggled past, "You've got a *long* way to go." I didn't need to be reminded how far away the Tetons were, but when I realized that he just meant to the top of the pass, which was only a half mile away, my discouragement took a new downturn. "Thanks a lot, buddy." I growled under my breath.

When I topped Chief Joseph Pass, I couldn't even muster a silent "Ta Dah!" If there was some grand, expansive view, it was obscured by rain and my dark mood. The exhilaration I'd anticipated in cresting the summits of the three Bitterroot passes had been thoroughly drowned out. I felt cheated. In deepening inner and outer gloom, I began the switchback descent, dropping 1,200 feet into the Big Hole Valley. Concentrating on the slick road, I watched in dismay as wet grit spattered onto Sunny's frame and into his gears. I hated Sunny being dirty; I worried about a breakdown. And now there was not even the usual reward of cruising downhill. Once again the impulse to quit was looming.

At the bottom of the grade I pulled into an empty parking area. It was just a place to stop. I didn't even care that there was some sort of historical marker here, which I usually greeted with interest. I leaned Sunny against a log post supporting a sign. I didn't bother to read it, but for what felt like the first time that day, I looked up.

The stark beauty of the Big Hole Valley before me was stunning. The "hole" was surrounded by gray-blue mountains fading away in the distance. The flat pale valley stretched between them—a half-million acres, sparsely covered with dry grasses and sage. As I gazed at the vast space before me I felt very small, and momentarily distracted from my misery

After a few minutes of taking in the immense valley, I turned to read the sign commemorating the Big Hole National Battlefield. "On August 9, 1877 gun shots shattered a chilly dawn on a sleeping camp of Nez Perce. By the time the smoke cleared on August 10, almost 90 Nez Perce were dead along with 31 soldiers and volunteers." *So that's how Chief Joseph Pass got its name.* Right where I was standing—in the southern part of what is now Montana—the U.S. Army had finally caught up with the Nez Perce, who were trying to escape to Canada to avoid being forced onto a reservation. After a fierce battle, Chief Joseph had surrendered. His farewell words live on: "Hear me, my chiefs! I am tired. My heart is sick and sad. From where the sun now stands I will fight no more forever."

The historical remnants of despair and death rose from the basin like a mist, merging seamlessly with the rain and my own gloom. The vastness of the valley, the sorrow of defeat and death on the battlefield, and my own depression opened up a cavernous space inside me.

Into that space rushed all my fears. *How can I possibly get to the Tetons?* Bound in with my search for God, this was the one big thing giving my life meaning. I slipped further into inner darkness. The dreaded "*I can't*" chorus sprang to life. *What if I* can't *make it to the Tetons? What if I* can't *fulfill my promise to God? And what about being Christ's bride?* I looked at the soggy bridal bouquet on my pack; it drooped, hanging as wet and lifeless as I felt. *What if He breaks off the engagement because I can't complete my task? What then? Maybe I should just let a truck smack me and be done with it.*

I was back on Paul Tillich's "ultimate boundary line"—that place of self-condemnation and rejection that adds another devastating layer to despair. Tillich's understanding and guidance had saved me before. But now, swallowed up in the immense empty space of the Big Hole and the sad and deadly story of its battlefield, even Tillich's wisdom was lost to me.

The thought of failure sat like a lead stone in my heart. Water ran steadily off my packs. My clothes and sleeping bag would be soaked. The rain would take off all the lubricant on Sunny's chain and gears. I could almost see the rust growing on his components. A dark, tempting thought came to life—a complex mechanical failure and breakdown would put an end to my misery. I would get a lift in a warm car to a place with a good bike repair shop. I would be reasonably justified in a not-quite-accomplished mission. I would say to anyone who asked if I'd made it to the Tetons, "Yes, well, uh, almost. I pretty much made it. Sunny had a mechanical breakdown and I had to get a lift, but I was only a couple of days away." *But what would I say to God?*

I hovered over my folded map, trying to keep rain off it as I studied the route ahead. I almost laughed when I saw the next marked habitation. Ten miles east was the town of Wisdom. Maybe there was something there for me—some great insight or confirmation about why I was riding my bike in the rain in Montana for God. Or at least maybe there was a warm café.

I turned away from the monument, determined to reach Wisdom. As I moved on down the road, the construction worker's words rose in my mind: "Oh, you've got a *long* way to go." Every few pedal strokes they turned over in me again, making the distance feel interminable. A rainy hour later I arrived at the sign for Wisdom. I veered left off the main route and followed the straight gravelly road past a number of old weathered wooden buildings. It looked like a movie set for a Western. I fully expected to see horses tied up to hitching rails along the street. Moving unsteadily on the rough road, I was keenly aware of more grit spitting up into Sunny's vulnerable mechanical parts. Fifty yards ahead, I could see the end of the street, and beyond that nothing but open range. *God, please let there be a café!*

I rounded a corner to see a few cars parked in front of a restaurant. *Oh, thank you, Lord!* And, unbelievably, there was another loaded touring bike leaning up against the front. I parked next to it. Inside, a quick look around told me exactly who the bike traveler was—a solo young man looking even more miserable than I felt. After a sympathetic nod and a few mumbled words of soggy, half-hearted greeting, I took a table on the other side of the room. Clearly we both wanted to be left alone.

The inside and outside of the café were the same—gray and chilled. The waitress came up to my table with a suitably cool greeting. She looked at me like I was dripping blood on her floor rather than water. "I'd like a piece of apple pie with two scoops of vanilla, please." I wanted sugar. I didn't care that the ice cream would make me colder. In my heart a small five year old was curled up in a corner, hugging her knees, sobbing.

I noticed a pay phone by the door and considered calling Paul to come get me. We'd worked out arrangements a couple of days earlier, and by this time he would have arrived in Jackson Hole and would be waiting for me. Why should I keep up this struggle? Hadn't I learned that God wanted me to take care of myself? Inside me, that understanding was fighting mightily with the determined pilgrim on her quest. I glanced over at the other bike traveler. *Do I look that bad?* I must have because when the waitress brought my check, she mentioned that there was a lodge open in the town of Jackson, Montana, nineteen miles south. *I am not going to fall as low as that guy! I can do this!* I stopped eyeing the phone and ran my forefinger over the empty plate to get the last licks of sticky, sugary goodness. I collected my wallet, wet rain jacket and hat, nodded to the drooping fellow, and shoved open the door into the chilly afternoon. I climbed back on Sunny, and we headed for that small bright spot on a gray horizon—an indoor place for the night. Maybe that was the gift of Wisdom.

That dark afternoon the road through the Big Hole was utterly and absolutely still, so quiet I could hear a car approaching from miles away, the sound of swishing tires on the watery road filling the immense space all around. The sounds I made—breathing, pedaling, sniffling—were huge and loud. It was scary and unnerving to hear how, though I was so small, the sounds seemed to fill up the entire Big Hole. The rain was falling only intermittently now. From time to time a hazy sun glazed the pale landscape with light. I turned over the pedals with a dull, monotonous motion, as if I were cycling on a perpetual motion treadmill. The road was flat, but I was in a climbing gear to minimize the resistance. I pretended God was sitting behind me on my packs, urging me on, but I can't say I really felt His presence. And I certainly wasn't in touch with the "God above God" that Tillich had inspired me to reach for.

With the chill in my bones and my eyes turned inward, my heart, rather than opening and embracing the space and beauty of the Big Hole, was feeling forlorn, alone and scared. Other than directions to a lodge, I hadn't found anything in Wisdom that would balance the despair with hope, the dark with light. I knew I once had an understanding of how those opposing forces were of equal value, how one implies the other, but that was completely gone from me now, swallowed up by the silence and space. If someone had come along and said, "Oh, I see you're in a very dark space, but of course without the *un*pleasant times there would be no pleasant ones," I would have first stared blankly and then perhaps attacked with my flimsy tire pump. So it was breath by loud breath, stroke by slow stroke, that Sunny and I made the nineteen miles to the Jackson Lodge just before the black storm clouds let loose another deluge.

Out of the ominous silence and misery of the Big Hole, I walked into the large open hall of the Jackson Lodge. Warm air washed over my face like ointment soothing a wound. I gave a sigh of relief as I leaned Sunny against the wall just inside the front door, hoping nobody would mind. I didn't want him out in the rain. The great room had a massive hardwood bar to my right just off the entryway. The connected lounge contained a few small tables, comfy leather chairs and couches, a pool table and dining area. Log beams crisscrossed the ceiling. Brass lamp chandeliers hung over the pool table and dining room. Huge antlers decorated the walls. One wood paneled wall was dominated by an enormous fireplace, the hearth and stone lintel blackened by soot from countless roaring fires, one of which was currently warming me just by my looking at it.

Several people were hanging out at the bar, laughing and talking their way through the late afternoon gloom. All conversation stopped when they saw me. Everyone stared, not unkindly but with considerable curiosity. Could I pull myself out of this deep interior space enough to engage in ordinary conversation? I'd often found that when I'd been alone and quiet, or in some deep part of myself for a long stretch of time, it was like I'd gone down a rabbit hole, and finding my way back above ground was uncertain and tricky.

I walked over to the end of the bar. A middle-aged woman greeted me cheerfully. "Hi, I'm Jenny," and pointing to a tall, lean man serving drinks, "This is Glenn." I got the sense they were the owners. "What can we get for you?"

"Hi, I'm hoping you have a room for a night." My teeth were chattering a little. "Sure, Hon," Jenny assured me. As she checked me in, she asked where I was from. I noticed everyone was listening as I told her briefly how I'd come to be there. "Oh my, what a trip!" she exclaimed. She proceeded to introduce me to the "audience"—Rose, from Rose's Cantina across the street, a couple of local fishermen, and two middle-aged guys touring by motorcycle from Nebraska. Everyone nodded and smiled at me. Conversation started up again, and to my relief, I easily joined in.

We all had something to say about the miserable weather. Someone offered that it was probably not that good to have hot weather for biking because you would get too warm. With great feeling, I blurted out, "Oh, I would *love* to be hot!" To my surprise they all cracked up. I could feel my cheeks flush as I realized how my comment had sounded, but then I fell into laughter along with them. It made me happy that I could still laugh.

Once the downpour had stopped, Sunny and I followed Jenny outside to another building a short distance from the lodge. My room there was another old-time cozy place like the Three Rivers Motel. There was an old wooden desk and chair, two springy beds with bright red bedspreads, and a large multicolored area rug made of woven rags. The best things about the room were the *two* electric heaters, both of which I turned on full blast. Under the circumstances, I forgave myself the excessive use of energy and turned the wall thermostat up to eighty degrees. I tried but couldn't squeeze another degree from them. After I'd baked in front of them for a while, I dragged myself back to the lodge and sat at the bar with a beer. Exhausted and depleted as I felt, I still welcomed some easy conversation with the owners.

Glenn told me with great pride that he was a former Marine. Even at fifty-something he still had that military look about him: very short hair, straight posture, a well-weathered face. I felt content to listen to stories about his background and whatever else came to his mind, which included a firm belief in a You-can-do-anything-if-you-want-to attitude. I appreciated the idea. I wanted to believe that, but though I didn't mention my doubts to Glenn, I wasn't sure it had proven true in my experience,. I had wanted to be married to one man for my lifetime, but that hadn't worked out. I hadn't been able to be the manager of Mudd's, much as I had wanted to succeed at that job. And I had barely managed to get to the Jackson Lodge, mentally, physically, and spiritually. When Glen asked me about my route, I told him I estimated it would take me another five days to reach the Tetons. Much as I wanted to do that at the moment, I wondered if I actually could.

As I finished my beer, I found myself thinking about some friends in Bozeman, Montana, 176 miles east, too far off my intended route to visit. My plan was to travel directly south the next day, toward Yellowstone National Park, four days away. But I wanted to say hello and tell them what I was doing. And I suppose I knew I'd be cheered up by their familiar voices. I went out to the pay phone in the entry hall.

Pam and Bill were delighted to hear from me and amazed that I was on a bike on my way to the Tetons.

"How *are* you? Wow! What a trip! How is it going?"

"Well, I'm a little tired...It's been cold...and rainy a lot...I'm headed for Yellowstone tomorrow."

Despite my attempt to sound upbeat they must have heard the exhaustion in my voice,

"Why don't you come over to Bozeman? We'd love to see you and put you up for the night. And then we'll drive you down to Yellowstone. After that you'll just have a day's ride to the Tetons."

The proposed plan would shorten my journey by one day. *Would God mind? Would I feel guilty that I hadn't ridden every single mile? Well, I've already "cheated" and taken a car in Oregon so it's not exactly a pure cycling trip as it is.*

I was too tired to resist their offer, and at this point I seriously doubted I could even make it to the Tetons on my own steam.

"That sounds really great. I would love to. I should be able to get there in three days." Somehow, eliminating a sixty-mile-day's ride felt more like cutting a couple of hundred miles off from my remaining journey, and gave me a huge boost. And the idea was better than calling Paul to come get me, which would feel like a complete bail-out.

Four more days total and I will be in the Tetons. I can do this.

The next morning came in cold and cloudy, and before leaving my room, I soaked up every single precious BTU I could from those beautiful, beige electric heaters. I took Sunny, all packed up, across the street to Rose's Cantina for a breakfast of hotcakes with homemade jelly. Still deeply tired and depressed, I gave myself another pep talk: *Four more days. Only three days to Bozeman. Then one more day. One less day than I thought. Piece of cake. C'mon.* I forced myself out of the warm café and onto the bike.

Sunny and I immediately pedaled onto a grade that I could see would take me out of the Big Hole. *Maybe it will take me out of my own big hole as well.* From Rose's the grade had looked like a gradual, no-big-deal climb. It was apparently so inconsequential that it had no name on the map, no elevation indicators. I'd even been able to make out where the grade leveled out some as it neared the top. A promising view.

As soon as I began to climb, a headwind hit me. And then it began to alternate with a crosswind. And, of course, it started to rain. I couldn't tell if the grade was really steep or whether it was just steep *for me*. It was probably less than a six percent incline, but it felt like twelve. *It shouldn't be this hard! This is not a steep grade! What is the* problem?" I felt so bleak and so low on every kind of energy that even a downhill grade would have been a trial at this point. I strained for every pedal stroke.

The rain did not last long nor was it hard, but it drove me over the brink of my tolerance and stamina. I could not stand one more bloody pass in the rain in a fucking headwind. I was only halfway to the top when I started to cry. My huge effort was barely moving me forward. It was pathetic. Pitiable. *How am I supposed to get to the Tetons if I can't even get to the top of this stupid, measly grade out of the Big Hole?* When I finally inched to the top I doubled over the handlebars, sobbing. I felt unbearably helpless. I had nothing left.

"What do you *want* of me?" I wailed at God. "You can have Puppy and Sunny. I don't have anything more to give you. You already have my life...! Are you even there? If you are, take it all if that's what you want."

Sorrow poured out of me. I sobbed and hiccupped tears and air and grief. Snot and spittle blended with the water from my yellow hat and dripped onto the wet road. If I had dismounted at that moment, I might have dropped to my knees, curled up on the pavement, and cried till I died or was hit by a truck. I felt utterly bereft and beaten.

Where was God now when I was so alone and broken? I felt utterly abandoned by Him, and yet utterly incapable of proceeding on my own. Years later something I would read from St. John of the Cross would help me understand what I was going through. He said, "In darkness and pain God is calling us to surrender, to trust in Him." I believe that God allowed me to fall so completely as I did on that pass in order to realize I was nothing without Him. Thomas Merton says, "To get to the core of God at His greatest, one must first get into the core of himself at his least." I had nowhere to turn but to Him for help. And even though I did not feel His presence, something in me somehow reached out, without words, even without faith. He would help me keep going.

Eventually the wailing subsided. I felt like a huge wave had passed through me, and I was left empty of emotion or thought. I'd climbed 1,000 feet from Jackson to the top of the pass at 7,400 feet. I looked out ahead of me at the open road and open country. I slipped one foot...and then the other...into the pedal straps and shoved off for Bozeman, and hopefully the Tetons.

I descended from Big Hole Pass into another huge, pale valley. Not so vast as the Big Hole, this one was more like its little sister but every bit as silent and breathtaking. The low sage grassland reached out toward mountains all around me. The black two lane road was lined on both sides with endless stretches of barbed wire—a sure sign of big cattle country. Not one car, not one beat-up, old ranch pickup passed me in either direction for fifteen miles. I had the land all to myself and was glad for it. There wasn't even a breeze, only me, quietly pedaling in my lowest gear on a flat grade under low, gray skies.

Ever since I'd begun the descent, my herpes lip had been heating up. I licked the swelling, throbbing flesh as I pedaled. Despite that stress, a song came to mind. I could hear the voices of Peter, Paul and Mary inside me, and I sang along to myself: "This land is your land, this land is my land," over and over and over, The inner song and the sound of my rhythmic breathing filled the expanse of silent and open rangeland.

When I was midway through the open valley, the sun found its way through a break in the mass of gray clouds. The landscape suddenly lit up as if the house lights in a dark theater had been switched on. The pale landscape came to life, and life stirred in me. I felt bathed in a heavenly glow of heat and light. Until that glorious moment I hadn't realized how starved I was for sunshine. As the warmth began to penetrate my body, I calculated that it had been nine straight days of little or no sun, and a lot of rain. No wonder I felt I was running on empty. My "solar panels" had failed to gather enough rays to keep the batteries charged. And now my inner lights too were finally switching on, along with a glimpse of renewed energy.

When I rounded the next bend, I found myself staring at the bobbing, furry hindquarters of about fifty brown cows being herded by two cowboys on horseback. It was a comical sight but perplexing. They were blocking the entire road. I couldn't pass on either of the rough shoulders for fear of puncturing a tire. I didn't have a horn, and I hadn't thought to pack a cattle prod. I slowed to within thirty feet of them wondering how far or how long they'd be chugging down the road, with me dodging wet, sloppy cow pies as we all poked along.

I noticed a car behind me slowing as it approached. As it pulled hesitantly past me, I instantly conceived of a strategy. "Sunny! Follow that car!" He leapt into action. The sea of bovine butts parted as the car blared its horn. I stayed within a foot of the car's bumper as we passed through the moving river of cows muttering low complaints of indignation at being pushed aside. Barely breathing, I kept my eyes riveted on the car, hoping that it would not stop suddenly or speed up and leave me caught between those thousand pound bodies of beefsteak. After a couple of exciting and odorful minutes, all six wheels of the convoy made it safely through.

God must have thought I deserved a break from cold, wet weather, because the remaining three days it would take me to reach Bozeman were mostly sunny, and dry. On several occasions I simply stopped for no reason except to savor the sunlight and its warmth. The days were easy and uneventful, and I found warm motels for the nights, as if affirming the decision to change my route. In retrospect, it's clear that each time I overcame a challenge or obstacle, or after an insight had given me renewed strength and confidence, I would have two or three days of respite and ease. Unfortunately, the flipside of the pattern also seemed to be true.

On the day before my rendezvous with my friends, that challenge-to-ease ratio tried to kick in. My map hadn't shown a pass over the Tobacco Root Mountains, but the grade leaving Virginia City continued upward—on and on. *What's the deal here? Why wasn't this indicated?* Cursing the inept mapmakers, I silently lodged my complaints with them. I didn't like surprises like this. I wanted to know what was going on, and what lay ahead of me. I hadn't had time to prepare myself. I didn't like being reminded how little control I had over my situation—or how unpredictable my life was.

I dropped into my lowest gear and kept the pedals slowly turning over and upward, one mile, two miles, three miles. A half mile more and I pedaled into the kind of surprise that made it all worth it. At the top of the grade, I was exhausted and ecstatic. I could see forever. It was not raining. I wasn't cold. I had made it to the top of another pass. Spellbound, I gazed down at the Madison River, named by Lewis and Clark, and the pale valley surrounding it. I let fly countless "Ta Dah's," one for every summit I'd reached without being able to muster any enthusiasm, and then some. Each "Ta Dah" was a brightly colored balloon of exuberance and joy that floated happily over the Madison River Valley. I wanted to zoom down the grade in utter

exhilaration, but I couldn't stop jamming on the brakes to take pictures every quarter mile. My high spirits continued into the evening when I was ensconced in another cozy motel with an adjoining café.

View from the Tobacco Root Pass

The next day's ride seemed to be a reflection of my rapidly changing emotions. What my friends had said was "a pretty flat route into Bozeman" turned out the next day to be Montana's version of the Ozarks, where Carol and I had faced an exhausting roller coaster of a road. This sort of terrain is like a sine wave, the "smooth, repetitive oscillation" made by sound waves, ocean waves, light waves. The operative word here is "repetitive," and it drove me mad. The upgrades of these Montana waves were steep—maybe nine percent so I had to go all out to reach the crest of each land wave. But before I could catch my breath and recover from the stress in my leg muscles, I was down at the bottom jamming on the pedals to climb the next grade. Each inch took every ounce of concentration and energy, though I managed to reserve just enough to curse those oscillations.

And to sing. About twenty miles from Bozeman, still in that up-and-down, up-and-down mode, I began singing "Jesus Walked this Lonesome Valley," "Glory, Glory Alleluia," "Onward Christian Soldiers." With ten miles left to go, I resorted to a version of "Om Mane Padme Hum." The last few miles required desperate measures.

"Ninety-nine bottles of beer on the wall, ninety-nine bottles of beer. Take one down, pass it around, ninety-eight bottles of beer on the wall. Ninety-eight bottles of beer on the wall…"

A few more miles went by. Up and down, up and down. *How many more miles of this torture?* "Thirty-six bottles of beer on the wall, thirty-six bottles of beer…"

There weren't many bottles of beer left on the wall by the time I reached my friends' house where I gratefully accepted a chilled bottle of the real thing. With great pleasure I absorbed their warm welcome—the hugs, the hot shower, the questions, the concern—and their offer to put my dirty clothes into the washing machine. The day was topped off with a real home-cooked meal, which included my first-ever elk meat and a decadent rhubarb cream pie.

As I lay in bed appreciating Pam and Bill's loving, attentive hospitality, and the exuberance of their young children that so lifted my spirits, I thought back to all the people who'd helped me on my journey in different ways: a wave, a thumbs-up, a ride to get me off the Umatilla Bridge, travel tips, a loving place to rest, interest and admiration for my journey, molasses cookies. Each person had buoyed my spirits and kept my pedals turning. It was as though God had not only kept me from harm, but had also arranged for support and encouragement along the way. It had all brought me to Bozeman, just a day's car ride and a day's bike ride from completion of my assignment from God. I drifted into sleep with a huge sense of relief—almost disbelief—that I was almost there, that I had made it.

13

THE TETONS

I sucked in my breath.

"Sunny, look! There they are! The Tetons!" I whispered, as if I thought the distant vision I beheld through the towering pines would break like a piece of glass if I spoke any louder. After forty-two days and over 1,500 miles by bike (and another 500 by car), the power, the splendor, the magic and the physical reality of seeing the Tetons hit me as though I'd been shot in the chest with a canon. My heart opened and soared. This first view was just a glimpse of their jagged silhouette. As I kept riding, the peaks disappeared, but, unbelievably, I had seen the end of my journey.

The previous morning—a gray drizzly one—my friends and I had piled into their small olive-green station wagon with Sunny strapped to the roof. I'd loved having a warm, cuddly three year old on my lap for most of the trip. During a break in the light rain in Yellowstone we'd stopped for a picnic lunch along the way. Then they'd dropped me off at Old Faithful Lodge, leaving me full of energy and anticipation for the final day's ride to the Tetons.

The day had begun cloudy, but I was so excited to be close to my goal that I would have been able to ride through a hurricane. For the first three hours I rode through the chill and shade of Yellowstone's dense forest, crossing the continental divide three times, barely blinking an eye or breathing hard on the upward grades. When I emerged I saw that, miraculously, the day was sunny, the blue sky spotted with many, unthreatening white puffy clouds. What was threatening were the bulbous RV's on the narrow two lane road, but I held my position and they simply had to wait until they could safely pass, as if I were a slow car. As I sailed downwards out the south entrance to Yellowstone, I was full of gratitude for the gift of our National Park system. I still had about twenty-five miles to ride before the end of my day and the end of my journey, but I knew it would be a gradual descent through this magnificent park.

The road in Teton National Park wound through bright green meadows dotted with yellow, red, and purple wildflowers. Intermittently I'd be back into stretches of forest, but each time I emerged, there would be the great mountains growing closer. I'd passed through a short stretch of one of the park's many summer construction zones without so much as a grumble. (In Wyoming the locals say there are four seasons: almost winter, winter, still winter and construction.) When the Tetons were fully in view, and the pavement smooth, it was hard to keep my eyes off them and on the road. I was mesmerized by them, magnetized to them, hypnotized by them even more than I had been as a teenager when, unbeknownst to me at the time, I had fallen in love with them.

At 3:45 in the afternoon I arrived at the Jackson Lake Lodge and a full view of the Tetons. Just a few miles farther and I would reach my rendezvous point with Paul. But first I wanted time to be alone, time to savor the moment, to be with the experiences of the last forty-two days. I locked Sunny to a bike rack outside the lodge and walked through the large glass front doors. At the sundry store just inside I bought a package of Grandma's Chocolate Chip Cookies—my favorites on the road—and went upstairs to the bar. It opened onto a spacious wooden deck facing west to the mountains. I settled into a deck chair with my beer and cookies. A little white butterfly fluttered about me. It was June 18, and it was warm enough for me to be wearing only a t-shirt and shorts. I'd made it! I'd done what I'd fervently wanted to do, and most profoundly gratifying was that I'd done what I felt God wanted me to do.

As I stared in disbelief and wonder at the Tetons, a few of the challenges I'd overcome drifted through my mind like scenes from a dream, or a nightmare: the panic of a dangerous encounter on my first day out; the road from Nubieber to Klamath Falls—that cold, windy struggle and all that rage and pain about my mother, inherited wealth, not feeling entitled to my own needs or the good things of life; the Big Hole of despair and discouragement, the endless rain and cold; the disappointment at the top of three wet, socked-in mountain passes; the close encounters with navy blue wheat trucks. I had always found just enough strength and courage and the grace of some supportive allies to keep going. And undoubtedly God too had kept me going.

With beer and sun warming me, wonderful memories also drifted by. I chuckled again to remember blurting out, "I would love to be hot!" and how everyone at the Jackson Lodge had cracked up. I smiled to remember the euphoria of topping a pass in the sun; the fun of herding cattle by bike; the joy in racing a train along the Columbia; the unexpected connection with my new friend Josh, and the glorious days with him among the volcanoes; the thrill of being blown by that tailwind eighty miles in a single day, and then the great adventure crossing the Umatilla Bridge—the struggle and then divine intervention; the exuberant gratitude and praise to God that erupted from deep within me as I sat staring out at the Columbia River after so much goodness had befallen me.

As I sat absorbing the sun and the Tetons on the deck of the lodge, it almost felt as if those forty-two days had never happened. But I knew every mile and every experience was deeply embedded in my being.

I looked at my watch. It was five o'clock. *Time to go.* My beer and the cookies were gone, and the little white butterfly of the Tetons was still dancing around me. I was reluctant to leave the intimate connection I was feeling with the mountains and the sun. While I was looking forward to seeing Paul and so grateful to be met by someone I loved, I was also deeply absorbed in finding my own way in both my outer and inner worlds. How would he affect me? Would I be able to stay up if he were down? Even though I had taken steps to separate from him, both with Josh and in myself, I still didn't trust my ability to stay in touch with myself. Would our relationship be different now, after all I'd gone through?

I roused myself with some effort, took the empty glass back to the bar, and in a dreamy state walked down the wide staircase of the lodge. People drifted past me, as if in another world. When I reached Sunny, I slowly unlocked the padlock, coiled up the cable, put it into my front pack. I straddled my bike for a few moments before I put first one foot, then the other, into the pedal straps. As I rode slowly through the parking lot headed for the highway, I realized with amazement that Sunny had traveled 1,500 miles without so much as a flat tire, no breakdowns, not even a chain slipped off the gears. God had surely taken good care of my bike too.

After a few slow miles I pulled up to the lodge where Paul and I would be staying. I took a deep breath and knocked. Paul opened the door. "Ginia!" he beamed. He wrapped me into his body, holding me tight. We held each other like that for a long while. In spite of my misgivings I was elated to see him and burst into happy tears. As always my heart totally opened to him. My soul rejoiced to be with him, to feel the love that radiated from both our hearts and surrounded us. When we finally looked at each other, I saw he had tears in his eyes as well.

We got my bike inside and unloaded my gear, and began settling in. Within an hour I'd come down with chills and a fever, and my stomach started cramping. Was it that my body was finally able to give in to its fatigue and stress now that it was safe to let go? Over all those miles it had slowed me some but had never let me down. Maybe it was all those chocolate chip cookies with beer instead of real food. Paul was very concerned and attentive. He brought me a little soup for dinner, and I went to sleep under a pile of covers and blankets.

I slept most of the next morning and awoke feeling surprisingly well. No more fever, no more cramps. I had an urge to get my hair cut—to do something normal—and I'd seen a beauty salon at the Jackson Lake Lodge. I told Paul I'd be back in an hour and drove Sparky to the lodge. Sitting in the chair, enjoying the scalp massage, listening to the snipping sound of the scissors was a delight. When the women in the salon asked where I was from, I told them how I'd come to be there. I still could hardly believe I'd made the trip, and the women were incredulous. "You have to go upstairs to the gift shop to talk with Mary. She climbed the Grand Teton at age sixty-two."

Mary was happy to tell me about her amazing feat, a climb she had made with her daughter. *Wow, what a way to start into Old Age!* As I listened, I got that familiar "uh oh" feeling in my gut, and knew I was making some kind of promise to myself to do the same thing when I turned sixty. It was a triumph I would indeed celebrate twenty-five years later.

That afternoon Paul and I drove the sixty-mile loop around the park, taking in the Tetons from every perspective. I sat quietly in the passenger's seat, grateful to have nothing to do but stare at my beautiful mountains. Every angle was powerful and perfect, but the one that moved me most deeply was the front-facing view, the spellbinding image you see on postcards and in books—the jagged spires of the Tetons rising at a ninety degree angle off the floor of the Jackson Hole Valley to a height of 13,770 feet.

We stopped at the roadside turnout across from this view. The park display named each peak, but I knew them already As a camper I'd memorized every spire of the Cathedral Group: Middle and South Teton, (those were easy), Teewinot, (that name was always the most fun to say), Mount Owen, (named after William Owen who organized the first documented ascent of the Grand Teton in 1898), Cloudveil Dome, Teepee Pillar, Buck Mountain, and the great Grand Teton. I stood transfixed by those peaks, their power and unimaginable beauty blazing directly at me. It was as though they looked straight into my soul. With the sun directly on the face of the mountains, I could see the crags, the crevasses, the ravines that carry snowmelt steeply downward all summer long, the sharp shapes of boulders and massive rock formations, the slopes of bright, white glaciers. It is the view my sister and I were blessed with for six weeks during several summers as we camped and rode our horses directly beneath the Grand Teton Range.

Back in Sparky, we continued our drive. When the road crossed Cottonwood Creek, we pulled over and scrambled down the slope. We wandered alongside the water; my feet crunching the gravel I remembered from camp days. Through the flickering cottonwood leaves, I could see the mountains sparkling. Those happy memories of a content, carefree thirteen year old merged with the delight and gratitude of a thirty-five year old woman. As I had twenty years earlier, I cherished the treasures of this place.

One of the most special experiences of my camp days had been riding our horses to the Chapel of the Transfiguration for Sunday services, so I especially looked forward to visiting it. As we pulled into the parking lot, I felt a new sense of anticipation. *Would this have anything to do with going to the Tetons as Christ's bride?* The words about this that I had heard before leaving on the trip were still completely mysterious to me, and I hadn't thought too much about them during the journey. Getting through wind and rain hadn't been very conducive to feeling like a bride-to-be. But it had crossed my mind that if anything were to be revealed about my nuptials, it might be at the Chapel of the Transfiguration.

Chapel of the Transfiguration

I walked slowly up the pathway toward the small log cabin structure. Built in 1925, it is not much bigger than a single car garage. I paused in the entrance hallway. Paul followed me in. The church was empty. I walked past the four rows of log wood benches on either side of the aisle and took a seat in the first row. Paul sat next to me. The Chapel was just as I remembered. A large picture window behind the altar frames the Grand Teton. The cross, with vases of flowers on either side, sits squarely in the middle of that magnificent view. I gazed out the window absorbing the quiet, the spirit and beauty of the place.

I had done what God had asked me to do. *Here I am, God, here in your house. I made it.* In my heart this moment truly marked the completion of my journey.

With the silence and peace of the Chapel within me, we stood and walked back down the aisle and outside into a bright day. Nothing dramatic had happened. No voices. No visions. Nothing more dramatic than having made it to my destination. And that was enough. Would it have been different if I'd been there alone, without Paul? But that didn't matter as I walked quietly out of the Chapel with only the knowledge of my success and the specialness of this place in my spirit. I had fulfilled my promise.

Two days later, on the day Paul was to fly back to California, my GI tract had another violent revolution that sent me to the hospital for tests. Paul cancelled his flight to stay with me. Back at the hotel, I found that lying down was the only tolerable position while my stomach was under siege with extreme cramping. The doctors had checked for the bacteria giardia, but there was no sign of it. Once again I concluded that it had to do with the stress of the bike trip. Looking back it gives me pause to see how my time with Paul was bracketed with stomach cramping. I'd been ambivalent about seeing him again, but I was distressed to see him go. It might have been circumstantial and inconsequential, but I know the body can reflect things we are unable or unwilling to discern through our intellect or emotions. I was happier on my own, but he was still my love, still my touchstone to God.

In the morning I was feeling better, and we drove to the airport for Paul's rescheduled flight back to the Bay Area. I thought for a moment that I'd manage a tearless parting, but when the plane took off and disappeared into the sky, that familiar feeling of losing a little piece of myself welled up and overflowed. I drove back to the hotel in a solemn mood.

For the past two nights, Paul and I had taken a hotel room in Jackson Hole with a beautiful view of the Range. I made myself some tea and sat on the porch to be with the Tetons. In the presence of my beloved mountains, the sadness of Paul's departure began to fade away, and the fullness of my own experience and the pleasure of being in my own company returned. It was still somewhat unbelievable to me that I had successfully completed my journey, but looking over at Sunny leaning against the wall I knew that it was true.

I couldn't honestly say that I had found God in the conclusive way I'd anticipated, but over the course

of the journey, without a doubt God had sustained and protected me, and that was a way of finding Him. I was willing to accept now that the quest to find God was apparently a much bigger mystery than just arriving at my destination in the Tetons. And I was content for the time being to continue following my heart on this mysterious journey.

The Tetons and me

14

VISION QUESTING

I was alone in the wilderness. No Sunny as a companion, no maps or destinations, no place to go—alone in my interior wilderness for the three days and nights of a Vision Quest. Early that morning my guide John and his family had dropped me off at the trailhead leading into Bear Creek Canyon. I was back in the Bitterroot Mountains, this time carrying a backpack with a tarp, rope, my sleeping bag, matches, a Swiss army knife, my journal, and some water. Besides that I had only the clothes I wore, my watch, and Puppy Jr. "We'll be here and praying for you to have a fruitful time," John had said. "Let yourself be open." They'd hugged me and waved goodbye.

I crossed the rushing Bear Creek on all fours, crawling along a broad fallen tree, then hiked up the canyon along a rocky trail that climbed through pine forest and over jumbled rock fall. Although I was happy that the day was sunny and eager for this adventure, I felt nervous. *What's ahead for me? Will I get some direction for the next steps in my life? Will I be okay? Is this safe? Will this time have anything to do with my still-persisting desire to find God? And what does that mean anyway?* With unanswered questions filling my mind and butterflies in my stomach, I hiked along keeping watch for the "right" place to camp for three nights. After what must have been a couple of miles, I left the trail and headed through the sparse forest of pine and brush. About a quarter mile in, I came upon a grassy shelf, about the size of a tennis court cradled between two granite cliffs. The cliff walls angled toward each other like two sides of a triangle, opening at the narrower end into an endless view of distant mountains.

I decided to put my campfire in the middle of the little meadow and my sleeping area tucked into the woods about fifty feet away, at the "base" of the arrow. I tied up the tarp to the tall pines, laid out my sleeping bag, and neatly arranged my few possessions. John had given me a Tibetan prayer flag, and I tied it to one of the ropes. It felt like a sign of my prayerful and peaceful intentions for being there, and also a kind of protection. Around my firepit I made a small circle of stones and gathered wood to stack in a neat pile nearby.

Next I built the Medicine Wheel. John had told me about this Native American spiritual practice of creating a circle of stones based on the four directions, radiating out from the sacred center. Each of the points on the wheel had spiritual and psychological meaning, and John had suggested these might be helpful in contemplating my life journey. Laying down stones, I carefully formed a circle about four feet across, with stone "spokes" reaching out toward what I'd approximated was north, east, south, and west. When the sun dropped over the cliff to the west, I made some adjustments to align them just right.

All the while, as I was building the Medicine Wheel, I kept hoping and praying that this ancient process would help me find the clarity and direction I would need when I returned to my life in California. Attaining my outer goal of biking solo to the Tetons was deeply satisfying, but my thirst for God was still unquenched. What did that mean? What was I supposed to do next? And what would it be like to return home?

Once my "house" was in order I went to scope out the neighborhood. I returned to the trail and walked up a little ways to see what was there. When the area promised no diversion or excitement, I turned around. I meandered over to Bear Creek, and for a while rambled over the rocks alongside the rushing water. Then I walked back to camp. I'd run out of things to do, and it was only two o'clock. Nothing remained to distract me from the growing reality that I was alone on a Vision Quest. I didn't even have the pleasure of looking forward to eating, not even nibbling a little carrot or having a scant cupful of juice. At the local diner that morning I had managed, with great effort, to restrain my voracious food demons from pigging-out on the "Cattleman's Pancake Breakfast." I didn't want to negate the value of the fast. The idea was to be as empty as possible in order to allow for incoming visions.

As I sat alone, empty, and visionless, I began to wonder why I had been so eager for this experience. After over a month of demanding inner and outer work on the road, why hadn't I checked into a nice resort spa instead of signing up for yet another challenge? And what, if anything, did this have to do with my search for God? But the inner urge that had so strongly drawn me to the Vision Quest was the same as that which had led me to take my first bike trip, to create Mudd's, to journey to the Tetons. Following my heart was the only way I knew to go about finding God. I listened and followed my heart's inner call, and no matter how scary or hard or uncertain, there was always a sense of rightness and peace. So here I was, alone in the wilderness. I don't know what I'd expected, but I was deeply surprised that when I had what I'd so urgently wanted, I felt panicked and anxious.

To ease the growing sense of claustrophobia, I turned my attention to the view of the far distant mountains. Still I felt trapped, like a self-incarcerated prisoner on a beautiful terrace of Montana wilderness. The coming seventy-two hours alone stretched before me like a blank white canvas. I could see nothing to put on that canvas but empty long days and longer lonely nights. I wished I'd just gone back to California with Paul.

I got up and headed back to Bear Creek. At least there was activity there. I sat on a rock, perched above a particularly fast and roaring stretch. The water was falling dramatically over big boulders into the dense woods below. I felt—and was—so utterly alone, except for the pesky fly that kept buzzing around and lighting on my arms and hands. What if I didn't have a vision? What if fear, loneliness, hunger, anxiety, and panic were all I could look forward to? Maybe I would never return from this mountain, never see my friends or loved ones again. Specters of cold and starvation and death arose from some dark swampy mire within me. Tears and fears poured through me like the water rushing past.

I knew these fears were all unfounded, because if I really couldn't bear it any longer, I could bail out simply by hiking the two miles back to where John and his family were camped. I could also get John to come looking for me. We had a safety set-up—beside the trail where I'd turned off in search of a campsite, I had built a stone pile. I was to place a new stone there every day to indicate to John that I was okay. All I would have to do is not leave a stone there tomorrow morning, and he would come looking for me and take me back to "civilization."

Despite these thoughts, leaving my mountaintop was not really an option in my mind—no more than quitting my bicycle trip before reaching the Tetons had been. I'd made it through the temptations then. I could do it now. The point of the Vision Quest was to allow whatever might arise from my innermost being. Maybe something terribly painful would come, or something beautifully pleasant; maybe something hopeful or something depressing. I knew I was supposed to be willing to accept it all, including bothersome flies.

In the midst of my tears and confusion, suddenly I thought I heard the river ask, "Why are you crying?" Maybe I'd already entered an altered reality. Without thinking, I answered, "I'm so alone and afraid." With exuberant splashing, pounding, thundering, crashing and the throwing of thousands of diamonds into the air, the river replied, "You're *not* alone. See, here I am. Creek!" "Oh, well, hello then," I whispered. I didn't want anyone to hear me talking to a creek. And that fly—it also suddenly looked like company.

Feeling slightly less lonely, I decided to return to camp, where I once again found only empty time and space. How could I handle seventy more hours of this? Do something! I began by starting what would become my daily routine of yoga and walking meditation. After stretching for a while, I walked slowly and silently around my terraced meadow for as long as I could bear. Then I added in singing meditation. The hymns and songs and prayers bubbling up from inside me felt like more company, almost as if my singing voice was another being.

Finally I lay down to just rest, to let be, and to wait. I thought of all my friends back home, and I spoke silently to them, one by one, telling them why I was grateful for their friendship and what they meant to me. It was soothing to imagine talking with them, to see them looking at me. Maybe I'd felt that alone and without company, I was disappearing, because I could see how connection with another person does one essential thing—it confirms one's existence. A person or animal responding to us makes it obvious that we are in fact here. Maybe Creek too—and Fly—had confirmed my existence.

By the time the sun went down and the last light of day faded from the sky, I was feeling calmer. Too tired to build a fire, I was only too glad to crawl under my tarp and tuck myself into my sleeping bag. I dozed off thinking, *Won't my stomach be surprised tomorrow when nothing falls into its ever-ready clutches?*

It struck me as entirely magical that the ball of light that had dropped from view over the western cliff at 8:00 p.m. appeared over the eastern cliff at 8:13 a.m. The ants and mosquitoes and I all responded to its warmth at the same time. They had far more to do than I had, and I envied their busyness and purposefulness. Only my mind was active. After less than twenty-four hours I was prepared to say that I was not the sort of person who was meant to be a yogi who meditates for years on a mountaintop in the Himalayas. During those two years in the maelstrom of the restaurant business, I had seriously considered that a life of solitude might be in my nature, but now I was sure this was not my destiny. I would have to find a balance between contemplation and activity in the course of my daily life.

There. I'd already had a vision!

At 11:45 a.m., I walked slowly to my rocky beach where, despite feeling apprehensive that some hiker might come by, I undressed completely and dunked my head into the river to rinse my hair. My scalp froze on contact with the snowmelt water, but I resisted the urge to leap out. After a quick rinse I lay out to bake on the warm rocks. Two butterflies came to investigate. Though their black and white wings were torn and frayed, they were lively and playful. I could almost hear them saying to me, "Look, we are battered as you are, but we are full of life." After doing their accordion wing dance on the rocks nearby, they lighted on my body, dusting and tickling me. I felt like they were making love to me, like I was being kissed with God's lips. As they touched my stomach, my legs, my breasts, the aches and pains and cold bones left over from my bicycle journey felt warmed and healed. I thought of them as messengers from God, come in understanding to care for me. I named the place Butterfly Beach.

When I got up to put my clothes back on, I felt shaky and suddenly devoid of energy, as though it had been swept away by the rushing water while I was lying on the creek bank. Despite the wobble, I set off downstream for what I was now calling Fly Falls, about half a city block away. It was unnerving to have to stop and rest every few feet, and by the time I arrived, I gratefully dropped onto my already favorite boulder beside my friend Creek. Amidst the mesmerizing thundering and chaos of the waterfall plunging into the forest below, I sat in a mindless, enchanted daze. The water, in its violent churning, drowned out awareness of everything but itself.

As I sat absorbed by the roar and wildness of Creek, I recalled that John had said that one of the purposes of the Vision Quest was to bring myself into the present time by releasing as much of the past as I could so that I would allow new directions to come forward. It was intended to be a time of passing over a threshold, of putting aside the hurts and burdens of the past, and opening to the feelings and visions that might come into the cleared space.

Right then and there I decided to do a releasing and letting go ceremony. I collected a pile of little twigs from nearby fallen branches and returned to my rock. Each twig would represent some haunting, burdensome mistake of the past. I held the first one in my hand—for my former husband. I asked his forgiveness for my failing to stay with our marriage and for all the hurt that I had caused him. I cast the burdened twig into the foamy waters cascading down the canyon, and imagined it being carried into the Bitterroot River and finally into the sea. I cast another twig as I asked forgiveness of my friend and business partner for impulsively firing his wife and our friend from the restaurant.

Fly, who was still accompanying me, reminded me of a painful memory from my camp days. My friends and I would capture the huge flies that bit our horses so ferociously, and cut off their legs or their wings. I cast several twigs asking forgiveness of those horseflies for my cruelty.

A twig was not enough for the deep pain and sorrow I felt about the death of my beloved young horse, Aki. I felt personally responsible for his death, and I decided to do a special ceremony later by the campfire.

After I cast the remaining twigs and sat a while longer, I rose from my boulder. It was late afternoon, and I was feeling weaker still. I slowly made my way along the trail, stopping to place a rock on the designated pile to let John know I was okay. I wished I could have split a rock in half to say I was just sort of okay—I was firing on only a few cylinders. When I got back to camp, I noticed that the two butterflies had followed me.

My sunset yoga and walking meditation were exhausting, but that evening I was full of song. Well into the night I lay on the grass with my head propped on a log, singing old camp favorites to myself and to the quiet wilderness. *Michael Row Your Boat Ashore, Kumbayah, 500 Miles, Where Have All the Flowers Gone.* I also made up a silly little Vision Quest song to the tune of *We Wish You a Merry Christmas*: "We wish you a happy Vision Quest...and a safe journey home." Around 10:00, the first star appeared, a little pinprick of light in the deepening blue sky. I tried to stay awake—it was so beautiful, so captivating—but I kept nodding off, even with the uncomfortable gnarly log under my head. I was glad to feel tired. When I crawled into my sleeping bag, I realized it was the first time since I'd stopped biking every day that lying down didn't start my feet twitching with unused energy.

In the middle of the night, I climbed out of my sleeping bag to pee. Even though it was late June, I could see my frosty breath dissipating into the cold night air. The stars were resplendent, filling the sky, but I could barely stand straight to see them. My legs felt like rubber. I managed to stumble about twenty feet from my tent and held myself up with my arms as I squatted. On my way back, I tripped over the small rocks of my Medicine Wheel and barely managed to stay upright. Once I was back in bed my insides began to feel like they had been taken over by squirming, noxious jellyfish. My heartbeat was heavy and fast, but it wasn't in my chest. The throbbing was in my belly. What if something was terribly wrong? I still had a full day and another night to go. In my mind I composed a note to leave on the rock pile: "If I'm not down to your camp by nine two mornings from now, you should a) send the cavalry, b) send a dog sled, c) send calories."

The morning was gray and dripping with rain. *Oh, please, no more rain!* As we'd agreed, at dawn, I managed to get to the rock pile, hefted a stone on top—with no note—and retreated back under the tarp to my sleeping bag. I still felt terrible. I assumed I was weak because my body was also in a process of detoxifying from lack of food. Based on my past fasting experience, I knew that the malaise would pass. At least I hoped it would. I was determined to stick out the Vision Quest to the end, even if that meant staying in my sleeping bag for the next twenty-four hours. And, anyway, there was no way I was going out into the cold rainy day. I'd had enough of that. A large horse fly routinely attacked me, diving at my face until I was raging at him. "Don't you know I don't like you!?" I swatted back at him as ferociously as I could. *So much for kinship with all life.* I felt a little guilty for not being able to accept *that* fly as another companion.

A break in the clouds eventually encouraged me to get myself upright. I looked at my watch: 1:30. I felt like a rag doll with no stuffing. I managed to pull myself up and stumbled onto the trail headed for Fly Falls. Slumped onto my rock, I sat watching water rushing over the boulders. It occurred to me that Creek, although wild and free, had a course it must follow. What was *my* course? How was I to spend my time and energy? *Could I please have another vision!* But instead of a rainbow appearing in the sky, or some great insight, the clouds piled themselves thickly over the sun again, and a wind came up from the southwest, whipping up mist off the foaming, rampaging waters of Creek. Visionless, I tottered back to camp, noticing that my guide had been to the rock pile to leave his acknowledging stone.

I decided to build a fire even though it was only 3:30 in the afternoon. I felt chilled and emotionally empty, and I knew it was time to face the pain and sorrow of Aki's death, to move past the guilt, if possible. I tore a couple of pieces of empty pages out of my journal, crumpled them up and placed them at the bottom of the carefully stacked wood in my firepit, then shakily put the lighted match to it. As the flames flickered into the dry wood I'd pulled from the bottom of the pile, I drew closer, glad to feel the little bit of heat

Beautiful little Aki. Born of a mare I'd had for some years, sired by a national Arabian champion, he was born one muddy spring day, looking exactly like my first childhood horse—a light bay, with black mane and tail, and four short white stockings. Here was my childhood Blaze come into my life all over again. I was thrilled. My husband and I raised Aki with the tender loving care we gave all our animals. Aki would have slept on our bed if we had let him in the house.

I trained him as best I could, considering that all I knew I'd learned at camp in the Tetons. I was the first person to ride Aki when he turned six, and I worked with him as much as I could for a year. But I knew my horse skills were limited, and I didn't feel safe to let other people ride him without some further training. So when he was seven, with great reluctance I decided to send him to a local training stable to be handled by a professional trainer. I trailered him there myself, and in spite of great hesitation on his part, I convinced him to go into a small, dark cell they called a stall. Aki had never been enclosed in his life. He had never been away from home. In tears I left him there, knowing how scared and confused and alone he must feel.

This was within a month of opening Mudd's restaurant, and with all the intensity of that project, I had very little time to visit him, even though he was always on my mind. I talked with the trainer at the beginning of Aki's six-week training period, and not again—until one Sunday afternoon three weeks later. The phone rang, disturbing the silence of a much needed peaceful day-off at home.

"Hello, Virginia?"

"Yes?' I recognized the trainer's voice. I couldn't imagine why he was calling.

I'm sorry to bother you on a Sunday. I'm sorry to call you." There was a long pause.

"I went to saddle Aki this morning, everything seemed fine, but then he just lay down and died." I couldn't speak. I couldn't believe what he was saying.

"I can't understand what was wrong," he went on. "He seemed healthy. Everything was fine."

I had no words, no feelings.

"Uh, what would you like me to do with the...body? Do you want an autopsy?"

I said no immediately. I couldn't imagine cutting Aki up.

"I'll bury him in one of our fields then. I'm sure sorry." He hung up.

And that was that. Aki was gone. I was in too much shock and pain to even think about going to see him before he was buried, or to have some sort of ceremony.

If only I had gone to see him more often. If only I hadn't sent him away at all. In my heart I felt he had died because he was lonely and sad, and he missed his home. If only I'd paid more attention to how he was feeling. If only I'd paid more attention to how *I* had been feeling, which was that I missed him and needed to visit him. If only...if only.... But now he was gone, and I believed his death was my fault. Of course, without an autopsy there was no way to know if a physical problem had been the cause of his death, but I knew I had let us both down because I was too busy to attend to him and our relationship that I cared deeply about.

Aki's death happened three years before my trip to the Tetons. I'd carried this sorrow and guilt since then, and I didn't know how to forgive myself or how to put it behind me. I hoped that now, during the Vision Quest, I could heal this somehow. I'd asked John if he could find some black horsetail or mane I could take with me into the wilderness, and he'd brought me a slim braid of long black horse hair, which I'd tucked into a little pocket in my knapsack. While the fire crackled I sat cross-legged with the braid in my lap, stroking it as if I were stroking Aki's own mane, and my own breaking heart.

I sobbed convulsively. John had also given me dried sweet grass and sage for a Native American cleansing and purification rite. I lit it now and waved the smoke over "Aki's" tail and over myself to purify any negative energy, and to bring in the Holy Spirit to bless us. I felt compelled to add a little of my blood to the offering of sage and sweet grass, but though I poked my finger over and over with my Swiss army knife, I couldn't get even one drop to come. Perhaps Aki didn't want me to bleed anymore. Eventually the tears stopped flowing. Using a stick and my knife, I dug a small hole in the ground by the fire. I curled up the strands of "Aki's" hair in a circle and laid it inside, crumpled up some of the sage on top, and filled the hole. It was done. I felt empty but calm. I sat quietly for a long while by Aki's "grave," wrapped in the fire's magic and warmth, recovering from the emotion of "burying" him.

Suddenly the flames were whipping in all directions and the wind was sending sparks flying toward the early summer forest. I immediately passed from peace into a state of sheer terror. The entire Bitterroot Wilderness could be set ablaze by my small campfire, and I was the only one there to deal with it! I began imagining myself running from tree to tree trying to put out pine needle fires. After two and a half days of fasting I was barely "running on fumes," so I knew my efforts would be pathetic and useless. The panic increased, and before long, in my mind, I had the whole forest burning.

I could hear the voice of my mother warning me I would be forever damned if I fell asleep while smoking in bed. One time as an early teen on my way back to boarding school, I had indeed smoked in bed. I was at the home of one of my mother's friends, who was putting me up for the night. I was ultra-careful, but...I thought I'd seen a little spark go somewhere. I turned the bed inside out, took the mattress off the frame, and then stayed awake all night for fear of setting the woman's house on fire. This memory fanned the flames of my fear, and I began remembering the Southern California wildfires that had nearly burned down the family ranch.

Whoa! Stop! Get a grip! The forest is not *on fire. Calm down!* I did my best to breathe normally and to study my situation with a rational mind. I watched the sparks fly—they all disappeared before they got anywhere near a tree—and it *had* been raining. I didn't want to put the fire out. I was cold, and I loved the smoke and heat and ashes blowing into my face. It was not an illegal fire, (though that was hardly the point), and it was in an open area, in as safe a place as a campfire could be. *It's okay. It will be okay.* My heart rate began to slow back down. I allowed myself to look out into the late afternoon sky. While keeping a vigilant eye on the wind-blown flames, I watched the clouds moving in layers in different directions—the higher ones toward the northeast, the lower ones to the east. Other dark gray and billowy white clouds were sitting peacefully, unmoving on the horizon to the south, in my window between the cliffs.

As my fears diminished, a sense of awe and gratitude rose up in me. It was all so intensely beautiful. Only God would create such a magical spectacle! God had directed me to this Vision Quest, and I had followed. He'd brought me to this wondrous place, and everything was okay. I felt inspired to make up my own version of a campfire song: "Rolling home, rolling home, by the light of the silvery mo-oo-oo-oon. Happy is the day when it's God who rules our way, as we go rolling, rolling home."

Around 6:00, I said a thankful goodnight to my well-behaved fire, thoroughly doused it, and cuddled into my sleeping bag. I tilted my head way back so I could stare into the sky out the open end of the tarp. Absorbed in the enormity and intensity of the universe and its movement, I considered that over these three days at the end of June, I had been witnessing the actual rotation of the heavens from west to east, or rather the earth's rotation from east to west. It gave me a dumbfounding sense of my relationship to the cosmos. Me, the ants, the trees—all of us ever so tiny here on the earth—were moving as an infinitesimal part of the great whole universe. *Where does it end? Or does it? What awesome order pervades this enormous scheme!?* As I lay there in wonderment, my mind felt like it was exploding in a hopeless attempt to embrace the infinite universe.

Then it occurred to me that it was only illusion that told me I was looking *up* at the heavens. In reality I was as likely to be looking *down* at the heavens. Maybe I was actually hanging upside down, glued to the earth, as though there were Velcro on the bottom of my sleeping bag to keep me from spinning off into space. This was a scary and shocking position to contemplate.

While it was easy to explain that this phenomenon was due to the law of gravity, that was a small matter compared to the bigger questions that then arose in my mind: *How come gravity? Who created gravity? What enormous power of intelligence, imagination and creativity has fathomed such a wild and brilliant scheme as this universe? As this earth?* Staring into the starry night, I was overwhelmed by the immensity of the unimaginable cosmos. I felt infinitely small, like one of the little pinprick stars above me. Yet at the same time, I felt an intimacy with it all. I had a deep, inexplicable knowing that Love created the universe, that God is Love, that God just *is*. Tucked into my warm sleeping bag under the canopy of the infinite galaxies, I could *feel* that Love radiating and vibrating around me. I felt so full and fulfilled, and yet…and yet, I realized I still felt something missing in my awareness of God? *What more is there? What more could I be looking for?* I drifted off to sleep, content for now with knowing I simply didn't know.

From time to time I awoke to gaze at the changing position of the heavens as they rotated above—or below—me. Awake when the sky began to lighten, I literally counted the minutes before the sun rose over the eastern cliffs at 8:03. This sunrise would mark the end of my three-day Vision Quest. I would step out of my warm cocoon, free to return to "civilization."

I had just enough strength to pack up, check to make sure the campfire was cold, and say my farewells to the mountaintop. When I reached the trail, I waved goodbye to Creek, which I couldn't see but could hear and feel. I said a quiet goodbye to Fly and the two butterflies as though they were all present to see me off.

The pack was heavy and wobbled me back and forth as I walked carefully down the trail, not wanting to twist an ankle or to fall with so little energy to catch myself. I rounded a curve and was elated to see the log "bridge" over rushing Bear Creek, the last obstacle before I'd reach to my friends' camp. I had made it. I was "home." I had managed to be with the loneliness, the empty time, the fears, the sorrows, the physical trials. I had found inner resources to help me through those difficult times and emotions. I had made new friends. I'd had some useful insights. I had witnessed and been a part of the moving life of the planet and the universe. I had seen and felt God's hand in it all. And I had *not* set the forest on fire! I still wasn't sure how all this might guide my life back in California, but I had a deep sense of change, and I trusted that would make a difference.

I was so weak that, afraid the weight of my pack would topple me into the roaring creek a few feet below, I dropped it on the bank before crawling across the log. At their campsite, my friends greeted me with warm hugs and smiles. I could feel my smile as big as a watermelon slice—if only my face were wide enough to contain it all. John skipped over the log to retrieve my pack, and they led me into the Medicine Wheel they had created. We linked arms and John offered a prayer of thanks to the Great Spirit for bringing me home safely. We gathered our belongings, said farewell to the place, and walked a short distance back to the trailhead and their car.

In the early morning I woke from a dream. It was my first night back from Bear Creek Canyon—and my last night before driving back to California. I looked around to orient myself. I was lying on a sleeping pad on a twenty foot square platform where John and his family made their summer home in the mountains. It held everything they needed: a wood cooking stove, a small round wood table with four chairs, sleeping bags, and a box for a few clothes. A canopy floated overhead like a circus tent. The others were still asleep and I drifted back into the dream.

My closest woman friend, her husband, and I are at a ski resort. The man's name is Danny. At the top of a ridge overlooking a wide bowl of delicious, pristine powder snow, we snap into our skis. Danny takes off into the bowl, headed toward another ridge lower down on the far side. A snow-packed road runs parallel to the ridge. On the other side is a drop-off.

Danny begins to pick up speed. He bangs into another skier, knocking him down, and races onwards. We watch with rising alarm. He looks out of control, and his speed is increasing with every second. Fortunately there are no cars coming on the road. But my friend and I look on in horror and complete helplessness as he continues on toward the ridge at top speed. Even before he sails over it, his skis are in the air and we know it is all over for him.

We take off into the bowl, and when we arrive at the top of the ridge, there are already a few people looking over the edge. Far below, amidst jagged rocks and steep snow banks, lies Danny's body. It is not possible that he could have survived such a fall, yet, miraculously, Danny is rising. But I know it isn't the old Danny. It is a new Danny. We watch as he climbs back up to us. "Whew!" is all he says when he reaches us at the ridge top. Later, we all sit in a lodge around a toasty fire, drinking and relaxing. I propose a toast to his rebirth, to the new Danny.

When I opened my eyes, I wrote down the dream. I knew from dream work in therapy that every character in a dream can be seen as an aspect of oneself. Of course, I most related to the old and new Danny. I felt I'd been given a glimpse into the elemental force of the mystical death and rebirth experience. I would have to die to my old ways before I could be reborn into new ones. I would have to let go of attitudes, images and stories of myself, and beliefs about my world that no longer served me or simply weren't true. On the Vision Quest, I had let go of some of my pain, sadness and guilt from past experiences. And even though I had not yet reflected deeply on my bike journey, I knew I had let go of many things. I knew I had been reborn in ways I had yet to discover and integrate.

After tearful farewells to my friends and promises to stay in touch, I packed up my truck and headed down a dirt road out of the forest toward the highway. The dream simmered inside me like a flavorful rich stew. Perhaps this was my "vision," a promise of rebirth if I just let go and have enough faith to go over the edge. Is that how I would come to God? As I turned onto the paved highway, to retrace the path of my journey to the Tetons, I had a sense I would find out.

15

ON BLISSFUL HIGHWAYS

I rode up this grade, with a bad leg? In the cold? In the rain?
I was sailing down the west side of Lolo Pass in the comfort of Sparky. What a marvel motorized travel was! We glided along the road—effortlessly, smoothly, magically—mile after mile. With just a slight adjustment of my foot on the gas pedal, a minute rotation of my hands on the steering wheel, I could stay squarely in the middle of my lane, any cracks or lumps in the pavement cushioned by shock absorbers. From time to time I looked in the rearview mirror to catch a glimpse of Sunny lying on his side in the back, taking a well-deserved rest. He had never failed me, and he and I together had made it up this long, steep grade that even in my truck required some careful navigating. No wonder it had been so painful! I allowed myself to take in with unabashed pride what I had accomplished. A little voice inside popped up to remind me that in grade school I'd learned it was a No-No to vote for yourself. Screw that, I thought, and continued to "vote" for myself at every turn, and applauded myself to boot.

Three weeks had gone by since I'd nearly been killed by wheat trucks on Route 12 crossing Idaho. So much had changed that it looked like a different place altogether. It was now the end of June, and the weather was calm, the skies clear blue, the temperature thirty degrees warmer. Based on everything people along the route had told me, this was the typically mellow weather I should have had.

My inner landscape felt equally unfamiliar. That the bike trip was over hadn't entirely sunk in yet. And the Vision Quest was still simmering inside me. Along with that, I still hadn't found God, and I still didn't know exactly what I meant by that. Even though I had experienced the Infinite Love that is God under the starlit sky on my Vision Quest, something was still missing. I had gone to the Tetons as Christ's bride, but we had not married. Maybe the trip had been a time of testing. Maybe I had gone as Christ's *fiancée*, and we'd been in an engagement period to see if we were meant to be bride and bridegroom. Really, I had no idea what was going on. I only knew that my search must continue, but that I had fulfilled my promise to bicycle to the Tetons alone. I was saturated with the immense satisfaction of that accomplishment.

I slipped the soundtrack from the movie *Yentl* into the cassette player and skipped ahead to one of my favorite songs. It is sung by Barbara Streisand, in her role of the young woman who has broken free from the strictures of the Old World, as she sets sail aboard a ship of emigrants on their way to America. As she stands at the bow of the ship, the wind in her face, New York harbor in sight, she sings, "Though it's safer to stay on the ground, sometimes where danger lies, there the sweetest of pleasures are found." The words I had sung in anticipation before the trip, now carried in them my own truth and the richness of experience.

Bicycling to the Tetons had indeed been dangerous, given how vulnerable I was as a solo woman cyclist. And what I had overcome and changed in myself had certainly become "the sweetest of pleasures." I had proven myself to be strong and capable. I'd overcome inertia and, with action and determination, fought for my life in the face of a potential rapist and wildly careening wheat trucks. I'd bravely crept into my little tent alone many nights. I'd been willing to accept the sweetness and support of a kind stranger. I had gone all out to get Sunny and myself over the Umatilla Bridge, but then had reached out for help when I needed it. I had fought my way out of despair by going on in spite of it. And I had ridden my bike 1,500 miles to the Tetons—all by myself, all on my own—and arrived in remarkably good shape. It was all something to sing about! I sang along with Yentl about "the things you can't imagine if you've never flown at all."

I could now imagine so much more. As I sang "If you can fly, then soar," I felt as if I were joining the flight of that eagle I liked to imagine above me, the one whose silhouette was painted on the dark blue hood of my truck. The sense of power, confidence, and awe filling me elevated the drive along Route 12 into a passage of euphoria. Our voices rang out as we flew past the Three Rivers Motel, along the banks of the Lochsa River (not a wheat truck to be seen!), past the Snake River, through the Blue Mountains, and into Walla Walla, Washington for the night. What had taken me seven days to bicycle through took eight and a half hours of driving in a dreamy state of contentment, fascination, reminiscence and amazement. It was, perhaps, the first taste I'd ever had of bliss.

I thoroughly indulged myself until noon in the pleasures and amenities of Walla Wallan civilization. In the college town coffee house where I had my favorite pancake breakfast, the atmosphere was lively—the waiters bustling, the conversations at crowded tables buzzing, the cappuccino potent. Energized and satisfied, I walked along the main street until I found an instant-service photo shop, where I left six rolls of film to be developed in the next hour. I came upon a wonderful variety store and walked out with an armful of novels and poetry books. I'd also been attracted to a book by the Trappist monk, Thomas Merton. It must have been the first word of the title—*New Seeds of Contemplation*—that caught my eye. *New.* Yes, I felt new. The whole title seemed to offer me a new world. And the fact that Merton was a religious man might mean he could shed light on my own journey. This was the first of many books by this great spiritual teacher that I would find invaluable.

To my collection of new books, I'd also added a Sunset travel guide to New Zealand. My friend Gerry in Chico, who had first inspired this solo bike trip, had mentioned that it would be fun to bike there. I had no idea what might be next in my outer journey, but a world of possibilities seemed to be opening up before me. I trusted God would tell me what He wanted me to do. Maybe it would be New Zealand with Gerry, maybe it would be a trip to the moon.

An hour later, sitting in the front seat of Sparky, I slowly went through the stack of 163 photos. I stared at the images of me as if I were looking at someone else. Three of them—taken sequentially by Paul as I had ridden away from him, embarking on my journey in early May—show a vulnerable-looking, small-framed woman with a pixie haircut, peering bravely into the unknown, leaving comfort, security and love behind, as she recedes from view down the empty road. In another photo, taken by my Portland friends on the day they sent me off up the Columbia River Gorge, I am straddling my fully loaded bike and looking back at them, as if to say, "I'd love to stay, but I gotta go." Most of the pictures were those I'd taken myself of my trusty companion Sunny in various poses: leaning against the guardrails above the many rivers we traveled along— the Columbia, the Clearwater, the Lochsa, the Bitterroot, the Madison; at the top of the Tobacco Root Pass; and, my favorite, Sunny's front end following the furry butts of a herd of cattle.

With a little plastic basket of golden raspberries on the seat next to me, I headed west out of Walla Walla to continue retracing my bike route. I ate the berries slowly, one sunny, sweet globe at a time, as I drove through a landscape that here too bore little resemblance to the land I had passed through a month earlier. The Washington wheat, a dark lush green in early June, now sported blond beards atop pale green stalks. Squared-off fields of bare brown earth alternated with fields of golden wheat covering the landscape like a patchwork quilt. I stopped periodically to immerse myself in the dry summer heat of eastern Washington: the yellows, browns, and golds of dry, crackly grasses; the sweet scent of sage; the crunch of the gravel underfoot; the shrill singing of crickets pulsing through the land and air.

Rejoining the Columbia was like meeting an old friend. I sailed alongside the wide muddy waters for several hours with the piano concertos of Schumann and Grieg pouring from the speakers. I winked my headlights and waved exuberantly at an eastbound freight train, which returned my greeting with a joyful whistle. Truckers returned my blinking headlight salutation with their own flashing headlights as we sped past each other. I laughed and smiled my delight all day long, moving through an ethereal cloud of goodness and joy and happiness. If the day before I'd traveled in a state of bliss, on this day I was in a state of rapture. I was amazed that such joy was possible in the world, and most especially in me.

Mt. Adams and Mt. Hood rose up through hazy afternoon sunshine. I could hardly wait to surprise a certain friend, but I decided to give myself another night in my own blissful company first. On the map I'd found an unknown but promising campground at Lost Lake in the hills surrounding Mt. Hood. I drove with ease across the Hood River bridge over the Columbia—just a slight breeze rippling the wide waters—and wound my way into the hills, passing through the lush, dense forests of pine, rhododendrons, and pale green, lacey ferns dripping with moisture. Every now and then the beauty was marred by an obscene patch of an old clear-cut, its ugliness and debris trashing the landscape. I cringed as I drove by. At least Josh's log company hadn't done this. At the campground I backed Sparky into a spot with a view of the lake, had a tailgate picnic dinner, and soon fell asleep with the moon throwing a silvery band of sparkling light toward me from the water. I felt like I'd been led to a little piece of paradise.

The next morning I waited until the sun was on the lake before setting out on a hike up Butte Trail. I'd always found the pull toward unknown grand views, and huge expansive spaces irresistible. And that morning I felt drawn upwards by some powerful magnetic force. The trail led immediately into the forest and began to climb. After a long, steep first mile over dark, moist earth and through thick ferns and rhododendrons, I hit a series of switchbacks for another mile. Sunlight filtered through the tall pines and alders, and at one point I glimpsed a view of Mt. Adams through the trees. The state of pure grace that I'd felt the past two days carried me higher.

And then the trail abruptly ended in a tangle of fallen trees and brush. But through the thicket of vines and dead branches I could just make out Mt. Hood. *There has to be a better view.* I scrambled over a pile of wood and decaying lumber, pushed my way through a knot of dead branches and brush and pine... and was brought up short. Before me, in all its splendor and glory, across the valley rose Mt. Hood. I was on a ledge extending out over a wide, thickly forested canyon. Nothing but a few clouds stood or flew or breathed between me and this great mountain, which seemed to be just a couple of miles of empty space away. I felt riveted to the spot in astonishment and awe and wonder, as if I were beholding an angel or seeing the Pacific Ocean for the first time.

Stunned, I made a quarter-turn to my left, and there was Mt. Adams before me, equally majestic, only slightly farther in the distance. Caught in a spell, I felt as if I were pinned to a wall, with two mighty giants bearing down on me. When I managed at last to extricate myself from their grip, I made another quarter-turn to my left and, unbelievably, *another* snow-capped volcano rose in full view. Mount St. Helens appeared before me like a vision in a dream. And the spectacle was not yet over. Another small counter-clockwise turn brought me face to face with one more snow-capped peak—Mt. Bachelor, the farthest from me to the south.

Dumbstruck, I felt as if the mountains were blasting me with an invisible power. Suddenly I was no longer standing but sunk to my knees, sobbing. Each time I glanced up at Mt. Hood, a new wave of wailing overtook me, as if I was being struck again by an unseen force. *How can I be crying in the face of such beauty and magnificence?* I crouched in the dirt with my head in my hands, wailing like a wounded crazy person. I wanted to throw myself off the butte. I wanted to give myself to the mountains. I wanted to launch myself like a bird into the wide open gulf that lay between Mt. Hood and the place where I knelt. I wanted to fly into that open space before me.

Mt. Hood

A small, wordless, restraining force kept me on the ledge, as though I was being held to the material world by one of the tangled vines behind ne. My sobbing abated, leaving me drained and empty of feeling. With one last, almost painful half-glance at all four volcanoes, I turned toward the bramble of bushes and dead wood, pushed my way through to the trail, and headed down the mountain, stunned and uncomprehending. Without speech, without thought, without emotion, I put one foot in front of the other.

Over the next two years I would struggle to make sense of what had happened to me on that butte above Lost Lake. Something in me knew that the urge to throw myself into the abyss had been a desire to surrender completely to God. But there was more to it than that, and one day I would understand.

I parked Sparky between the barn-sized stacks of cut timber and settled myself on the tailgate in the sun to wait. Trucks piled with logs roared into the mill yard amidst clouds of dust, unloaded at the log chute, the drivers pausing for brief conversation, then headed out again at the same urgent pace. In the yard men in plaid shirts, bright suspenders, and yellow hard hats worked efficiently to handle the constant flow of incoming logs. A water truck routinely circled the area with a fan of water to keep the dust down. By the time the noon whistle wailed into the sap-scented air, the truck I was waiting for hadn't yet appeared.

I was not impatient. I basked in the sun and the warm glow of memory and anticipation. Josh had been a steady friend and support during my journey; our phone calls had kept me going. They had also brought us closer together. It was not passion I felt for him but a deep tenderness. Our unusual bond had become a shiny treasure in my life.

As the comings and goings at the mill continued, I reached for Thomas Merton's book. One passage particularly grasped my heart: It begins: "For when our minds and wills are perfectly free from every created attachment, they are immediately filled with the gift of God's love." And then a little farther in the same paragraph, a quote from the New Testament: "Everyone who has left his home or his father, or his mother, or his wife for my sake shall receive a hundredfold and shall possess eternal life." That really got me. Ever since the dream of penetration by God, then falling in love and leaving my home, my husband and animals, that mysterious urge to find God had been driving my life. So often since I had launched myself on this quest, I felt that I was crazy, that I was on a wild goose chase, or jousting with windmills like Don Quixote, dreaming the impossible dream. Here was Thomas Merton, and Jesus, telling me that it was understandable to want God so desperately, to throw everything away for God. Merton goes on, "To desire God is the most fundamental of all human desires. It is the very root of all our quest for happiness."

In this one short paragraph I was being given reassurance, comfort and guidance. I was not crazy for having taken this path, and I would not be crazy to continue following it wherever it took me. At least to Thomas Merton my quest made sense, and I felt immense gratitude for his words and his insight. Even though I hadn't thrown away every "created attachment"—whatever that meant—I somehow knew that everything I'd done on my spiritual journey—leaving my home and marriage, engaging in the relationship with Paul, taking the trip to the Tetons—had been part of my path to God. For now I didn't need to know all the answers. I didn't need to know why I had gone on the bike trip as "Christ's bride" even though there hadn't been a marriage. I didn't need to know what the ski accident dream about death and rebirth meant for me. I didn't need to know why I had been so undone by the volcanoes earlier that morning. At that moment, with Thomas Merton and Jesus supporting me in my quest, I had all I needed to feel I was on the right track.

An hour and a half and two freight trains later, a certain Peterbilt pulled into the mill. The pleasure of the surprise when Josh saw me was off the charts. We hugged and smiled and laughed and hugged some more. It was everything I could have hoped for: a surprise that worked out, and both of us were thrilled with our reunion. After he unloaded his logs at the dock, we climbed into the cab above the growling engine for a last run of the day up to Trout Lake. The level of our delight could have powered the Peterbilt all the way up the grade.

It was the Fourth of July weekend, and we spent all four days together. Even though I was sure we both had a gut feeling that we were crossing—not joining—paths, not destined to be lifelong mates, arriving back at his little farm felt like coming home to me. Rowdy and Laddie bounded up to greet me, and Charlie the cat brushed back and forth against my leg. The place was steeped in peace. The chatter of cicadas and crickets filled the warm summer air. The aspen trees fluttered like strobe lights. The creek chuckled merrily among the willows below the house. Mt. Adams, full of magic, rose in the distance at the north end of rolling golden fields.

As Josh and I watched the Independence Day fireworks flash and crackle over the Columbia River, I remembered how Carol and I had celebrated the completion of our cross-country bike trip in 1978 with a view of the Washington, DC fireworks from a small boat on the Potomac River. The success of both trips filled me to the brim. All those things my mother and my culture had intended me to be—weak, incapable, mindless, powerless, subservient, and a victim—were just not happening. *Alleluia!* I had broken free of so many of the limitations I had accepted and imposed on myself, that I rejoiced as if I'd escaped from a long jail term.

"Welcome to California: Sacramento—292 miles. San Francisco—352 miles." As I passed the large green and white highway sign on Interstate 5 just south of Ashland, Oregon, a bus flew by me with black smoke pouring from its tailpipe. The air had a hazy, smoggy quality to it. I suddenly felt sick to my stomach at the prospect of returning to California. I was tired of California, tired of the suburban area I'd lived in for fifteen years, tired of the same routes traveled, the same views. Much as I loved them, I didn't want to see the brown hills and green oaks. The last place in the world I wanted to drive into was Sacramento, and the thought of beautiful San Francisco didn't feel much better.

Near Mt. Lassen I turned off the interstate and onto the route I'd followed when I left California. I cruised upgrade along a familiar tree-lined road. Despite my sense of awe at how far I'd cycled alone, bewilderment and angst were growing stronger in me. I pulled into the very same rest area where I had stopped on the last clear warm day before the weather had turned so cold and foul for the remainder of my bike journey. I felt confused and disoriented. With such an array of experiences in just two months, my grasp of time and reality seemed to be falling apart. It was as though some fat rubber band, which had been holding together a neat little package of order and understanding of the way the universe works, had snapped. All of my mental belongings began to drift away into space.

By the time I landed back at Gerry's house in Chico, I had little desire to trade adventure stories, share feelings, or even to relate much—to anyone. I was floundering deep in my own turbulent world. We had planned for me to stay for a few days, but returning to California and nearing home was making me feel like a squirming fish caught in a net on a boat deck.

The next morning as I started the truck, ready to leave, I rolled down my window to say I was sorry. I felt bad to be so uncommunicative and for changing our plans so abruptly. "You know, the trip is over," Gerry said soberly, knowingly. As I pulled onto I-5 for the last leg of my journey home, I knew very well that the bike trip was over but that the bigger and deeper journey was not.

16
PRAY FOR YOUR OWN DISCOVERY

It took me three weeks to unpack. I'd unloaded Sunny right away, but I put off pulling gear out of my panniers. That would bring a certain closure to the trip that I was not ready or willing to have happen. I missed the euphoria I'd enjoyed on the road home. I longed to be immersed in that state of grace that was so new to me. I wanted more time in those intoxicating waters of bliss and rapture. But I had plummeted from grace into turmoil and confusion. Now back in the world I had bicycled away from, my days and nights were filled with questions: *Where am I? What am I doing here? Do I fit? What am I supposed to do now?* I was missing the road, missing Josh, missing a sense of purpose, a goal to strive for, and most of all, I was missing myself. I was missing who I had been before I set out, and I was missing the person I had become

My entire inner life had been radically rearranged in the course of my journey. Before it, I'd had a certain picture of who I was, not always comfortable but familiar. Now it was as if all the nicely assembled pieces of the jigsaw puzzle image that was "me" had been thrown up in the air and tumbled back onto the floor, landing in complete disarray. I couldn't reassemble that previous picture because I was no longer the same person, yet I had no idea what the new picture looked like. I had made my way through countless interior miles during those hundreds of road miles, but now I was lost to myself.

I had a hard time relating or connecting with people. It was as if we were speaking different languages or had come from different planets. Everyone but me seemed to know who they were and what they were doing. I wanted desperately to be a part of others' lives again, to feel okay, to feel loved, yet most of my interactions with people were strained and awkward. I felt like an ostrich in a herd of deer. Much of the time I was tramping through a septic tank of foul humor, fighting to stay out of ever-looming depression. In stressful social interactions I sometimes feared muriatic acid would come shooting out of my mouth instead of words. But much as I wanted to connect I mostly wanted to be alone

Constantly being crabby made me angry. Feeling like an alien made me angry. Not knowing what I should be doing made me angry. Not knowing who I was anymore made me even angrier. Feeling like a helpless foodaholic made me feel hopeless. Being painfully uncomfortable inside my own skin made me feel as crazy as an alligator in a dog crate. Nothing I did alleviated the emotional turmoil or the pain in my heart. One of the daily inspirational messages I was reading told me if I could overcome the inner conflict, I would be rewarded with growth. When I was on my back with a bloated stomach, or sitting on the pot straining with constipation, or crawling on my virtual knees through dark rages, I simply wanted out of my living nightmare. I wanted to return to those blissful states I'd felt on the road—and not being on the road in that euphoric space made me angry. When I wasn't raging at God, I was filled with longing for Him—and not finding Him made me angry and anxious.

And then there was Paul. He had returned to my home in the Bay Area, which we'd been sharing before I left and where he had lived while I was gone. So arriving back home also meant returning to him. While several times I'd tried to tell myself it was over between us—and he and I had talked of this—it wasn't happening. I could see the threads of our lives unraveling, but we both kept hoping that we might pick up the ends and weave them together in a new way. So when Paul asked if he could use our house as a base camp over the next few months, I said yes. Maybe something would change, maybe it would finally work out for us. Maybe as well as my doorway to God, he was the life partner I hoped for.

Wishful thinking. When I wanted to be alone, which was most of the time, his presence drove me up a wall. I resented having to be pleasant when my mood was so foul. One evening he was standing at the kitchen sink preparing dinner. Paul always looked graceful to me, like a dancer, even while washing carrots. The window over the sink looked out over the dry, grassy pasture that I hoped would be full of horses one day. Then he innocently asked, "Love, would you like a salad or a vegetable for dinner?" I nearly went ballistic. I was holding a head of cabbage and had to make a great effort not to throw it at him. I managed to mumble, "I don't really care, Paul. Whatever you make is fine." On another occasion he came home from a short trip earlier than expected. When I saw his little red station wagon pull into the parking pad, I was thrown into a blinding rage. Helpless in the face of my emotional turmoil, I prayed intently, and thankfully God put some kindly words in my mouth to greet him as he walked in the door. But I was weeping inside myself. I loved this man, and yet sometimes I couldn't stand being around him. I didn't know what was going on or what I should do.

Maybe even more confusing was the fact that things weren't *all* darkness and confusion. Times of contraction and darkness were interspersed with times of expansion and lightness. Suddenly the memory of my success at getting to the Tetons would lift me up, and at the crest of the wave, I could tap into the sense of accomplishment, the strength, the confidence, the sense of infinite possibility for my present and future days. I would find myself feeling ecstatic. *I'm thirty-five, and my life has just begun.* With a renewed sense of purpose I'd reach out beyond my cloistered world, especially to the ongoing re-vision of Mudd's and Crow Canyon Gardens. Even though I had turned over operations to my wonderful business partner, he was eager to have my involvement in developing the new and bigger picture. I welcomed working with him, planning educational programs, plotting garden layouts, talking over the kinds of menus that would bring more garden produce into the restaurant.

Although my moods went radically up and down, I continued to be in the best physical condition ever. I loved seeing my lean, strong shadow on the pavement as I biked. At times I was unaware of anything below my elbows as Sunny and I sped—more like floated—over the suburban roads. I could run several cross-country miles over the ridgelands and still have energy to spare. I loved seeing my taut and shapely muscles in the mirror. I loved seeing the veins on my tanned arms, traceable and pulsing with energy and life. I loved being thin—I was 108 pounds. One friend said I looked like an ad for a Biafran hunger charity, but I felt like one of the athletes competing in the 1984 Olympic games in my hometown of Los Angeles that summer.

The intense physical exercise dissipated some of the crazy internal energy that plagued me. When I could feel myself sliding toward a sinkhole of depression, I'd tell myself, *Just do something. Hang a picture. Write a letter. Type up your notes from your travel journal. Look at pictures of New Zealand. Look at a map of the United States so you can plan your next road trip.* Even before arriving home, images of a cross-country road trip in Sparky had been calling to me, and I'd been planning to make this happen in the fall. Thinking about being back on the road would always lift my spirits, and traveling about the country increasingly felt like what I should do next. Following my heart's desire and impulses was all I knew to do in my search for God.

I wished I knew more specifically what I was looking for. I wished I could find some step-by-step instructions for my search. That search though continued to be as vague and mysterious a desire as it had been when I first determined that I wanted to find God in my waking life. I had not found God in the depths of the Big Hole or in the radiant splendor of the Grand Teton or the Bitterroot Mountains. I had not found God through my love for Paul; that had been a doorway, not the end of the search. If I had found God, the yearning in my heart would have ceased. But the hot fire of longing was still present. All I knew to do was to keep following those inner impulses and interior directions. I would keep looking even if it took me my whole life.

One morning, with the house blessedly all to myself, I climbed the eleven narrow oak steps to my "perch," my little office, the room of my own. It felt like the compact room at the top of a lighthouse or like a forest lookout tower. An eight-foot long plate glass window framed the huge live oak just outside and beyond that, the oak-studded, grassy ridgelands. The entire room was little more than a hundred square feet, and the small alcove opposite the window was just big enough for a double futon mattress on the floor. I curled into this cozy space with my underlined, creased and faded copy of Merton's *New Seeds of Contemplation*.

"Ultimately the only way I can be myself is to become identified with Him in Whom is hidden the reason and fulfillment of my existence," Merton wrote. The words jumped off the page. *Identified* with God? I had already read these lines several times, but suddenly something I hadn't gotten before was opening up to me. I read on: "Therefore there is only one problem on which all my existence, my peace and my happiness depend: to discover myself in discovering God. If I find Him I will find myself and if I find my true self I will find Him." My breath caught for an instant and my heart leapt with hope. This was a clue! I felt as if I'd been driving down a seemingly endless road in a foreign country, hoping to get to a certain place, and Thomas Merton had stepped into the road, flagged me down and handed me a map. "Here, take this. It might help."

Merton was describing me and my own search. I *had been* discovering myself, ever since I'd gobbled up that infamous plate of scrambled eggs at my mother's house on March 15, 1976, eight years before. But I had become so fixated on *finding God* that I'd been considering my own growth and personal changes to be secondary, almost beside the point. Now here was Merton telling me the two were *inseparable*. One of his chapters in this book was even called "Pray for Your Own Discovery!"

My eyes were riveted on words of that single paragraph, as if they could bore through the paper and find God right then and there. My mind was jumping up and down. What did it mean to *identify* with God? Would that be the same as saying I wanted to *be* God? If so, how could I *be* what I couldn't imagine or define or understand? How could I be something unfathomable, intangible, amorphous, so infinitely huge? Wouldn't it be arrogant and presumptuous to want to *be* God? Much as I was confounded by Merton's words I now deeply and suddenly knew that I wanted more than just to *find* God. But what would that mean? What was beyond finding Him?

I lay the book down, my mind swimming in a vast space full of questions and hope. In that empty moment, a song came into my mind: "To Dream the Impossible Dream..." from *Man of La Mancha*. Was I a hopeless dreamer like Don Quixote? Was my quest for God an impossible dream? How ironic that my search for God had actually started with a very tangible dream. But I didn't want to "dream the impossible dream;" I wanted to *live* my dream. I wanted my dream to be real.

The song went on playing in my mind: "To reach the unreachable star...." Was I trying to reach an *unreachable* star? I recalled how strongly I'd been drawn to the name of an actual road in Montana that leads into Glacier National Park. The name on the map was "Going to the Sun Highway." Was God the sun, the "unreachable star"? As I contemplated those words, I realized I could do nothing but take heart from Don Quixote's resolve, which was also mine: "This is my quest, to follow that star, no matter how hopeless, no matter how far."

I took up the book again and read on, diving into another chapter, "The Mystery of Christ." Maybe this could help me understand why I went to the Tetons "as Christ's bride." Maybe this could give me a clue to who Christ or Jesus was to me. I'd pasted that image of Jesus in my *Teton Traveler's Guide,* hoping I would learn to understand the words beneath, "I am the way, the truth and the life." But I was still puzzled.

Merton's chapter only opened up more questions. I reached over and pulled another book from the shelf, *Grist for the Mill* by Ram Dass, the Harvard professor turned spiritual teacher. I'd read it a couple of years earlier when I was trying to understand the same question about Christ. I vaguely recalled that Ram Dass' deep understanding had appealed to me. I rifled through the pages, looking for the part I'd underlined. One of his students asks: "How do you interpret statements like, 'No man comes to the Father but through me?'" Ram Dass answers:

"In the *New Testament* are these the words of Jesus or of the Christ? You have really at least two beings in that one being. One of them is Jesus who is the Son, a form of the Father made manifest on Earth. 'I am in the Father; the Father is in me.' Then there is the Christ, which is the consciousness out of which that form is manifest...."

Things were beginning to fit together. That Christ is the *consciousness* of the Divine was consistent with what I remembered Paramahansa Yogananda saying in *Autobiography of a Yogi*: "The Son of God is the Christ or Divine Consciousness in man." This notion of consciousness suggested a different way to see Jesus and to understand him as the Christ. So what did this mean for me?

Tucked in my little alcove, I struggled mightily to understand who Christ was in my life. Back to Merton: "...the mystery of Christ concentrates the rays of God's light and fire to a point that sets fire to the spirit of man." Had it been Christ then who had inspired in me the realization of the divine *I Am* when I had raged about the newspaper article? Was it Christ who had infused my heart with praise for God when I sat by the Columbia River and those words arose: "How beautiful is Thy Name"? The clearest, and maybe most challenging for me of Merton's words were: "...all experience of God comes to us through Christ...." So there was the "way" part of "the way, the truth, and the life." Did this mean that it was Christ consciousness I saw in Paul? If this were true, then Christ was even more vital to my finding God than I'd thought. And maybe that's what marriage to Him was about. I was looking for clues about what to do and where to go to find God. If that meant marrying Christ, I hoped I would learn how to do that as well.

I closed my eyes and lay back on the futon. I couldn't take in any more for now. I got up and returned the books to a special place on my desk, descended the stairs, and hoped I could get into a sociable space by the time Paul came home.

In early September I loaded up the back of my truck. The nature of the car trip across the country to the East Coast was now well-formed in my mind. It was to be an aimless journey for the most part, retracing portions of my bike route, with visits to a few friends along the way. I figured I'd be gone about two months. Sunny lay in the back surrounded by a box of books and assorted writing materials, a box of miscellaneous gifts to leave with people along the way, and a duffel bag with a basic traveler's wardrobe. In a basket on the front seat, I perched Puppy Sr. (he was not too old for car travel!) and Puppy Jr., so they could enjoy the view.

As always, it was hard to say goodbye to Paul. He would continue to stay at "our" house, and we planned to keep in touch as I went along. I was sad to leave him but eager to be on the road...and to be alone. His expression was the same as it had been when I'd pedaled away from him the previous spring—sad and resigned. Once again I felt grateful for the space and support he was giving me to continue my inner journey. He always wanted what was right for me in my life even when it was not what he wanted for himself.

"Goodbye, Love," he said as we held each other. "Have a good trip and hurry home."

My own sadness lasted for about a half hour. As soon as I pulled onto I-5, my spirits bounced upward like jumping beans. I was relieved to leave California, relieved to be alone, and excited to be unfolding a new adventure. Some of my favorite words from Merton echoed in my mind: "…you only have a vague, unutterable sense that peace underlies the darkness and aridity in which you find yourself. You scarcely dare admit it to yourself, but in spite of all your misgivings you realize that you are going somewhere and that your journey is guided and directed and that you can feel safe."

As I drove north, I felt completely at ease, willing to be led I knew not exactly where, but ready to discover more about God and about myself, to follow my star "no matter how far."

On the road again

17

GIFTS OF GOD'S LOVE

Something was happening to me inside, something wonderful. Ever since leaving California I'd been in a blissful state again. Just being on the road had taken me out of the confusion and gloom that had been dragging me down. My happiness affirmed that I was once again on the right road. I was on the next leg of my journey toward God, and I apparently had His blessing for this drive across the United States. Yet unknown to me, along the way I would be showered with gifts that could only come as a result of all those inner miles I had already traveled on my bike. Some of them would be in the world around me; the most deeply unexpected and astonishing would be right inside me, but the two were intimately connected. Inside and outside—in these gifts there was no separation.

The first time it happened Josh and I were driving together through the Hood River Valley. It felt like a dream, but it wasn't. I'd arrived the night before, as part of my planned journey, and today we were doing one of our favorite things together—exploring the beauty in his "neighborhood."

I was staring out the window, grateful that Josh was driving the jeep so I could be free to lose myself in the scene around me. The straight, two lane road was sweeping through thick forests of tall ponderosa, cedar and fir, open meadows, then past small villages, little log cabins, old run-down farms, new mobile homes. Everything was interesting and new to me, and I looked around like a child in Wonderland. At the end of the corridor of tall pines, Mt. Adams rose up, transfixing me with its power and beauty.

And suddenly it wasn't the volcanic mountain anymore. Instead a crystalline palace in the Himalayas, with snow-covered slopes and jagged points and peaks, was soaring many thousands of feet into the air. Shimmering lights of pink, rose, cobalt blue, and lavender vibrated within a surrounding aura of yellow, turquoise, and pale greens. Pulsing with color and energy and light, the palace soared into the heavens. *What am I seeing?* It was as though I had opened a child's fairy tale book and stepped into an exquisite illustration of a heavenly kingdom.

In another part of my mind, I flashbacked to my early twenties—hippie days—when hallucinogenic drugs had expanded my perception of what I normally saw. But no drugs were in play here. I'd read about people with special abilities who could see auras around people and things. Maybe I was seeing Mt. Adams in that parallel universe. It felt the same way as when I'd suddenly found myself in that vast and unknown spiritual dimension after falling in love. I knew now that the divine and earthly realms existed simultaneously, and maybe a door between them had just been opened up to me. After a few minutes, maybe even seconds, the vision faded, but the magical mountain remained permanently aglow in my mind. And my eyes remained open to a deeper inner vision.

The next day was Sunday, the end of my weekend stopover with Josh on my route east. We'd gone out for a drive in the early evening. All the colors were muted and soft. The air was hazy with the pale light of the setting sun. As we headed up the road toward Trout Lake, I noticed a structure like a monorail track running alongside the road. When I asked Josh what it was, he pulled over and we climbed out of the jeep. He explained that it was a flume, a structure that was built to carry logs down from Trout Lake to the mill twelve miles away. The flume was a couple of feet wide and made of metal, like a huge pipe cut in half lengthwise. It was chest height, supported on a wooden framework of crisscrossed two-by-fours, and it ran in either direction as far as the eye could see. Beautiful, clear, gurgling water several inches deep flowed down the channel. The setting sun was reflecting a salmon-color light on the far edge of the trough, making the tiny, chuckling river look like the liquid version of a rainbow trout.

I was filled with the sound and the sight of the water rushing just inches away from my body. Suddenly this rainbow trout flume with its rushing stream was *inside* me. It was as much a part of my body as my blood vessels. The whole twelve miles of rushing water was inside me, as were the forests surrounding the flume, *and* the Columbia River where the water headed, *and* the mountains where it came from, *and* the mill and the mill town, *and* Hood River Valley, the volcano country, the Cascade Mt. Range, the Pacific Northwest region. Bigger and broader and wider, it was all part of me. It was all *inside* me. I had no skin to distinguish the point where I stopped and where it all began. The boundary had disappeared, not only right here but the boundary between myself and the entire universe! Dazed, I climbed back into the jeep, and we rode back to Josh's home in silence.

I had no idea what had happened. I'd never experienced anything like that and had no idea what it meant. I was so stunned it didn't even occur to me to wonder, until much later, if this inner vision had anything to do with God, with *finding* God. These gifts of inner vision were so dramatic and astonishing that I just tucked them away carefully, reverently inside me.

The next day I pulled tearfully out of Josh's driveway, suspecting that we might never see each other again, even though we promised to stay in touch. More than anything else my road trip was about following the call to find God, and I set out to continue my journey east.

I followed the now familiar Clearwater River into Idaho, and when it merged with the Lochsa River, I greeted her too like an old friend. Not far from the Three Rivers Motel, a refuge that now seemed so long ago, I pulled into a rest stop. The rushing water of the Lochsa captivated me, diamonds dancing on its surface, the happy sound filling every inch of space in my consciousness. Then suddenly there it was again, that opening into another dimension. The only way I can describe this one is that I felt like one of those fold-out party decorations, the kind in which paper about a half inch thick is held in the shape and image of a pumpkin or turkey. When you unclip the sides, the colored tissue paper inside unfolds outward into a three-dimensional object, 360 degrees of pumpkin or bird. I felt like I'd been unhooked and slowly begun opening outward, taking in more and more of my surroundings until I had taken in the entire universe. What I identified as "I" had disappeared altogether. "I" now contained the universe, just as "I" had at the flume. Everything "out there" lived *inside* of me! I was one with everything. No separation. No boundaries. No "I." No "other."

Deeply moved and full of awe and wonder, I climbed back into Sparky and slowly pulled onto the highway. I didn't know what these experiences were about, but I felt profoundly blessed. They were so far out of my normal way of seeing the world that they had to be gifts from God. As I drove along, I remembered Thomas Merton's words about being "filled with the gift of God's love" when we are free of "created attachments." I had let go of many beliefs and stories I'd told myself about who I was, about my lacks and limitations. After the successful completion of the bike trip, I was emptied of some of these old images of myself, and freer than I'd ever been to discover new ones and, perhaps as Merton talked about, to discover God in the process.

Though I didn't understand this at the time, maybe because I was so receptive to new things, God had been able to open my eyes and heart so wide to reveal His presence. I had *been* something of God. I had merged with God. I had *identified* with God. But there in the Hood River Valley, and by the Lochsa River, that remained just a look, a clue. When the experience was over, God was still Someone or Something I was pursuing, though at the moment with a deep and delightful sense of peace.

Through the vast and rugged landscape of Montana, the hum of Sparky's engine mirrored my own inner steadiness. I felt utterly confident that being alone on the road was where I belonged. The magical beauty of the land in fall colors was a constant delight. I was open to everything. I felt like a magnet, attracting new experiences and insights. By the time I reached the Tetons that evening, I felt as if I'd been pushing a shopping cart down the aisles of a colorful market bazaar. The aisles had names: Amazing Beauty, Personal Revelations, Big Ideas, Moving Experiences, Random Treats. For the remainder of the journey items from these aisles would continue to fall into my cart, filling it with the gifts of God's love.

After three exquisitely beautiful fall days of hiking and biking around the Tetons, I left my Holy Land feeling sad and wistful. As I drove north, I watched the mist-shrouded mountains in my rearview mirror for as long as I could. The uneventful day got me to eastern Wyoming by sunset, and I decided to stop and take in the view. I was sitting on the hood of Sparky, absorbing the peaceful evening, when I once again entered a magical kingdom. A freight train, its engine gleaming and headlight beaming, was coming toward me through the oceans of dry grass. The setting sun was reflected in Sparky's deep blue paint, and all the vast world glowed. As the train thundered past me, through me, in me, I felt once again flooded with the wonder and power and beauty of it all. The gifts seemed unending. Back on the highway, I floated onward, keeping an eye out for dinner and a place to stay for the night.

After so many days of non-stop amazement, I suppose a come-down was bound to happen. As I was eating dinner in the coffee shop of a truck stop motel, Loneliness showed up. The sunset was gone. The freight train was gone. It was just me sitting in a booth by the window having dinner alone, staring past my solitary reflection into the dark night. A hollowness began opening up inside me. My heart seemed to be caving in. My chewing sounded like a loud washing machine running inside my head. I felt like I was heading into a creepy forest in the pitch dark with unseen dangers all around me, like I was about to fall into a camouflaged pit set to trap a bear. Was there a way out, a way to escape? The answer seemed to be no, and I let go and entered the yawning space that was opening up inside me.

The very moment I stopped thinking about escape and let the hollowness just be, something shifted—in a big and unexpected way. The vast and scary space began to take on a kind of intimate, loving quality. In place of the emptiness, I began to feel every cell in my body waking up and hatching like a newborn chick emerging from a brittle shell. The emptiness became a poignant, almost painful, waking up to the reality of being alive. Instead of the gaping hole I felt an immense presence that was the being I called "me," so tiny and yet filling up the universe.

When I emerged again, I was still seated in the coffee shop, with dinner on a plate before me. My heart was beating full tilt, but the empty hollowness inside me was gone. I felt "me" with an intimacy I'd not known before. With gratitude I acknowledged yet another gift of God's love, this time a useful lesson. If I stayed with a painful situation, some good thing might come of it—some insight, healing, or awakening. Whatever was happening to me, it certainly was expanding and deepening my sense of who I was and how I lived.

Finding I could pass through fear and pain to love and aliveness made me as eager to investigate new places inside myself as I was outside on the open road. It was all a big exploration, and I began to feel that I was up for anything I might encounter, in one realm or the other. I went upstairs to bed, a happy stranger in a strange land.

I was in a state of grace as I left the glorious fall colors of Michigan and drove across the Mackinaw Bridge into the foreign land of Canada. Since leaving home, my days had filled my inner shopping cart to overflowing with revelations, challenges, treats, and deeply touching experiences, and I was eager now for my next adventures into the unknown. The beautiful suspension bridge I was on reminded me of the Golden Gate back home, only much longer in span. It deposited me on Canadian soil and I happily headed for my next destination, Niagara Falls. By late afternoon I was halfway there. The light was diminishing as the sun set, and rain began to fall in a steady sheet. Suddenly I was finding it hard to see, and this was *not* the beginning of another experience of altered sight. It was turning dark, but not just because the sun was going down. The region I was driving through was growing increasingly urban and industrialized. A brown, choking smog hung in the air that was already thick with rain.

Needing gas, I pulled off the highway at Hamilton and into a gas station. A scraggly young man emerged from the station house, looking as depressed as the weather. I felt like I'd entered into a scene from the movie *Bladerunner*, set in some generic urban scene of the future where there is no sun, where it is always raining, smoggy and gloomy. I left the station and crept through Hamilton from stoplight to stoplight, feeling the heaviness in the air. Even the squirrels I spotted in grassy spots along the road seemed blackened by soot.

I had no idea where I'd stay for the night and no idea where I was. I could barely see road signs. *What if I inadvertently drive into a dangerous section of the city?* The heavy spirit of the place was oppressive, and an inner darkness to match the outer began to close in on me. A tiny tearful voice inside called out, *Help! Get me out of here!*

I glanced over at Puppies. My stuffed animals, whom I'd cuddled since childhood, were not only my lifelong friends but also a mysterious extension of myself. When I looked at them, I somehow saw me. But they were looking back with expressions of total acceptance and calm. They knew I could get on the right road, could take care of them on this strange and complex journey. "Puppies trust me," I whispered silently to myself. I was so moved by their trust—my own trust in myself—that I started to cry. I had managed to get us safely this far. I deserved our trust. *I can do this. I* am *doing this.* I moved slowly on, trying to find my way out of Hamilton.

In spite of the gloom and the challenge, I began to feel surprisingly cheerful and positive. I still deeply felt the oppression of the place, and yet there was a lightness in my spirit. What on earth was happening inside of me? I felt as if I had broken through an inner barrier to a deeper core within that would not be shaken by outer adversity. This was startling.

I'd always been ready to enjoy life when conditions were lovely and happy—sunny days, great bike rides, beautiful times of love and intimacy. But when things turned gloomy or sour, I clearly tended to go right there with them. Now here I was feeling light and balanced in the midst of darkness and fear. It would be some time before I would read anything about this kind of acceptance. Eventually it would especially be the Buddhist teachers who would point out that circumstances change constantly and are sometimes pleasant, sometimes unpleasant, sometimes downright awful. The goal is to be able to accept it all with equal calm, if not appreciation. With this inner core of acceptance intact, one can let go and move on to the next changing moment. Right there in Hamilton I was getting a glimpse of that possibility. In that moment this was just about as good as seeing Mt. Adams transformed into a crystalline Himalayan palace.

I was moving on through the dark and crowded streets when suddenly the road led into a complex of detours and construction zones. *I can do this. I am calm. I am strong.* In the midst of the maze, I saw a sign for Niagara-on-the-Lake. I made a quick, impulsive turn between orange construction cones onto the road. *Goodbye, Hamilton!*

The road led me into a tiny, quiet village where I easily found a cozy bed and breakfast on the main street. I fell asleep feeling guided and directed as Merton had promised I would be.

As I breakfasted with the two ladies who owned the inn they told me that Niagara Falls was only about twenty miles away. *I can bike there!* I ran up to my room to put on my bike shorts, filled my water bottles and pumped up Sunny's tires. I felt over the top with joy, gratitude and abundance as I cycled steadily up the gradual grade through sleepy, residential areas. Low rock walls, carefully and artfully crafted, lined the road. They had witnessed travelers' journeys to the Falls for decades, and now I was one of the pilgrims. Back away from the street, big houses were nestled among the trees. And these were no ordinary trees! They wore fluorescent autumn leaves, looking like billions of little wings that had been saturated in Photoshop—electric shades of yellow and orange, amber, rust, coral, salmon—colors I could not believe. They vibrated like a pulsing neon sign in Times Square. I biked joyfully through and over these crunchy colors.

Then there it was—Niagara Falls! Oceans of water poured over the cliffs, pounding into the river 170 feet below with thundering, deafening force, erupting in volcanoes of spray as it crashed downwards. Hollywood's greatest special effects achievements could never top this in a million years. And to think I had arrived at another spectacular place by bicycle! I asked a fellow tourist to take a photograph of Sunny and me as we stood against the railing, a barrier that fortunately prevented us from throwing ourselves ecstatically into the Falls below. With that treasure in my memory and my camera, and the water still thundering inside me, I headed back to town.

Me and Sunny at Niagara Falls

Before I left Niagara-on-the-Lake, I had a cappuccino at a small café, bought flowers for the ladies at the inn who had been so kind to me, and got directions for the town of Amsterdam in upstate New York. In the back of Sparky I was carrying a box of fragile family heirlooms from a family in South Dakota with whom I'd lodged one night. They had relatives in Amsterdam and had asked if I would deliver their treasures, which were too valuable and breakable to ship. I was only too glad to play at being a UPS driver and to have a special purpose to complement my mostly wandering travels.

Sparky and I rolled easily over the tree-lined country roads of upstate New York, alongside green meadows, through brightly colored woods, past small towns of quaint shops and picket-fenced houses. The dreamy quality of meandering through this fairy tale setting stirred further reflection on the past two days. I looked back at the oppressive darkness I'd felt in urban Hamilton, followed so immediately by the brilliance and pleasure of this day riding my bike to and from Niagara Falls. The two experiences were so extreme in their opposite natures that it struck me that I had just seen, and experienced in myself, two sides to the same coin, like night and day, darkness and light. The two were part of one whole. It was just a matter of flipping the coin; black on one side (Hamilton), white on the other (Niagara). It was Paul Tillich's "can't have the 'yes' without the 'no'" dramatically experienced in a real life circumstance.

Whatever side of the coin I looked at—whether it was light or dark, yes or no—the bottom line was that it was one coin, opposing aspects of one drama. I couldn't have one without the other. It was all one. Oneness. I followed the sequence of thoughts that flowed into my mind. The coin is God...The One is God... God is IT...God is all there is...God Is...Is.... No subject. No object. Just is.... Period.

Pure being-ness. Nothing and everything. Again I was reminded of the realization I had come to as I biked down Danville Boulevard in a rage over the newspaper article proclaiming me "the disabled heiress." At that point I knew I was neither this nor that, but *I Am*. But here on the road in upstate New York, the realization was that everything was neither this nor that, but *it is*. It was an equally stunning revelation. *I Am...It is.* My in-breath was not followed for several moments by the companion out-breath as this thought of one reality—Oneness—settled into my consciousness. Another gift.

I continued my contemplation as I drove along the quiet route through rolling farm country, with horses grazing in green pastures bordered by white rail fences. Why had the darkness and gloom of Hamilton had such an impact on me? The suffocating air, the rain, the urban congestion had borne down on me like a dark force. It reminded me of how deeply affected I had been, bicycling out of Nubieber into the cold, the gray, and the relentless headwind. The oppressive nature of both circumstances had made me think of my mother. In Nubieber I had railed against her for most of 120 miles to Klamath Falls, but now, in light of the "two-sided coin," I was realizing something different about her impact on me.

Much of what I had done in my life had been to get away from my mother's influence, to be unlike her, to do something different with my life. But right there driving along through green pastures, I got it that if she hadn't been the way she was—a precise model of a Victorian lady, feigning incompetence and ignorance, playing second string to the male sex, being sickly and without honest power, abandoning personal ambition or needs, rejecting emotions and problems—I would likely not have gone to such lengths to keep from falling into her grasp. If she hadn't been the way she was, I would not have been so driven to overcome these limitations in myself and to seek so intensely another life for myself.

How startling to realize that I could be *grateful* to my mother for her influence on my life! I was quite moved by this roundabout way of making peace with her. On the two sides of this particular coin, her negative made my positive. It was absolutely clear to me that the things I was most proud of in myself—my courage, my fierce determination to overcome dark forces, my inner and outer strength—were a direct result of who *she* was.

This paradoxical appreciation didn't mean I'd go to her and say, "Mom, I have to thank you for being such an evil witch. I truly appreciate all the trouble you made for me, because it has helped me to become a stronger, better person." The shift in consciousness was more a way into my own heart, a vision of how I could see our relationship in a more positive way. I also considered that if I had been born into her family in the social milieu of her day, I might have been just like her. *There but for the grace of God go I.* These gifts of God's love were taking many forms!

The train rocked and swayed as I happily snuggled into my tiny roomette on the Amtrak Crescent, bound for California. By the time I'd reached the East Coast I was tired of driving, and the idea of a long, dreamy train ride was most appealing. Sparky and most of my stuff got driven back home by a transportation service, while I sat back and let the outer and inner worlds unfold before me. I stared out the window of the Crescent, savoring the flames of fall colors as we traveled south. In the evening the trees of the Carolinas, illuminated by moonlight, turned to silver. I smiled at the leaves. I smiled at the trees. The trees smiled back at me. My reflection in the thick glass smiled back at me. The gifts continued flowing.

I had changed, and just how deeply continued being revealed to me. On an overnight stop in New Orleans, I'd taken a walk through the French Quarter. Passing by the window of an antique store, I was stopped dead in my tracks. Behind the metal, latticed burglarproof grill was an old-fashioned doll. Something about her grabbed me. She was an eighteen-inch Southern Belle, wearing a pale yellow dress of taffeta and silk, little white patent leather pumps, and a poufy matching hat. Her chestnut hair hung in ringlets over her shoulders; her porcelain face pale, bleached and dry as chalk. This was who my mother was, who I was supposed to be and, to a large extent, who I had been. This doll was most likely the picture on the puzzle that had gotten thrown up in the air by the bike trip. Maybe the new image was starting to assemble, but I still had a lot of questions.

As the train rocked along, I wrote crookedly in my journal, reflecting on who I was now and remembering with gratitude all the gifts this journey had bestowed. One day I found myself writing, "I am setting up treasures in heaven." Heaven! I had written "heaven" when I'd meant right here and now, on earth. This was big.

Ever since falling in love, finding myself dropped into the divine realm, I had felt an irreconcilable split between heaven and earth, human and divine, spirit and matter. For several years I sat painfully on the fence between the two, wanting mostly to be in the realm of spirit. But I now knew I had to find a way to live in both worlds at the same time. What I had just written confirmed for me that heaven now was firmly planted on earth.

This "descent" of heaven to earth had happened gradually over the past couple of years as I'd learned to allow myself to enjoy experiences of my earthly life. On my car travels I had been gifted abundantly with adventures, incredible landscapes, social pleasures, and many other gifts. I'd felt so full I thought I might drown in goodness. *Everything* was a gift. *Everything* had meaning. The sense that I'd had at the beginning of the trip—that I was following God's plan for me and would be taken care of—had played out a hundredfold. The divine kingdom was a part of the planet that I walked and rode on. The divine realm—the Kingdom of God—was inside of me, and the outer world was inside of me, and all was One.

As the train steadily clicked away the miles, I sensed that my time of wandering was over. I was ready to plant my feet firmly on earth. I'd been integrating what I learned on both the bike journey and the car trip, and I had a new vision of how to be in the world. My traveling had taken its course to a natural conclusion. And I was

New Orleans doll

so filled with the gifts of God's love, so filled with blessings, understandings and insights, that all I wanted to do when I got home was share these gifts with my human community and use them to be of service to my greater community, the planet.

This had long been a deep motivation for me, especially in creating Mudd's, so I didn't know exactly what I meant by this new impulse or how I might act on it. I had often read—and pondered over—spiritual teachers speaking of "manifesting God" in the world. As I daydreamed out the window, an image of how to do that appeared in my mind. I imagined one of those glass globe candles often used on restaurant tables. The little flame would be God, and the globe surrounding the candle flame would be a person. I wanted to be a clear glass globe—not smoky or covered with a netting or cute decoration—so the flame of God could radiate light without obstruction. I wanted all the gifts of God's love I'd been given to come through me. I wanted to allow more love, power and creative expression to radiate through me so that God, the God-force, would be increased in the world. For me, God was now the practice. I wanted to dedicate myself to that work. To practice God. I would just do that and let the rest unfold. The title of one of my favorite books came to mind—*The Practice of the Presence of God.*

Day and night the train was rocking me closer and closer to California and the next phase of my life. That night I fell asleep smiling. I had finally found my way to a deeper connection with God. I had learned so much during my Happy Wandering, and I'd lived in a joy so sustained that I thought it would continue forever. Never would I have imagined that the flame of God within me could go out and the Kingdom of God disappear soon after reaching home.

18

CALL OF THE INNER CHILD

ook, Mom, no hands! I was flying! I was in a state of ecstatic motion. I was rebirthing myself. If I could bike with no hands I could do anything! I had always envied the kids who could sit astride their bicycles, arms nonchalantly folded across their chests, riding smugly straight down the road. Yet even after biking thousands of miles as an adult, I'd still not been able to ride without holding onto the handlebars. But one warm, late November day, shortly after returning home from my Happy Wandering adventure across the continent, I decided it was time to take the leap. When I reached a slight downgrade on Danville Boulevard, I sucked in a breath and lifted my hands. Concentrating on my balance, I prayed and kept pedaling. I was upright and moving straight ahead! With this robust sense of confidence and well-being, I entered the holiday season, anticipating a lovely swan dive into the coming new year.

Since my return in mid-November. I'd been riding a surge of energy and vitality. I went to bed at midnight and was up again at 7:00. I had many meetings with my partner to envision the next steps for Mudd's and Crow Canyon Gardens. I joined the board of a Bay Area college that had an ecological education mission similar to our restaurant and garden venture. I got involved with other people of wealth who wanted to use their resources to better the world. I poured over financial statements to get a better understanding of my situation, and worked with my financial advisors to place my investments with more environmentally and socially responsible companies. I joined a "personal development group," based on the spiritual teachings of George Gurdjieff, which focused on one's mission, purpose, goals, and "the three lines of work"—service to the world, to others, and to oneself. I initiated contact with friends in a way I hadn't felt inclined to do for years. I wrote personal letters reporting on my bike and car adventures, and assembled an album of pictures and text entitled *Happy Wandering* to share my cross-country trip with others. I cleaned and re-inhabited my house and now welcomed the presence of Paul, who remained in the house after my return. I was reading voraciously in Gurdjieff and Merton, and the joy of also sharing a spiritual life with him spilled over into all my projects.

I biked everyday with more speed and pleasure than ever before. Sunny and I were like stars shooting along the roads of the San Ramon Valley. Sunny ran as smoothly as a Rolls Royce, and I felt perfectly in tune with him and with my own body. I breathed in a way that synchronized our movements and made us lighter and more powerful than we'd ever been.

And I pushed my limits at every chance. One day as Sunny and I flew down the road like paired skaters on an ice rink, a small pack of male riders appeared on the road ahead of me. Should I try to pass them? I was feeling strong and enthusiastic, but still, they were guys. Guys go faster. I had more endurance than speed. What if I failed? Would it knock me out of the high state of energy and confidence I was exalting in? My usual mode when confronted with any kind of competitive challenge had been to shrink back. This time I knew I would regret *not* trying.

Decision made, I dropped to a racing position, and we took off after them. I smiled to myself as I spun past the first, the second, the entire pack of riders dressed in their color-coordinated team bike wear. I pulled in ahead of them and maintained the superior position for the next several miles until we all arrived in town, where I turned right and they turned left. It was a rush as good as Niagara Falls. Even more exhilarating than overtaking the pack was that I had made the decision to not hold back, to go for everything I was capable of. I hadn't been afraid of trying even if it meant I might not succeed.

In every aspect of my new life, I felt as though someone had opened the release valve on the Hoover Dam, letting the Colorado River surge through my being. When people asked me how I was, I replied, with enthusiasm and conviction, "I feel great!" I didn't temper my response with a modifying ailment or problem, though I was aware how, in our culture, it is not cool to feel really, really good. It is better—a sign of our collective, shared humanity—to be up against something really tough, to be burdened by one thing or another, to be unhappy, to have bad things going on or to be worrying. Ecstasy is discouraged. Yet I was willing to take a stand for the sheer joy that was in me and proclaim it. I was drunk on my life, intoxicated and aglow with Spirit. My birthday in early January was the happiest I could remember as I celebrated the vibrant energy and unimagined possibilities of my own life, and the life of God in and as me.

I probably shouldn't have been surprised that my bubble of elation was popped by challenges that created inner turmoil, a cycle that I was familiar with. Though much in me was deeply new, the patterns of the past would still determine certain choices—and lead to certain consequences.

A few weeks after my hands-free victory, things began to unravel. The swan dive began to feel more like a belly flop. As the gray cold of winter started taking its toll on me physically and psychologically, my bike rides turned more into pain than pleasure. Simultaneously and predictably—as I might have known—my deeply happy reunion with Paul was being overshadowed as my surge of vigor and life came up against his silence and his energy that felt to me constrained and repressed. Once again I reached my breaking point before Christmas and asked him to move out.

I celebrated the holy season alone in deep communion with the Christ Child. But soon after I began to feel that familiar driving, searching force. The terrible longing for God returned, taking over every minute of my day. I knew that Paul no longer was my link to God—I knew I didn't need him in order to find God. But I also knew that when I felt love in my heart, I felt closer to God, and my love for Paul definitely opened my heart. Somehow my longing to experience deep human love had something to do with my deep longing for Paul. From the beginning of our relationship I'd known that my love for Paul "had something to do with God." Years later I would find a quote from Jean Houston that would help make sense of my experience. She writes, "The breadth and depth of human loving both gives us the sense of what human-divine loving is about and instills in us the preparation for spiritual union." Evidently, loving Paul and being loved by him was still teaching me something I needed to learn on my quest. So puzzling as it was, I was drawn back to him, to that love that was leading me along my path toward God. Three weeks after Paul left, we were back together again.

But I was shocked—deeply, horribly, and painfully shocked—that I was again feeling so driven by that longing for God. On the road I'd had so many insights that seemed to be a direct connection with God. Why hadn't those realizations stayed with me? After all the gifts of God's love—treasures of heaven found within myself—how could I possibly still not know and feel that I had already found God! What hadn't I gotten? Why was I still searching?

Driven by this renewed longing, I felt a rising sense of desperation that only increased as I realized that the longing wasn't quelled by Paul's presence. In fact, his presence added another dimension of anguish. As usual, initially things went well. I tried to convince myself that we could live together. We both did. By the end of three months, the same old frustrations once again compelled me to ask him to leave. Why couldn't I accept that we were not compatible on some level? Why couldn't one of us just admit that this dream of a life together was a proven impossibility?

Most confusing of all was that the grace that had seemed so real during my travels across the country was gone. Where was the insight that all things—light, dark, good, bad, pretty, ugly—were just different sides of the same coin, the one coin that is God? Gone. Where was that inner core of equanimity in the face of difficulty? Gone. And here I was again, sinking to the bottom of some deep, dark interior pool.

Meanwhile, my visions and desires for Mudd's were coming up against the visions and desires of my business partner. During my absence, he had understandably made changes to fit his management style, and it was becoming apparent that I didn't fit in anymore. What was I supposed to do with my life if work at Mudd's wasn't an option? I was thrown into a full-blown identity crisis. Was I an entrepreneur, philanthropist, writer, pianist, designer, educator, philosopher? Maybe I was all of those, but what was my specific work in the world? I wished for the umpteenth time that I'd been passionate about being a doctor or a lawyer or a scientist—some straightforward career path!

I knew on a spiritual level that my deepest identity was the divine *I Am* I had been given a glimpse of. But I needed a human identity as well. If my seatmate on an airplane turned to me with a friendly smile and said, "Hi, I'm Joe. I'm in sales. How about you?" I couldn't very well say, "Hi Joe. I'm Virginia. I'm neither this nor that. *I Am.*" I had to be able to say, "I'm in the restaurant business," or "I'm an artist," or "I'm a secretary," or even, "I'm unemployed right now."

While this struggle to define myself externally was happening, a deeper, more complicated identity crisis was going on inside me—not only "Who am I" but "Who is the 'I' that is asking?" The word "I" itself felt increasingly vague and meaningless to me. It seemed there was less and less substance to the reality "I" referred to, because "I" was continually changing. In the work of self-discovery, in the act of "becoming," "I" was in a constant process of self-destruction and self-creation. There was nothing "I" could latch onto.

Eventually I would discover, in the words of my guide and mentor Thomas Merton, that this entity called "I" was just a mental construct that is evolving, and even dissolving, over time. But I hadn't yet found that insight and support for what I was experiencing. Not knowing who *I* was, feeling the illusoriness of that identity, not knowing what *I* should be doing even if *I* was not a solid reality made me uncertain and anxious. I had no idea what I needed to do now to find myself or to find God.

My anxiety caused me to start pushing again, and all those insights about slowing down had also disappeared. That desperate yearning to find God still manifested periodically as a compulsion to overfeed myself, and it compelled me to get on my bike and ride no matter what I felt and no matter what the weather was like. In January and February of 1985, the annual Tule Fog had oozed back into the San Ramon Valley where I lived, filling every square millimeter of space. The fog usually burns off by early afternoon, but that year it remained a constant presence. There was literally no sun—not one flicker of brightness or warmth—for twenty-eight days straight, only that cold, gray, creepy, invasive, suffocating, oppressive fog. The temperature of this thick presence was anywhere from the mid-thirties to the low sixties. Most days I rode out wearing four layers of clothes, telling myself that *should* be enough. It never was. I rode anyway, and the cold saturated me as thoroughly as if I'd fallen into arctic waters. Until one day when I was stopped in my tracks.

Help! Stop! You are *hurting* me!

Beneath the four layers of shirts and sweaters and jackets I was wearing, a tiny voice was trying to get my attention. I could hear it but I didn't want to listen.

"Can't you see I'm freezing cold? I am *miserable*!"

I kept pedaling.

"Can't you stop? Why won't you listen to me? You are *torturing* me!"

As the little voice continued its plea, an image came to mind of Edward Munch's painting, "The Scream." What I'd always seen in that painting was a little girl with her mouth grotesquely open, as big as a grapefruit, and her eyes wide with terror. Now she was inside *me*.

I arrived home that day miserable and cold. I turned on the kettle to make tea, placing my icy hands on the warm surface as the water heated. Within a few hours I was flat on my back, shivering in bed under a thick quilt. As I went from my bed to a hot bath and back to bed again, I tried to make sense of the little voice that had screamed at me on the road, again and again: "Please. Can't you *stop*?"

As I lay there thinking of Munch's painting, another image came to mind. I pulled myself out of bed and pawed through my stash of old family photographs till I found the black and white image I was looking for—me on my first birthday. This baby sits in a little wicker chair, beaming at the world as my brothers and sister—their arms full of gifts—look on. This was me!—pure, innocent, radiant, open and loving. She radiates light. She is the face of Love. She is most definitely "transparent to God." I had once been that child. Maybe she was still inside me. Maybe she was the child screaming out to me on the road.

I climbed back under the thick quilt and lay staring at the photograph. What had happened to that radiant being in the wicker chair? Where had she gone? Images from my childhood arose in my mind. I remembered how the doors of the living room were always closed when I practiced piano, so that the elementary music I made couldn't be heard in the rest of the house. The only time those high, heavy doors weren't closed behind me was when I was obliged to play for someone, like my creepy grandmother and others who sat dutifully on the couch and applauded politely after I'd muddled my way through a piece.

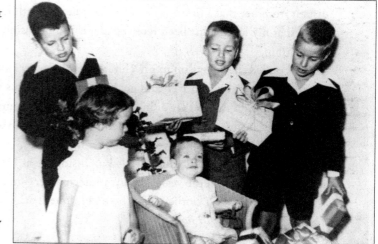

My first birthday

I recalled another time when I was about four. I was supposed to be napping, but instead, on the white plaster wall beside my bed, I'd made a small pencil drawing of a little man with a pointy hat seated on a bench in front of a small log cabin. My burgeoning artistic talent wasn't greeted with praise and appreciation but rather a flurry of distress and cleanup.

When had I been happy? When had this open and loving child been recognized and supported? I'd had fun with my sister, my brothers, sometimes my Dad, with my beloved "nanny," Ilse, and always with the animals. One of my favorite things to do was hang out in the kitchen with "the help" at their lunchtime. The two miniature white poodles would sit on a chair nearby. The cook, the housekeepers and Ilse would sit around the kitchen table, joking, laughing, telling stories of the "old country," just enjoying each other's company. One of them would always wrap an arm around me and pull me to her in a big hug. They were so real, so warm, so earthy and loving. But whenever my mother would come into the kitchen, all the laughing, chatting and joy would cease. I would feel obliged to slither off the lap I was on and leave the kitchen in a contrite, ladylike manner, as if I had been caught smoking in bed. I grew up very quickly, bypassing a lot of childhood, and was praised for being very "grown-up for my age." When I was eighteen, I was hired as head secretary of a congressional office in Washington, DC. By then my link to my creative, playful inner child was pretty much severed.

And then, many years later, we met Paul. My inner child *loved* Paul. She felt safe with him. The way he smiled at me—at her—was totally appreciating and accepting and loving. Sometimes he laughed like a child himself, and the innocence and purity I saw in him mirrored my inner child's own essence, although I was so distant from her that I didn't know that. And he received the love that poured from me and my inner child in a way that my love hadn't been received as a child. It was no wonder I had such a hard time letting go of the relationship.

I pulled the covers up to my chin and sank deeper into the refuge of my warm bed. I could see it clearly now. I'd always been so driven and goal-oriented, I'd been so "grown up" that I hadn't taken much time to just have fun or to do things that didn't necessarily produce something. I could name hundreds of incidents when I'd pushed this inner child aside in order to follow my own adult agenda. Even working so hard to understand and better myself made me sweep right over her.

A huge shame and sadness welled up inside me as I recalled her cries—my cries. Suddenly I was sobbing. I cried for all the years I hadn't protected her—me. I cried for making her ride in the bitter cold without enough warm clothes on. Why had I done that? Could I change? I prayed into my pillow: *May I be able to hear my little girl now.*

As I lay there quiet and empty, I actually thought I heard that small voice again. I *like* going for bike rides with you, as long as you keep me *warm*. What other things did she like doing with me? What made both of us feel lighthearted, free, and expansive? What could I do to make her feel safe and welcome in my life? Could I stop long enough when I was rushing around doing errands to say hello to a friendly dog? Could I skip a few steps during one of my long runs in the hills? Could I do something just for fun?

I felt something shift inside me. My prayer grew deeper and bigger. *Help me to learn how to love more.* As I prayed I saw something new. My search for God was also a yearning to expand my capacity to love—to love her, to love myself. Christ arose in my mind, and I could feel my heart open to this teacher of love. *Show me the way,* I prayed.

I climbed out of bed, and for the first time in three years I put on a recording of the Christian devotional music I'd found so soothing and uplifting. I was on my back physically, but I was on my emotional and spiritual knees before God. As the words and melodies filled my heart, I was flooded with love for God. Realizing how much I had ignored and forgotten, my heart opened in Love itself. I chose a special page in my journal, and in my best calligraphy I wrote: "The only thing that matters is God, Love & Loving God." Next to it I pasted a card with the illustration of a little girl about three years old hugging a rabbit.

A few months later, grappling with my food addiction led me to read a book that gave me a deeper understanding of how the appearance of this inner child was leading me on toward God. In *The Pregnant Virgin*, Jungian psychologist Marion Woodman writes: "The child who is our very *soul* cries out from underneath the rubble of our lives...begging us to say, 'You are not alone. I love you.'" Calling this the Divine Child, Woodman relates it to the state of pure being, the divinity within us. That's what I'd so clearly seen in that photograph—something of God in me. God and I had been one, right from the beginning.

The only thing that matters...

This realization set me on a fervent search to understand what it implied about my quest. For the next few weeks I felt like I was on a timed treasure hunt as I searched anxiously in my mind to understand this revelation. Something big was changing, but from what to what?

Under Merton's guidance, I'd struggled to understand what it meant to be identified with God, to know that by finding my true self, I was finding God. I had briefly known myself as the *I Am* that is God. In the Washington and Idaho wilderness I had dissolved into and merged with all the Universe, with God. On my way back from Niagara Falls, I'd known that everything—good and bad, dark and light—was God. I'd begun to understand how Christ was God and the way to God. It seemed I'd been arriving at God from many angles, led a step at a time. And now maybe at last the clues were coming together. But they were pointing to something new, something disturbingly new.

At first, I'd set out to *find* God. Now I saw that my quest was changing. Somehow, the photograph of my innate divinity at age one altered my heart's desire. I no longer wanted to just *find* God. I wanted *union* with God. *Union with God.* Trying to understand the enormity of what I was now seeking threw me into a panic. What could *union* with God possibly mean? The author of one of my spiritual books likened a person to a wave in the ocean that was God. I thought of other ways in which something was part of a larger entity, like a single note in a chord played on the piano, or a ray of the sun, which was an image that St. Teresa of Avila used to refer to her experience of union with God. These were helpful ways to imagine what I desired to be in relation to God. But these were just mental images. I couldn't fathom how to reach this place of *union* with God.

The "unreachable star" rose again before me. My search had been upgraded to a whole new higher—and seemingly impossible—level. *Oh, God. What must I do now?*

19

INNER AND OUTER HEADWINDS

"SPENCO 500" the flyer read in bright bold type. "The Ultimate Endurance Ride!" A little electric pulse had rippled through me the first time I spotted this announcement at the local bike shop. That was shortly before I'd left for my Happy Wandering drive across the country. It wasn't the extreme mileage (about the distance from San Francisco to San Diego) that grabbed my attention—though 500 miles had a romantic ring to it—it was that the miles were to be ridden *nonstop*. I imagined riding into the sunset, through the night, and into the dawn. This intriguing challenge had been rolling around in my mind for the past five months, and now here it was, right in front of me, again.

On the morning of the spring equinox, I stopped by the California Pedaler to pick up some spare tubes, and on the bulletin board by the door, kind of beckoning to me, was that flyer. I leaned in for a closer look. The 500-mile bike race began and ended in Waco, Texas, in early November, seven months away. With a little flutter in my stomach, I found one of the guys working at the Pedaler and asked about it. Tim pulled out a video from under the counter. "Here, take a look. Bring it back when you've seen it."

The video revealed that this "ultra distance race"—sponsored by the Spenco Medical Company, maker of sports medicine products—was considered by a prominent endurance cyclist to be one of the toughest of all sports competitions. He'd rattled off a list of events that included the Ironman Triathlon, The Race Across America (RAAM) and the Tour de France. My heart beat a little faster with a combination of fear and excitement. This race was a big deal! In its 1984 debut the previous year, 300 people had started and fifty-three had finished. The fastest man's time was twenty-seven hours, average speed nineteen miles per hour. The fastest woman's time was thirty-one hours, average speed seventeen miles per hour. Could I do that? Or anything close to that?

I hunted up my back issues of *Bicycling* magazine and stared at photographs showing the top cyclists at the Spenco 500 finish line looking like they'd cycled through a tornado. In one photo a skinny, bare-chested guy cyclist was passed out on the ground receiving first aid. The day of the race must have been pretty hot! Somehow instead of discouraging me, all of this only served to pique my interest. To ride or not to ride became a steady question in my mind.

What was I thinking? I'd just begun learning how to take care of my inner child, not to push too hard, and now I was considering an *endurance* ride? That child might like bike riding as much as I did, but such a major undertaking was not the same as a thirty-mile spin around suburbia. Would I be able to remain attentive and caring enough to hear her quiet voice and not run over her? Now that I was fully aware that she was a vital part of my search for God, I knew we would have to do this together or there would be a blowout bigger than a flat tire on a bike at thirty-five miles per hour down Mt. Diablo.

But an irresistible pull was churning deep inside me. The fact that the Spenco had grabbed my attention so strongly was an alert that got my full attention. This might be what I was supposed to do to continue my search. If I was trying now for the "impossible dream" of union with God, was that connected with training for and riding the Spenco 500? Would I find what I was looking for in Waco?

Clearly my incessant longing for God was wrapped up with my passion for cycling. Maybe on a bike I felt like I was getting somewhere on my quest. At least I was in motion, and it was something I could do as I waited and listened to know what God wanted next. I could also see how the strenuous physical effort of cycling took me to a deeper part of myself where I uncovered unconscious beliefs, hurts and feelings that needed to be healed or changed if I were to more fully "discover myself."

Of course I also had to think about what this race would mean for me on a physical level. I didn't consider myself a superior athlete by a long shot, but the Spenco 500 was not out of the realm of reasonable challenges for me. I'd ridden a few century rides, as hundred-mile rides are called. In fact, I'd arrived at the finish line of the Davis Double Century—200 nonstop miles—in Davis, California, in good condition and high spirits. Added to my resumé was my recent trip to the Tetons—and, of course, my ability to pass a pack of guy cyclists on the road and ride with no hands. Although daunting, cycling 500 nonstop miles was a challenge I could wrap my mind around.

I carefully filled out the one-page entry form and wrote my check for $100. I was committing to a big step, inner and outer. *No one but me will ever know that my longing for union with God will drive my every pedal-turn.* Nine days after watching the video, I posted the envelope to the race headquarters in Waco and started plotting my training strategy.

I began crunching numbers with the formula I'd learned in junior high school: distance = rate x time, d = rt. While I had no aspirations or fantasies about racing for the winning cash prize of $50,000, I did want a respectable finish, like being in the top ten percent. I thought finishing in thirty-six hours had a nice ring to it, which would mean an average speed of about fourteen miles per hour. I had no intention of being a straggler or the "lanterne rouge," the name given to the last place cyclist in the Tour de France, the one who suffers the embarrassment of being the "red tail light" on the caboose of the peloton train of riders.

As I was calculating rates and distances, I was reminded of what Charles de Gaulle said about how "the greatest distance we have yet to cover still lies within us." I had traveled thousands of miles by bike and had thousands more of training just ahead of me, but there was no way to know how far the inner miles would end up taking me. I could not have known that the more distance and speed I would cover in miles, the more intense would become the inner process of self-discovery, and the more intense my longing for God. Distance traveled would accelerate in both directions.

I loved thinking of myself as an Athlete. My painful history of falling down, flubbing gymnastics exercises, and spraining ankles was behind me. I was launching myself into a graduate course of mental and physical training that I knew was followed by the pro cyclists I read about, some of whom I would be with at the starting line of the Spenco 500. I studied how to train for high-level sports events like I was studying for a bar exam. I learned about carbohydrate loading, lactic acid buildup, slow- and fast-twitch muscles, how the body uses different nutrients. I went to a sports and fitness center to find out my body fat percentage. I learned that I shouldn't build up my strength and endurance too fast so that I wouldn't "peak" too early, which is athlete-speak for achieving top form just in time for the main event, and not before.

Besides my spiffy new cyclometer—measuring average speed, miles per ride, and accumulated miles— which was now front and center on my handlebars, I had Sunny refitted with lightweight wheels and tires to be a road racing instead of a touring bike. I made an extravagant purchase of a pair of honest-to-goodness cycling shorts. If you're going to straddle a two-by-four (which is what a bike seat can feel like) for hours on end you need shiny stretch shorts with a wad of chamois in the crotch. I hadn't bothered with clothes made specifically for cycling before, but since I was taking myself to another level of the sport, I needed to give myself every advantage. Flashy new shorts would surely get me to Waco!

The next step of my plan was to find a cycling partner. Within two weeks of advertising in the local cycling scoop, I was on the road with Geri, a soft-spoken gentle soul for whom I felt an instant affinity. She bore an uncanny resemblance to my cross-country partner, Carol, so I was pretty sure the Universe had arranged this connection. Geri was ready and willing to help me prepare for the Spenco race, and our weekly rides every Saturday, rain or shine, were vigorous, demanding and lengthy. They were also fun, and my inner child was content. We logged hundreds of miles on beautiful rural routes and up steep mountain grades. I was stretching my limits *and* taking care of myself.

Once again I was blessed with unexpected helpers. Besides Geri, my longtime Pen Pal from Down Under turned out to be my long-distance training coach. Alfred lived on the southeast coast of Australia and had first written to me when he read my book, *Across America on the Yellow Brick Road*. He'd cycled across Australia from the west to the east coast, much as I had done in the United States, and he regularly participated in races and riding events. Because he lived 12,000 miles away, was sixty years old, and married with grown children, I welcomed him as a valuable and safe confidante. Best of all, he had a deep spiritual understanding so I could even confide in him the dual nature of my training work. Alfred was the perfect coach.

This was before the days of instant emails, and so our letters traveling by post were like a correspondence training course. In my letters I'd go into great detail about the race, about Sunny (who'd been built specially for me by a renowned frame-builder, Bruce Gordon), what my gear ratio was, how I was trying to "spin" more by increasing my rpm so I would get less tired, all my cycling data, and my exercise regimen of biking and running in the hills. Two weeks later his response would arrive with specific ideas for building up strength, endurance and speed. His letters also spoke quietly of his faith in God's guidance and help.

Besides going out every Saturday for long rides with Geri, I rode every day on my own except Sundays. Day by day the odometer on my handlebars added up the miles. After my first full week of training, I'd logged 130 miles, up from fifty miles per week at the beginning of the year. By October I planned to be riding over 300 miles each week. It never occurred to me to estimate the total number of miles I would ride before the November first race, or what increasing my speed and miles—day by day, week by week, month by month—would add up to. If I'd known it would be 7,000 miles, I wouldn't have believed it. But the rigor of the inner miles would be an undeniable testimony.

You would think that after riding hundreds of miles into headwinds that I would have learned to cope with them, but I remained as resistant to them mentally as they were to me physically. It was probably my imagination, but it seemed like the wind was watching me and purposely changing directions whenever I did. So as I turned, it seemed as if I was *always* riding into a headwind.

I took this personally. They were in my face like an invisible gray wall that was always pushing against me, diminishing my speed, driving me backwards. As I dug into my reserves to fight them, they seemed to be responding, "Nyeah, nyeah, nyeah." At times the force bowed me so low my nose was touching the handlebars, and even that was nothing compared to how low they bowed me emotionally. I felt angry, resentful, helpless—and then angry at feeling so unable to deal with them. These headwinds still seemed to represent everything I couldn't control—Paul, my life circumstances, my reactions, my mother.

Even though I'd found a way to be grateful for how her negative force had influenced my life in a positive way, to my dismay I was still vulnerable to my mother's undermining comments. I knew I had to heal anything in myself that might keep me from finding God, but how long would this particular battle have to go on? Within a couple of weeks of my commitment to ride the Spenco 500, she called. It was almost as if the Universe had told her of my ambitious goal.

"You know, dear, you look so *weathered*, and I'm worried that you lack the *vigor* you ought to have at your age."

I'd visited her over the holidays a few months before, and after all my cross-country travels, I'd felt pretty laid back. I took it easy, rested a lot. Perhaps she thought (hoped?) I was ill, and she was calling now to give me the name of a doctor she wanted me to see. I certainly had plenty of wrinkles to attest to miles in the sun, so I couldn't argue with her about "the weathered look." But as I had just logged in another thirty miles that morning, I wondered about the "missing vigor."

Immediately I felt up against that same dark force I'd battled for so many years. Like facing a head-wind, I felt helpless before her. Shaken and demoralized by the phone call, I went for a walk, hoping to calm myself. One of my neighbors—an older gentleman named Frank—was out in his garden. "You look beautiful today," he said as he handed me a baby pink rose. I felt so appreciated for just being who I was, and grateful for his gift. God must have told him what I needed to feel good about myself again. It helped me make it through that particular internal headwind.

But God was also part of the uncontrollable. When I got right down to it, the search for Him wholly possessed and controlled me. I had been "called" to ride to the Tetons; now I was being called to another demanding challenge. I was following these deep inner impulses because those were the only clues I had for finding God. What else was I supposed to do? On some days I went along with these instructions willingly, put in the effort, clocked my miles, felt good to just do what I had to, a step at a time, not knowing for sure what it was all about. On other days, riding into a headwind, I felt angry and resentful at being told what to do. I felt like God was leading me about willy-nilly, like a puppy on a leash or a piglet with a ring through its nose. And even though I'd "chosen" to sign up for the Spenco 500, it wasn't like I'd had much real choice in the matter. I was on a monorail track to God with no way to get off now. I raged at the headwinds that were battering me, cursing the notion of free will, feeling it was either a joke or a lie.

The inner miles were building up. During the nastiest headwinds, I'd grit my teeth and tell myself that at least I loved my bike and loved cycling. Something had to keep me going for the next seven months, or at least until I learned what I was supposed to from the headwinds.

One day though, as I was riding into a particularly mean headwind, the cumulative anger at feeling so manipulated exploded. I was tired of God pushing me around so much.

"What do you *want?*" I yelled.

Silence.

I got angrier.

"You're always on my case. *Do* this! *Do* that! You're always ordering me around!" Even though I was willing to tear out my heart for God, nonetheless I didn't want to be told what to do. Even if I did pray to do God's will, I didn't want to be told how to do it. Like a petulant child, I pedaled on in a fury. I'd had it with God.

Day after day I'd go through this "headwind resistance" to God, then by the time I reached home, my longing for Him would overcome my defiance. Momentarily sheltered from the wind, I'd bow again to the deep inner call. At one point I found a book by Paul Tillich, *The Shaking of the Foundations*, in which he says it is "natural to hate the One who commands us and determines our course." At least Tillich understood what I was griping about, and I wasn't the only one who felt this way. Maybe it even meant I was on the right track somehow.

One day at the California Pedaler as they rang up my purchase, I started complaining to the clerk about the wind. Overhearing me, another customer, a lean, macho guy, said a little smugly, "I *purposely* ride into the headwinds. It makes me stronger. You have to have the right attitude." *Goodie for you!* I glared inwardly at the guy. It turned out he had ridden the Spenco the year before. I had to admit to myself that he had a point—I *did* have a bad attitude about wind. If I were going to keep riding, I would have to change something in myself.

On my way home, Merton's words popped into my mind again: "Pray for your own discovery." In finding myself, he promised, I would find God. Who or what was I supposed to discover in myself? Would tracking down the root cause of my deep aversion to headwinds help me find the self that would be finding God?

Meanwhile, to remind myself of why I was doing all this, I created two mantras to use whenever I hit headwinds.

Change me.
Change me.
Make me anew,
so that all I can do
I do through You.

Teach me.
Mold me.
Let Thy loving arms enfold me.

I can't say that cycling these mantras through my mind made headwinds a breeze, but they helped change my attitude, And it was a relief to hear something going through my mind other than bitching. Regaining at least some control over my reactions gave me renewed confidence and boosted my energy.

The headwinds had another positive point in their favor—focusing on them gave me a way to avoid the ongoing challenges in the rest of my life—at Mudd's and with Paul. I usually preferred facing winds and what I seemed to be learning from them. So I poured myself into the training. I pushed harder up hills and rode faster than was comfortable. I even found a spiritual rationale to support my experiments in increasing my pain threshold. Gurdieff's book, *Conscious Labor and Intentional Suffering* referred to spiritual and psychological practices that would eventually, ideally, free a person from limitations and attachments and bring about a happier, more joyful life. But I liked how his inner practices played into a popular slogan at the time—"No pain. No gain." I wrote Alfred that "at times, the pleasure and pain are so close as to become one and the same thing." There was a lot of pain, and I was definitely making gains. My strength and mileage were increasing. My riding was smooth and strong and mindless much of the time, and my "pain practice" and mantras were helping to put a positive spin on the headwinds. "Biking is being," I wrote in my journal. I became so addicted to my bike and to cycling that when I went to the east coast for a ten-day conference on sustainable living, I left before it was over because I missed Sunny.

I was like a racehorse with blinders on. Faster. Farther. Faster. Until one day my inner child spoke up.

"Can we stop, please? I have to pee."

"We did before we left home."

"I know but I have to go again. You promised to pay attention to me...."

"Yeah, okay, but it will make my average speed less than it would be if we didn't have to stop." I begrudgingly pulled over to a clump of bushes away from the road. As I climbed back on Sunny, I was brought up short. How could I have forgotten that she was part of God and that I wanted, and needed, to nurture her? On the way home I decided it would be good if I were less obsessive about logging in a certain number of miles at a certain speed each week. I still had five months of training to go. I'd ridden 1,612 miles, almost the equivalent of riding to St. Louis, Missouri from California. *And* I'd recorded my fastest speed of forty miles per hour on a downgrade, and broken my average speed barrier of seventeen miles per hour. I could ease up a little.

That week I initiated an anti-compulsion practice—Less About Miles; More About Style—and I adopted a catchy, favorite song by The Doors to accompany my bike rides:

> *Take it easy, baby, take it as it comes.*
> *Don't move too fast, if you want your love to last.*

The lyrics went on to advise me to "go real slow," that I would like that more and more. The final bit of counsel—"specialize in having fun"—I knew would appeal to my inner child so all during June we rode and tripped-out on The Doors. I was happy to be riding with more inner peace and pleasure, though it didn't necessarily slow me down. Sometimes as Sunny and I zoomed down one of the valley roads, I'd conjure up my childhood horse Blaze, who had been a racehorse but not quite fast enough for track winnings. He still loved to run however and, despite my mother's admonishments and handwringing, I gleefully raced with him across the pastures of the family ranch. When Blaze joined Sunny and me on the road, the three of us would race along together at top speed, flying as fast as we could. I could almost hear my inner child shouting with delight, *Wheeee! Let's go faster!* If this joy had anything to do with getting closer to God, then I was more than willing to let God push me around.

As the outer miles added up, I was driven deeper inside, and the flame of longing flared. The more miles I clocked, the higher the flame. Sometimes I felt consumed with the fire of yearning for God. At unexpected moments—gazing into the night sky at all the stars, listening to the ethereal electronic music of Kitaro—a force akin to a blowtorch igniting inside my chest would erupt into agonized loving and longing. This yearning sometimes became exceedingly frightening and painful. I felt as if my heart and breasts had been clamped and compressed in the vice-grip of a mammogram x-ray machine and the technician had left the room. The pain, and the fear of never being released, was excruciating. Loving God felt like having molten lava boiling up inside and exploding my heart. This made the love and longing I still felt for Paul look like a single grain of sand compared to the entire Sahara Desert.

At times I despaired that I would ever find God, let alone have union with Him. I felt eternally abandoned on earth, destined to never know what it meant to be truly home. At those times I would dissolve into anguished, convulsive sobbing. I would have thought I was going crazy, except for the companions I found in Ram Dass, Merton, and mystics of old—Teresa of Avila, Hildegard of Bingen. A small spiritual journal I subscribed to described this state perfectly as "the poverty of a great, raw, objectless longing." In my mind the object was God, but in my heart I really had no idea about what I longed for. In my journal I vowed, "I will ride over nails and glass, or die in the process, to satisfy my longing for God."

I carried on. To bring inspiration into my training program, every week or two I would browse the video store and ask for movies about people attempting great challenges or overcoming huge obstacles. I looked for films about people winning against steep odds and succeeding just because they wanted something so badly. These were ordinary people doing whatever it took to manifest their dreams or achieve their highest potential. *Chariots of Fire,* about the runner who said he could feel God's pleasure when he ran, inspired both my desire to succeed at the Spenco and to find union with God. *The Champion,* about the jockey who would not let cancer keep him from winning the Grand National horse race in Britain, encouraged me to continue despite any challenges.

One night I picked *The Black Stallion,* mainly because I love the physical grace and beauty of horses. I lay on my stomach on the futon bed in the TV room with my chin propped in my hands, just a couple of feet from the screen. I cried without reserve as I watched the magnificent black horse and his small human friend fly along the empty beach, splashing into the surf—boy and horse ecstatic and wildly free. Then suddenly I wasn't just crying, I was breaking open, not only moved by the astounding beauty I saw in the film but also by an unexpected longing for something I could only call "home." I found myself silently repeating, "I want to go home. I want to go home."

I was mystified and unnerved by the intensity of homesickness I felt. Something inside me was crying out desperately, but at the time I couldn't make the connection between wanting to go "home" and longing for God. But many years later, listening to a recorded lecture series, *Wild at Heart,* about Christ figures and images in literature, art, and film, I would finally understand. The speaker, former Mother Abbess of a Carmelite community and spiritual teacher, Tessa Bielecki, asks, "What image might arise for you in your own experience, something that happens to you that touches you to the core of your being? You don't quite understand it, but if you pay attention to what's happening to you, out of that mysterious initial stirring may come a very profound experience and reconnection with Christ." The wildness, the beauty, the intimacy of the horse and the boy, and their union, must have touched my own longing for connection and union with God and with the Christ I was beginning to understand as the way to Him.

Over and over I was being given clues to the mystery that was unfolding within me. Following my intuition to pursue my own private "film festival" turned out to yield even more clues than I'd anticipated. One Saturday night near the end of July, I was watching my favorite film *Yentl* again. On the screen Barbara Streisand, as my hero Yentl, was bursting into passionate song about "wanting more," about following her dream. The force and depth of Yentl's yearning, her passion for learning and knowledge once again moved me profoundly. The music and Streisand's voice went deep into me, and like endless waves crashing onto the shore my heart opened wide and wider as tears poured out of me.

In the midst of the film, I felt called to write in my journal. Having learned the importance of following such inner promptings, I picked up my pen and without thinking wrote: "Am I lover, beloved, Love?" Was I one, or all, of these? Then another question emerged; "Should I be longing for *myself*?" The questions were surprising and puzzling. As I sat bewildered, a voice inside me said, "My little angel, I *want* you." Who or what wanted me? Although these inner voices were so strange and far removed from my normal frame of reference, I no longer questioned them. They seemed to come from a deeper source within me, and I honored that.

I was too swamped by waves of emotion and longing to think about what I'd just written. Nor did I recall that my inner child had also led me to that realm of love several months before. At that time I'd written in my journal that sudden understanding: "The only thing that matters is God, Love & Loving God." The inner miles were heading right for my heart, but I was still in training and had a long way to go before reaching that goal.

As the film neared its end, and I watched Yentl on her way to fulfilling her dream, I was left feeling that my own dream was painfully uncertain, so vague and indescribable that maybe it was truly unattainable. But Yentl's yearning had once again triggered my own, and my longing felt like a volcano erupting within me. In the midst of the explosion, a powerful conviction arose in me. *I've been invaded by the Holy Spirit.* I had no idea where that idea came from, or what it meant. I had no idea what was happening to me, but the potency of that experience lasted the entire next week before receding into the back of my consciousness, to join the many other unanswered questions of the mystery I was caught up in. Whatever was going on inside me made my promise to ride over nails and glass look easy. All I knew was to keep covering the outer miles and trust where the inner ones were carrying me.

20
TRAINING FOR SALVATION

My spiritual path appeared to be purification through cycling, and my next step on it had the ominous and humorous name of the Markleeville Death Ride. As part of my training for the Spenco, I decided to do this 113-mile, nonstop ride over five mountain passes in the Sierra Nevada Mountains. That sounded challenging but minor compared to the Tour de France that would be taking place around the same time. To align my efforts a little more closely with that great event, I'd decided to set up my own "Petit Tour," starting with a two-day roundtrip ride to Sacramento, totaling 159 miles, and immediately following that with the Death Ride. So as 189 professional racers were covering 2,200 miles over the Alps and Pyrenees, across vineyard valleys and on toward the Champs Élysées in Paris, I set out on my California Tour, on which I would encounter a few vineyards and mountain passes of my own.

The most memorable part of that first leg of my journey was attaining the frightening speed of 49.2 miles per hour down Kirker Pass into the Sacramento River Valley. I loved the speed, taking the risk, pushing my limits, feeling the wind whipping around and past my head. I wasn't wearing a helmet—never had. It wasn't a rebellious thing; I just didn't like the cumbersome shell on my head. And thankfully I'd never had a serious accident. I knew I would have to wear one for the Spenco, but that day on Kirker Pass I reveled in my freedom as just another amateur cyclist.

The day after my return from Sacramento, Geri and I put our bikes in the back of the truck and headed to the Sierra Nevada for the Death Ride. The evening before the race we camped on the local ball field in Markleeville with hundreds of other cyclists. I was still riding high on my Petit Tour, but as the night closed in, my inner demons came out to play. Doubts crawled all over me like worms. "You can't possibly do this." "You're too tired out." "What makes you think you can ride over five passes?" I soon took up their refrain. *I can't. I can't. I can't.* My mother's message seemed to be winning again.

At the same time, however, a powerful—and frightening—determination rose in me. I *had* to complete the Death Ride. This was my assignment. If I didn't I would be letting God down. *What will happen if I fail? Will God be so disappointed in me that all hope for union with Him will be lost?* In the face of fear and confusion, I could feel myself sinking into the same shadow of despair I'd felt in the Big Hole before reaching the Tetons. I crawled into my sleeping bag in silent tears, not wanting to reveal my turmoil to Geri. I prayed for strength to complete the ride, to keep my pedals turning toward the goal. Before I fell asleep I surprised myself by somehow attaining a certain level of acceptance. Maybe my unspoken prayers had been heard, because a sudden peace came over me. I would either make the Death Ride, or I wouldn't. God would decide. I let go, and slept.

The next morning at 6:15, all one thousand of us gathered to wait for the starting gun, everyone in brightly colored shirts and helmets (which weren't required), straddling bikes of every make and color. Once turned loose, we all settled into the day's work. My body showed plenty of strength and endurance. I conquered all five passes with relative ease, and ten and a half hours later I arrived at the finish line to collect my deathly-gray T-shirt. My average speed had been just under eleven miles per hour. I was more than pleased with my performance, and Geri said she was now sure I could do the 500 miles in Texas. My Petit Tour had been a big success, and more importantly, I had fulfilled my desire to please God. It meant I could keep training and planning for the Spenco. I'd passed the test.

Three weeks later I "cracked," hit the wall, went into a slump. Suddenly I had little power and juice for riding. It was as though some inner fuse had blown and fried a bunch of my circuits. My average speed did not increase for several weeks, and my mood was sour. Feeling utterly unmotivated, discouraged and humbled, I slogged through my rides, eking out as many miles as I could with my heavy body dumped on the saddle. My considerable will power was useless to lift myself out of this state, which pissed me off. I knew that only God could grant me the lively power to ride, and all I could do was wait for Him to give that back.

Meanwhile I was caught in a never-ending cycle of hostility and gut-wrenching emotional outbursts. Every time I pushed myself a little harder physically, or when it was too cold or too windy, some painful emotion would erupt from the unknown depths: rage, anger, deep sorrow, loss, guilt, regret, remorse, shame, impatience, hostility, contempt, resentment, fear. Mostly I had no idea of the root cause of any of these feelings. It was as though a huge caldron was simmering inside me, full of all the emotions I'd never fully expressed. They were now all blended together into a toxic stew that regularly poured out of me.

One morning I found myself head-to-head with a brutal wind that was entirely ignoring my cute little anti-headwind mantra. As I fumed and trash-talked down the road, an ugly inner voice began jeering at my struggles. *Well, you'd better get used to it, hadn't you.* I was startled and unnerved. This mean, harsh voice was *inside* me. The level of hostility and self-loathing that came at me almost knocked me off my bike. It was as though I'd found a stinking corpse at the bottom of the well of my toxic emotions. I could *feel* the self-hatred as fully as if I had wrapped myself with this corpse like a shawl.

As I rode and railed against the wind, self-hatred oozing from every sweaty pore, I finally had to confront the reality that the cruel, ugly witch I saw in my mother was also within *me*. Jungians call this part of the psyche "the negative mother," and like my own mother, at every move she condemned and judged me. There was never a break. Only after I performed feats of heroic proportions—the Tetons, the Death Ride—did she relent and temporarily let me off the self-criticism and self-judgment hook. But she never really stopped hounding me, and that morning my struggle and helplessness in the face of headwinds had released her zealous negativity.

Never in a million years would I have expected to find such venom, such self-loathing in myself. As I pushed onward, I remembered that theologian Paul Tillich had talked about self-hatred as one of those psychological forces that threatens our very existence and can lead us to despair. I'd been there before, and I wasn't willing to go again. It was time to confront this inner witch. But how? I'd tried so many times before. What would work?

I'd recently read a book entitled *The Inner Enemy: How to Fight Fair With Yourself*. My battle was obviously a familiar struggle for others. The author, Dr. George Bach, describes how parents or teachers or our culture find fault with us as children, and with no authority to counter their opinions, we capitulate and unconsciously agree with their negative perceptions of us. We end up colluding with the enemy. Bach says that the remedy is to take an aggressive stance and banish, as best we can by whatever means, the enemy within.

Okay, I was going to eradicate this undermining, subversive, negative force. I screwed up my courage. "You are *outta* here!" I screamed into the wind that was the witch, my self-hatred, and my mother all rolled into one. "Out of my face, do you hear? Fuck off! No more Miss Sweet Cheeks. No more try-to-recon-cile-our-differences shit!" The outburst went on for a mile as I fought the wind along an empty rural road near town. "If you have nothing nice to say to me, then you are dead meat! And may you rot in hell!"

I suddenly felt calmer. Maybe I'd scared her. I gave myself credit for having had the guts to confront her, to confront the forces that held me down. Still vigilant, I rode on into the wind. Its power had not diminished, but I was able now to notice the fields of dry yellow grass, old barns and the occasional group of brown cows grazing together.

Without thought or warning, a few miles farther on, a voice arose in me, quiet but insistent. *The only place I want to be is with you, and you don't want me.* Inwardly I jerked as if I'd been burned. Who on earth was speaking these words? Where did *this* accusation come from? It wasn't exactly demeaning—more like an invitation. Loathe as I was to admit it, here was my inner child again, glaring at me with tears in her eyes. I knew she had every right to be angry and hurt. Despite my promise made early in the year to take care of her, I had again let her down. These past weeks I hadn't been attentive to her needs for lightheartedness and fun. I'd been grumpy and pissed-off because of my slump and the headwinds.

I could feel her slipping away from me. She was my *divine* inner child and a crucial link to finding God. What if I lost touch with her? Would she stay long enough for me to say, "I'm sorry, I'll make it up to you. I promise." Would she give me another chance? Oh, these bridges, these tenuous connections to God seemed so precarious! It was so hard to stay aware and conscious of myself. I had to keep renewing my intention and commitment over and over.

I dug into my pedal strokes with deep conviction and vowed out loud to myself, and to Sunny and the Universe, "I will find her again, and I will never let her go." There would be no more not taking care of her needs because I was too goal-oriented. I didn't have to stop or even back off my training program; I just needed to add more elements of nurture, and eliminate the elements of torture. I needed to appreciate and love her. I had to bring her back to me and be a consistent, safe place for her. It seemed I'd blown the lid off and found my inner child beneath, ready to teach me again. And somehow I had broken through the long slump.

With 4,000 miles on my odometer —and two training months left to go—I began September determined to try a new approach. I would let my body train *me* instead of trying to impose my fierce will on it. The idea rose into my mind like a still, small voice from within—there was a good possibility that God and my body were the same. I certainly did not want to offend God, so my new training program would be directed by my God-Body. If I wasn't feeling strong, I would take it easy. If I felt good, I would crank up the pace. I would put on or take off layers when my body said it was too cold or warm. I peed when I needed to, ate when I was hungry. Over the next couple of weeks, my riding began to grow strong again.

One warm, calm day as I pedaled easily along one of the local roads, some words arose gently and spontaneously from within me. I heard myself say aloud, "I know you want me." I did not know for sure what those words meant. At first I believed it was God speaking, affirming that He wanted me to find Him. I thought perhaps He was saying, in so many words, "Keep looking. Keep going." In retrospect, I could also understand these words as my divine inner child saying, "Even though you often overlook me and roll right over me, I believe you truly want me and that you are trying. I'll hang in here with you." Whatever they meant, an unusual inner peace filled me as I pedaled. Was the inner war really winding down? Was the wicked witch dissolving? My heart gave a little hopeful jump. A favorite song by the Beatles popped into my mind, and I began singing:

Listen. Doo dah doo. Do you want to know a secret? Doo dah doo.
Let me whisper in your ear. Say the words you long to hear…

I sang the final words "I'm in love with you" with a joyful and swelling heart. I wasn't sure if I was singing to myself or my inner child or both. But it didn't matter because being "in love" was a beautiful place to be.

During those first three weeks of September, I felt a new sense of myself, like that renewed feeling of being alive after you've been sick with the flu. And Sunny too was renewed. I took him in for a new derailleur and chain, and the mechanic "trued" the wheels again. "That ought to last you a while," he said as I wheeled Sunny out the door. If only my inner world could have stayed so reliably trued.

"I hate you! I despise you! I am sick to death and tired of you!" I was raging *again* at the cold, foggy winds of late September. I was raging *again* at God.

"Why are you making this so hard? How much more of this do I have to take? Give me a fucking *break*!"

I would scream at the wind, and then at God, then dissolve into convulsive sobbing, all of which left me more exhausted than the physical exertion of the training ride. It was as if a small firestorm would ignite in my chest and speed through my body, into my heart and brain, and then out my mouth. The putrid soup inside me kept boiling over. No matter how hard I tried to understand my emotions and control them, to overcome inner obstacles and learn the lessons I was supposed to learn, I kept falling into these toxic outbursts. I'd shriek into the wind, "This has *got to stop*! This is a stupid, useless pattern!!" But I couldn't seem to stop the pattern any more than I could stop the wind.

The worst of it was that I knew I couldn't possibly have union with God if I were so full of anger, frustration and hostility. One morning after one of my rages, a surprising and troubling question came to mind: *Was my salvation possible?* I'd never considered the idea of salvation before, let alone my own, but whatever it meant, I knew intuitively it was what I needed. Much later in another of Paul Tillich's books, I would find the words that described what I was longing for. Tillich talks about salvation as bringing together all the parts of ourselves—including the wounded and broken parts, our inner child, our unlovable parts—into one healed and whole "new being." That's what was happening to me, but I didn't really know it. I consulted one of Merton's books and found the definition of salvation to be: "to work out our identity in God." I found myself telling an interested friend that I was "working out my salvation," as if I knew what I was talking about or what I was doing or where I was going. Of course I didn't. I just wanted out of my misery. I wanted to find inner peace, even happiness and joy, and I knew that with so much anger inside me I would never get there. I would never find God.

And if I did, would He accept me? Maybe I was too far-gone, too much of an ugly duckling, too helplessly lost. Surely God wasn't looking for ugly ducklings! Surely God wanted only beautiful swans. Was I such an ugly and angry duckling that the possibility of being a swan was just too remote? Each day I'd return from another training ride plunged into a foul soup of doubt and despair.

All along I'd been assuming that the Spenco, and the training it required, would be my next step on the way—or at least a part of the way—to finding union with God. Now I wasn't sure. I was plagued by anxious questions: *Is my life to be endless wallowing in and spewing toxic waste? Even if I get to the Spenco feeling prepared enough, and ride the 500 miles, will that get me to my real goal? What are the odds that training another 1,000 miles will make a lick of difference in my quest for union with God?*

It began to look pointless, but I kept training anyway. I didn't know what else to do. Each day I got on my bike and rode through the endless muck of hostility and despair. Ironically, the last week of September, I recorded the highest mileage of my training so far—331 miles—and my strongest ride—eighty-two miles with an average speed of 17.3 miles per hour. At least I was going faster through the muck.

As I always did on weekday rides, at eight o'clock one morning I parked Sparky in front of my favorite coffee house and unloaded Sunny from the back. After my allotted miles I'd return to get a cappuccino and walnut cookie there. I pulled on my windbreaker, reset the odometer, swung my leg over the saddle, settled my crotch onto the familiar hard slim seat, and shoved off into the windy morning. The sun was in my eyes as I rode into the ranch country outside town—a mostly flat route with some rolling hills and dry creeks. I tried to stay focused on my cadence, but of course the wind was on the rise, along with my frustration. The rushing of the wind was so loud against my ears that I barely heard the quiet voice speaking inside me: *I want you to come to me*, it said gently. I burst into tears. This time I knew it was God calling me. In spite of my inner desolation, the wind, and the barren, overgrazed landscape I was riding through, a spark of hope lifted my spirits. Was He willing to take in ugly ducklings after all? Would He take me even with all my rage and anger, with my despair and hopelessness?

The beautiful words came to mind of the Bible passage that had kept me going on my way to the Tetons: *They will mount up on wings as eagles; they will run and not be weary*. God was calling me, urging me on, helping me even in the ugly inner state I was in. There was hope for me after all! I felt a surge of energy.

For the remaining thirty miles I dwelled on this sense of acceptance and hope, barely noticing the howling wind.

The next day I left the house feeling lighthearted. I "flew" up nearby Mt. Diablo—a climb of almost 4,000 feet—in record time. When I arrived at the steeply inclined parking lot near the top of the mountain, I almost got off to walk Sunny, as I always did. But this day the wings of eagles carried me right to the top. As I stood there, I savored the little ripples of hope rising in me. God was inviting me to come to Him. And my speed and strength were also on the rise. Maybe I could make it after all.

Like peeling away the layers of an onion, within a couple of days my eagle crash-landed, and I was once more in a foul mood. When I told my body worker about this relentless cycle, she asked me, "Who is not getting what she wants so that she keeps rising up in anger and tears?" There it was again. I was *still* not taking care of my inner child, not taking time to do fun things, to be happy. I vowed to make a specific time every day to ask how she was feeling, and then listen to her. I also committed to saying the daily affirmation my body worker suggested: *I am creating a loving, joyous environment for myself.* I promised myself as well that as soon as I returned from Texas, I would bring a pet into our lives. I *had* to learn to give myself permission to be happy. I *had* to take care of my inner child's needs. I *had* to learn how to be a good nurturing mother to her, and to myself.

Geri and me on top of Mt. Diablo

Two days later during my long ride, the temperature dropped and the icy fog rolled in. I could feel my frustration rising, but this time I was determined not to fall into a destructive response. As the cold gripped my body, I could feel an inner iciness grip my heart. I saw for the first time that I was also equating freezing weather with my inner / outer negative mother. I needed to separate the two. Wind and cold were wind and cold; they were not my mother. As I rode, I began to repeat to myself:

The wind is not my mother.
The wind is not my mother.
The wind is not my mother.
It is not my mother.
It is not *my mother.*

Chanting my inner mantra, I rode my assigned miles in a relatively neutral mood, staving off the usual anger. Again the next day, when the wind began to rip into me, I restarted my mantra: *It is not my mother. It is not my mother.* The farther I cycled with that mantra, the less the wind had its usual power over me. It was working! Maybe I had found a key to break the cycle of anger and diminish the power of my inner witch. In subsequent days when the cold, oppressive weather did not automatically activate her, I barely dared to think—maybe I have been set free!

Oh Joy!
I dove into the deep end of the pool and was instantly swimming in happiness, breast-stroking underwater for the entire length of the pool. I reveled in the coolness and magical resistance of the water as I dug my strong arms through it and felt my hair trailing behind me. I came up for air panting, then laughing and giggling like a six year old. I dove again, standing on my hands in the shallow end, somersaulting and splashing, glad no strangers were around so I could express every ounce of the joy I was feeling without being self-conscious.

My inner child was happy—we were with Paul for a two-night vacation. Even though our relationship continued in the same unsatisfying way for me, I was still in love with him. As long as I didn't ask for too much, he and I—and my inner child—had a wonderful time. Being with Paul still felt to me like coming home. He reflected what felt to me like my "true self," and projection or not, he always made me feel closer to God.

By the time I finally climbed out of the pool, the skin on my fingers was all wrinkly. My hair still wet, my heart still laughing, I twirled around the little sitting area in our cabin. In my terry cloth robe, I plopped down into a chair to write in my journal.

Oh, to remember what happiness is! To remember and greet Joy again. To recognize her as part of my life, that she has a right to exist, that she must *exist to provide balance to the suffering and struggle I am so proficient in. These feelings—coming from so deep—must be from God; they must be okay.*

What struck me was that I had personalized *Joy*; I recognized "her" as part of my life. Perhaps I was talking about my divine inner child, seeing her for the first time in her true nature. I was connecting again with the happiness and joy that I'd felt during my Happy Wandering. On my solo bike trip I had resolved, back in Klamath Falls, to accept that happiness was as much my birthright as anyone else's. But I'd fallen back into old patterns, and I needed to remind myself over and over again that it was okay for me to be happy.

It was early October, my last month of training. I'd planned to ride 1,300 miles in October before leaving for Waco. The hard-earned outer miles I'd ridden so far had shifted my inner life dramatically. I'd seen some of the most foul ingredients in my toxic soup, and some ways to disarm those emotions. I couldn't say if I had completely dissolved the inner witch, but I had learned ways to shrink her and make her sit in a corner. I'd ridden through my despair and now felt ready and eager to try my hand at the Spenco. No matter what happened I knew I'd done everything an amateur cyclist could do to prepare for the challenge. I didn't know if Waco would bring me union with God, but I had done all I was supposed to do. I'd learned how to take better care of myself and to bring more joy and happiness into my inner child's life and mine.

Still feeling Joy in my heart, I rode the next day into the Napa Valley, covering 104 miles in seven and a half hours. Yes, I was definitely pushing it, but I'd also made it into a "joy" ride by noticing all the horses roaming the golden, oak-studded fields, the flocks of black and white goats, the bounding, white-tailed deer, and the beauty of the quiet country roads. At one point, Sunny and I were at a high enough elevation to watch the fog rolling in from the ocean—soft, gentle, cool and soothing to the land below. I was glad to be seeing it from above, although now I knew that riding through it would not have disturbed me as it had in the past.

In mid-October I rode the Sequoia Classic, ninety-eight miles on the San Francisco Peninsula from the base of the Santa Cruz Mountains, over the crest, down to the coast, back up to the crest, and down through thick, chilly, moist fog into Portola Valley. By the final downhill run, my body was as stiff as if it had been put on ice, yet my spirits were still upbeat. I felt a great sense of accomplishment in both miles and mood.

When I got home, I removed the cyclometer from Sunny's handlebars. From this point on until the Spenco two weeks away, we'd be going only for joy rides. I'd completed my plan. I'd ridden that surprising 7,000 training miles, the equivalent of riding across the United States and back. And the inner miles I'd traveled were incalculable. I felt like a powerful force was carrying me to the Spenco 500. I told Geri that I thought the Great Race would mark the end and the beginning of my life.

Before leaving for Waco, I savored my final ride. I passed through a brief thundershower, and the road glistened as the sun beamed through the black clouds. In spite of the wet road splashing grit onto my gears and Sunny's clean yellow frame, I felt happy as a toad in God's pocket. As I rode I laughed with delight at this phrase inspired by a little pen and ink drawing Geri had given me of a frog peering out of the coat pocket of a mysterious-looking person. I chased the sun, smiling through the raindrops, and sang, "You are my sunshine, my only sunshine...." My outer arms were firmly planted on Sunny's handlebars, and my inner arms were welcoming my divine child and hugging her closely.

On October 29, the last entry in my training journal before leaving for the Spenco 500 was "I am winning."

21

NO SUCCESS LIKE FAILURE

"Oh Wow! Geri! It's *an armadillo!*"

It was two o'clock in the morning and raining somewhere in the hill country near Waco, Texas. I'd been cycling for twelve hours as part of the Spenco 500. I knew that Geri, driving the truck a few yards behind me, couldn't hear my excitement above the hum of the engine and the hiss of the falling rain. But I hoped she could see in the shaft of light from Sparky's headlights this strange prehistoric creature waddling across the road barely five feet in front of me. As I cycled slowly up the hill toward it, I watched transfixed as the gray creature that looked like a cross between a giant rat and a pig covered with armor disappeared into the pitch darkness on the far side of the road. There was no doubt I was in Texas!

Geri and I had arrived in Waco the night before, after driving 1,475 miles in thirty-eight hours. From the moment I'd slipped in behind the wheel of Sparky, my foot had been stuck to the accelerator and my eyes glued to the road dead ahead. After the first four nonstop hours, Geri had called me out for "relentless driving." Because I was feeling like a goal-oriented racehorse much of the time, it was hard to remember I was carrying not only a young rider—my inner child—who liked to look at pretty views occasionally and to putter around the interstate convenience stores looking at souvenirs, but also a human companion who liked to eat from time to time.

Getting busted by Geri slowed me down a little but not quite enough. Outside the remote west Texas town of Van Horn, I'd been pulled over by the local police for speeding. They escorted us to a tiny mobile unit in the middle of nowhere to meet with the Justice of the Peace. This all seemed a bit irregular, and we felt nervous. We were two urban babes, and they were three burly country cops. Thankfully they only wanted to give us a hard time verbally, and we drove away at fifty-five miles per hour, feeling flustered but relieved.

That evening at the race headquarters, set up in a conference room at the Waco Hilton, I'd signed in as one of 302 race entries. Many riders were in teams, and sixteen women were riding relay. I was one of only ten women riding solo. As we walked around the room, checking out the commercial offerings in the various booths, I was excited to recognize and meet some of my cycling heroes—international professionals and nationally known ultra-marathon superstars, the ones who ride the Race Across America and finish in nine days. I knew I wasn't competition for these pros, but I felt flattered when some of them looked me over as if I were a potential rival for the winnings. I just hoped to finish the race in no more than thirty-six hours. I suspected that I was the only one riding the race to find God.

The day of the race had dawned sunny and cool. But by 2:00 when we'd lined up for the ceremonial start at Baylor University, clouds had moved in, dropping the temperature considerably. I'd put on five layers of clothes, including knee socks, hoping that was enough. Cyclists with their bikes and scores of bystanders were milling around the designated starting area, which covered a couple of blocks mid-campus. A twenty-foot replica of a Dr. Pepper can loomed over the check-in tables beneath a "Spenco 500" banner spanning the street. I felt calm but excited as I strapped on the required helmet. *This must be what an armadillo feels like.* Little did I know that in a few hours I might actually catch sight of one.

At the start line

The loud retort of a pistol cracked the air, and we'd shoved off. Though we all felt like racehorses chomping at the bit, a police escort restrained us as we passed through the city streets. At the Spenco plant all the employees had been out to wave us off. Elementary school kids lined the street with outstretched hands that we high-fived as we cycled past. It had been a festive send-off. After six painfully slow miles, we reached the city limits and were released to go spinning into Texas hill country. By that time a steady drizzle had descended upon us, and the wind had kicked up. Now the real work began, what I'd spent the past seven months preparing for, in inner and outer miles.

At the beginning of the route, the country was mostly flat. Fields of grain lined the two lane blacktop highway; small houses dotted the landscape; tall, dark telephone poles stuck up into the gray sky like a long row of toothpicks. Occasionally we passed through a corridor of trees on either side of the road. Through the flat, gray filter of rain everything appeared dreary and colorless.

I was somewhere in the middle of all the cyclists, and watched as some riders grouped together, while others went off on their own or with one or two others. Teams were clearly distinguishable with their matching outfits. A couple hours out, my pace matched that of a young guy and we rode together for several miles. We were talking amiably when suddenly there was the unmistakable *pffft* of a punctured tire. My companion wobbled his bike onto the side of the road. I pulled in behind him.

"Do you want help?"

"No, thanks. I can handle it. You go on"

"You're sure you're okay?" I was reluctant to leave. He didn't have a support crew like many of us had. Even though fixing a tire is a one-person job, I knew I'd appreciate company in his situation.

"I'm fine. Really. You keep going. Good luck."

I said goodbye and set off alone.

My support crew was Geri, driving Sparky just a few yards behind me, keeping steady with my pace. Sometimes when there were no other vehicles on the road, she'd pull up along my right side and we'd visit a bit until an approaching car would send us back into single file. By 5:00 p.m. I'd cycled through the first forty miles of headwinds and rain. I was dripping wet and although my rain jacket kept my torso dry, I felt chilled. This was not what I'd expected—or hoped for.

"It's going to take a minor miracle to get me through this ride, Pardner," I said to Geri as she pulled alongside me again.

"Just keep on going," she said. "You're doing great."

Ten miles later I'd reached the first check-in point and feed station, which was in someone's garage attached to a farmhouse. A dozen cyclists were wandering about in the inner recesses of the garage, chatting, chewing, or staring off into space. I signed in and went to pick up a peanut butter and jelly sandwich on Wonder Bread, an apple and a banana. As I ate the sweet, sticky, spongy sandwich, I did a quick assessment: I'd put some decent miles under my tires so far but was not exactly feeling relaxed. I had a long way to go. Not wanting to linger and get more chilled, I put the fruit in my pack for later on and, still chewing, set off again.

During the next fifty miles my sagging morale began to pick up. It was comforting to see other cyclists looking as wet and subdued as I was. *If they can do it, so can I.* I picked up a rhythm and the miles went by. *Take it easy, baby. Take it as it comes.* I began to relax and settle into my pace and the spirit of the ride.

At about seventy-five miles, I noticed that my right calf had begun tightening up, but I didn't pay it much mind. When I arrived at the 100-mile feed station, I took some time to massage my leg. I couldn't seem to stretch or work out the cramped muscles, but I trusted it would be okay. Through all those thousands of training miles, I had been slowed down by emotional pain but never physical ailments, so I figured it would eventually work itself out. I'd saddled up again and pushed off. It was about 9:00 and by then plenty dark.

Sparky's headlights blazed across the road from a few yards behind me. The steady hum of the engine in the night was soothing as I stroked the pedals. Geri was playing my favorite music on the stereo, driving with the window open even though it was raining. I felt deeply supported by her in every way. Inside my mind I sang along with Peter, Paul & Mary, ("500 Miles"—what else?), Kenny Rogers, the Beatles (*"Doo Dah Doo"*), and The Doors ("Take it easy, Baby"), riding on the waves of the music that had accompanied me through so much during my months of training. My entire attention was riveted on the road and turning the pedals, propelling myself forward.

That's when I saw it—the armadillo—shuffling across the Texas highway in the middle of the night. This strange and somehow noble creature formerly seemed almost mythical to me. But here it was, in flesh and helmet, right in front of me! Maybe it was worth seven months and 7,000 miles of training just to see this famous Texas icon. I pedaled slowly on, imagining the comings and goings of the armadillo and other mysterious night creatures who lived beyond the wide swath of Sparky's headlights. Maybe they were all watching the race.

It was cold; it was raining; I was using my lowest gears—the ones reserved for very steep climbs—just to get up the endless string of moderate grades in the Texas hill country. My right calf felt like a steel rod had been inserted in it from my knee to my toes, and each dark hill I climbed seemed to rise twice as far as it fell. Every down-stroke felt like an electric shock hitting that steel rod. When I'd dismounted several miles earlier, I was shocked that I could walk only on tiptoe on my right leg. *What is going on? How can this be happening?* The rain and cold and wind—my nemeses during training—no longer were getting in my way. In spite of the difficult conditions, I really wanted to keep riding. My heart and soul were in the ride—all 500 nonstop miles of it. The very fact that I was feeling that way was a triumph.

But something completely unexpected was happening. My body was saying, "No way!" I had learned I could change my attitude, but I felt helpless to fix my body. At the 210-mile point, sixteen and a half hours into the ride, with just a bit of light in the gray sky, I rode toward yet another hill. It seemed to rise higher as I approached it. When I reached the base, I stopped dead. It felt to me like a wall rising up before me. *This can't be the end of the line....* But there was no way I could pull myself and Sunny up another grade, even with Pachelbel's Canon in D Major playing at full volume behind me. My right calf would not turn one more rpm. For me it would be the "Spenco 210." Geri pulled alongside me.

"Pardner, I can't make it any farther. It hurts too much."

Slowly I dismounted. I couldn't tell which was worse—the pain in my leg or the disappointment of having to quit. I started crying. My body had always been so reliably steadfast and strong. It was such a fluke that my leg had seized up. I might have expected emotional trouble, but since the race began I'd not uttered or thought an angry word against the headwinds, and my inner witch and nay-saying demons had all kept their mouths shut. God had wanted me to do this! I had done everything "right" in my physical training and emotional purifying and peacemaking. I felt as if I'd been sabotaged. It didn't make sense! I felt robbed of this opportunity to please God, and to accomplish something big. I knew I could have made all 500 miles. Still in tears, I climbed into Sparky, relieved to end the painful riding but confused and frustrated and disappointed at this defeat.

The sky grew slowly lighter as Geri drove us solemnly back to race headquarters. The spacious conference room was as busy as it had been the evening before. A lot of tired-looking riders were milling around a food table, gulping coffee and snarfing cookies. I obviously wasn't the only one who didn't make it, but that didn't make me feel any better. I lined up with a few others to check in so they'd know I'd abandoned the race.

"That was bad out there," the guy behind me muttered.

"The weather had started out so well," another beat-looking cyclist chimed in.

"Yeah, I wanted to keep riding, but my leg seized up." I said. "I guess it was the cold,"

When the woman checking us in said that some of the top contenders had abandoned the race even before I had, I felt a little better. As we were leaving the room, the race organizers handed me a light blue commemorative t-shirt with the "Spenco 500" logo emblazoned on the front in bright red and orange graphics. I accepted it with a tired smile. At least I'd have a memento to show for my efforts and proof that I hadn't just dreamed the whole thing. I would later find out that of the 302 riders who started, only thirty would finish.

I telegrammed Alfred, my dear cycling coach: "Weather conditions, physical breakdown, Spenco 210 in 16.5 hours. Disappointing, but feeling ok. Details to follow. Love now." If we'd had email at that time, I might have sent out the same message to the friends who had been cheering me on. As it was, that one telegram was all I could manage.

Geri and I didn't talk much about the Great Race—or the Great Failure—on the drive to Denver where she was catching a flight back to California. She wisely didn't bring up the subject though it filled the car like a giant turd. I was in a kind of tired daze, recuperating from the physical effort and trying to digest what had happened. We stopped for the night in Leadville, Colorado, an appropriate name for how we were feeling. We walked around the still snowy town and took a short bike ride to give us emotional space from the ride and the disappointment. We reminisced about all the great training rides we'd taken, and how our friendship had grown. The next morning we drove quietly to Denver, and after a tearful parting at the airport curbside, I began the long drive home alone.

Geri and me in Waco

I whizzed past the steady flow of 18-wheelers on I-40 through New Mexico and Arizona. Since leaving Denver, I'd continued in a reflective state of mind. All those months and miles for an event that had passed in a flash! Even though I could still feel the effects of the race in my body, and images of those pre-race and race hours replayed over and over in my mind, it was almost as if the race had never happened. In early September I'd written in my journal: "If I don't finish 500, I'll eat my chain." I smiled now at the cavalier humor and confidence I'd felt.

I hadn't accomplished what I had so ardently and wholeheartedly prepared to do. Yet as I continued driving, I began to notice, to my amazement, that I had not then, nor was I now, beating myself up for this failure. And I wasn't about to take so much as a lick of my chain either! I'd kept expecting my inner witch to serve up a barrage of negativity for my failing to complete the 500. But she didn't show.

On the contrary. The only voices I heard inside were full of support and appreciation. I actually felt *good* about myself. I had earned my place on the start line with so many pros; I had trained adequately enough to have a legitimate shot at completing the race. I had done my very best, had covered a fair part of the course, even more than some of the pros. To my great surprise, I was accepting myself in spite of failure! And not only *accepting* myself—I was *proud* of myself. As I drove through the desert, I was actually feeling joyful. Had 7,000 miles of painful inner work freed me from self-abuse and condemnation?

On top of this unexpected and rather radical reaction, I began to see that it was the best "failure" I'd ever had. Suddenly I understood the paradoxical truth in the words of one of Bob Dylan's songs: "There's no success like failure, and failure is no success at all." Of course I had wanted to succeed as a cyclist, but if I had, I would have felt compelled to commit myself to an ever-greater cycling challenge, like the Race Across America, an event I would have no business even thinking about competing in. But the part of me that always felt compelled to do something bigger and better—to quiet the witch, to prove something to myself or somebody, to win someone's love, to find God—might have just considered that as the next thing to do.

It also occurred to me that while I was clear that God had assigned the Spenco to me to train for and ride in, He never said I had to *finish* it. It hadn't occurred to me that God might have *wanted* me to fail. Before leaving California for Waco, I'd had an intuition that the end of the race would be a "pearl of great price." Though I hadn't come any closer to reaching my heart's deepest desire—to find and have union with God—maybe making the commitment and going through the process rather than reaching the goal was the pearl of great price. Maybe what I'd needed to learn about union with God wasn't at the end of the race in Waco. Maybe it was in simply following His call. Maybe it was in the 7,000 miles of headwinds. Maybe it was in this moment of accepting my failure without condemnation. As I'd written in my journal, I was winning.

22

THE PROMISED LAND

I was having a beautiful dream.

In it I was not trying to go anywhere at top speed. I was not contemplating taking on a big project, or in the midst of some demanding task. I was not pushing myself to complete a daunting feat. I was not homesick. I was not driven to find God. I was not longing for God. In this dream I felt like I had reached the unreachable star.

The most beautiful part of the dream was that it was playing out in broad daylight every day, and I was wide-awake. I'd been home for three weeks after the race, and the dream was still running continuously. Based on past experience, I kept expecting the painful intensity of longing and homesickness to return, the way headaches or back pain you've suffered with for years can abate for a short time but return with a vengeance. The crash after my return from Happy Wandering—the shock and disappointment to realize then that I was still searching for God—seemed the norm. But these deeply peaceful days had stretched into weeks, until I began to believe, and to feel, that something in me had profoundly changed.

There was never an "Aha!" flash of understanding, never a definite moment when I exclaimed, "Oh God, after almost ten years of searching, I have found you at last!" Nor did I think about Merton's directive, "Find yourself and you will find God." I didn't think about whether I'd found myself or not. There was only a surprising euphoria that had grown like a balloon being slowly inflated and rising within me, proclaiming, "I am no longer looking for anything!"

What was the reason for this dramatic shift? The only thing I could think of that could possibly have changed my interior landscape so radically was that I had accepted myself in failure. Had the "salvation," which at one time had felt so impossible for me in the face of the toxic stew of my anger and self-loathing, actually come to pass, bringing the joy and peace of mind and heart I was now experiencing? The last place I would have expected my salvation to come from was loving myself at a time of failure. I thought of how Merton said that working out our salvation "...is a labor that requires sacrifice and anguish, risks and many tests." Had everything I'd been through been part of that working out of salvation? Had I passed the tests? Had I awakened to my "own identity in God," as Merton puts it? Had I been made whole through self-love, all the parts of myself brought together?

And did this mean then that my alienated inner child had also been redeemed? She had been fearful of doing and saying the "wrong" thing, but we were no longer at the mercy of the inner witch, and I had discovered the essence of the nurturing mother in myself. And with my acceptance of failing, I had said to both of us, "I love you no matter what." During these magical days at home after the Spenco, I was finding it hard to distinguish between my adult and my inner child, which made me feel that we two were united at last. I felt playful and light and unafraid. And since I knew this inner child was also a link to the divine, I felt even more encouraged that I had also accepted that God was within me, not some external being I had to pursue. My loving gesture of self-acceptance had transformed my entire interior life. Now I understood what I hadn't known on my Vision Quest when I felt that everything was love—that same love was also *inside* me. I was almost embarrassed by this simple explanation, but I knew it was true.

In a state of wonderment, I gradually acknowledged that my search for God was over. After all the years of struggle, I now basked everyday in the warm inner glow of this new, unexpected, and deeply peaceful inner reality. It was as if the sun had risen within me. For so many years, after those bland scrambled eggs at my mother's house, I'd felt as though I were adrift in a little boat in the midst of violent, stormy seas. After that dream of God coming to me, I'd fallen in love with Paul, then I left my home and my marriage to find God. The all-consuming desire for Him had been the burning fuel propelling my storm-tossed boat forward. There had been brief periods of happiness and calm, yet I'd always felt I was still on a journey, still on my little boat out at sea. And the lulls were invariably followed by violent storms of ever-deeper, more intense self-investigation, and a renewed, more passionate longing for God. Until now. The lovely dream I was in continued every blessed day for weeks on end. My boat had pulled into a calm, safe harbor and docked. For the time being, I wasn't asking what was next.

My inner world wasn't the only part of my life that had undergone radical change. I'd decided to sell Mudd's and Crow Canyon Gardens. I was letting go and moving on. Fortunately my business partner was ready to do the same.

"Well, my friend, it's been quite a journey," Kerry reflected quietly, as though he were watching a beautiful sunset. We were sitting on the patio on the south side of the restaurant overlooking the gardens. I started to get teary thinking about letting go of my "baby," our collaborative work together, and the vision we'd brought to life. We agreed we'd done a lot to make people more aware of living in harmony with the earth. And we'd served thousands of beautiful and delicious meals with produce from our own garden.

I was still concerned that I might have to resign myself to a new owner who wanted a meat and potatoes concept. "Do you think we'll be able to find someone who will carry on the vision of this place?" I asked Kerry.

He was always calm and thoughtful, even in times of change and upheaval. "Let's put the word out to the Universe. It's all we can do. I'm positive something good will emerge."

Eventually we would sell the garden portion of the property to the City of San Ramon to be preserved as a productive garden, and the restaurant would be purchased by our manager who, over the next twenty years, carried on the spirit of the project.

Perhaps the biggest change of all was in my relationship with Paul. We'd arranged to meet in Palm Springs on my drive back from Texas. As always, we were happy to see each other, but this occasion marked the end of the painful pattern that had gone on for years. Paul wanted to end our sexual intimacy. He said he'd given up hope that I was going to come around to being satisfied with all aspects of our relationship, and he wanted to move on. He'd gotten involved in another relationship with a woman, whom I knew and thought very highly of, and I understood—intellectually. But emotionally, it was a blow, a harsh reality check. Paul had been such an integral part of my life all during this profound time of change and discovery. He had been my link to God and had helped carry me to the place I was now at in myself. I felt sad at letting go of the hope that somehow a full and lasting relationship could work out with this man I loved so much. I was hopeful that we could still be friends.

In contrast to all the other wrenching and disorienting separations Paul and I had gone through, this one did not throw me into longing and despair. That alone was testimony to my solid connection to God, on my own, without Paul. Further affirmation of this profound change was that the emotional challenge of separation from him did not throw me into a major, or even minor, food binge. The addictive force had continued to diminish over time as my journey to find myself and find God had progressed. Though I didn't feel it at the time, Paul's decision would prove to be a gift, releasing me to continue on into my own life's call.

Other circumstances in my outer world were changing as well. On the road home from Waco, I'd checked out Boulder and Santa Fe as potential places to live. I felt done with the Bay Area and with the long period of struggle and growth I'd passed through there. I was ready to let it all go and launch into a new "career." Writing and publishing *Across America on the Yellow Brick Road*—years before Mudd's and everything that followed—had been such rewarding and enjoyable work that I decided I wanted to make books of various kinds for the rest of my life. I wanted to learn how to print letterpress (the old technology of applying type to a page with lead letter forms) and how to bind books by hand. My research revealed that there were teachers I could study with in the Southwest. Little did I know what would be in store for me before that vision would come to pass.

Advent arrived, those magical first twenty-four days of December that lead up to the birth of Jesus, the incarnation of God. In my new state of being, this Advent became more than opening the little windows of a calendar each day to reveal a pretty winter scene. I began to have an uncanny feeling that Christ was actually coming. Although I hadn't thought much about Christ since my journey to the Tetons as His bride, I still wore the ring that had signified to me our engagement. And now my already open and peaceful heart was stirring with a new awareness of Him.

Once again I found myself grappling with who was Christ? And who was He to me? For one thing, I was confused by all the names He was known by—Jesus, Jesus Christ, Christ, the Christ. Did each name mean something different? And how was I to think of Him in my very personal connection to Him? I reread Ram Dass's insight about the historical Jesus being a manifestation of Christ consciousness, "the consciousness that acknowledges the Living Spirit." For me that "Living Spirit" was God, the Divine Presence. And I read Thomas Merton who calls Christ our "inner partner," and "our other self." That sense of such a close relationship with Christ would help evolve my relationship to Him from that time onward.

I trusted that I would grow in understanding who Christ was and what my own relationship was to Him. For now, it seemed there were many ways to envision Christ, and I resolved my confusion by deciding I would use His many names somewhat interchangeably. Whatever name I chose, I would mean God manifested in the man Jesus.

But I was still left wondering why I had been so drawn to Christ in my search for God. Merton says, "All experience of God comes to us through Christ." Had my longing for God put out a call to Christ? I remembered that the Episcopal liturgy often ended with "through Jesus Christ our Lord." It was true that because Jesus was a human being like me, I could more easily identify with Him than with God. Was Jesus Christ now my link to God, just as Paul had once been? Did *finding* God through Christ mean *union* with God? Given how complete, full, and peaceful I felt already, what more could God have in store for me?

As the days of December unfolded, I became immersed in a totally extraordinary, unimaginable mystery. Advent was real. Christ *was* coming. Christ was coming to *me*. It was as if I were standing on a subway platform and could feel the subtle thunder of the approaching train as it began to fill the cavernous space of the station and shake the platform floor with ever-increasing intensity. Closer...and closer...

One day I was nestled in my cozy alcove reading when I came upon a short poem by Thomas Merton.

Make ready for the Christ, whose smile, like lightning,
sleeps in your paper flesh like dynamite.

My whole body prickled as though the electricity from that lightning had just passed through me. I even glanced at my skin as if expecting it to burst into flames. I put down the book, immersed in that image of Christ's smile sleeping in my flesh. I didn't quite know how to make ready for the Christ, other than what I was already doing. But Merton seemed to know what he was talking about. Elsewhere he'd said that Christ concentrates the rays of God's light and heat to the point where He sets fire to the spirit of man. I knew that fire, I'd been in it before. Would it come again? Just the thought of it was so explosive in me that I went out for a swift bike ride to dissipate some of the energy.

The further into Advent we went the more my whole being was irradiated with ongoing explosions of Christ's love. Instead of the blazing fire of longing I'd felt for so many years, I was now overwhelmed with the roaring fire of love. It was a constant presence, whether I was running errands, washing dishes, or writing in my journal. My body was filled with hot, orange-glowing coals that radiated waves of heat and love to me, for me. I had never felt such love before—many times more powerful and profound than I'd ever felt from or for Paul. I felt as if I were in a bubble, curled up like an embryo, floating within love, and the bubble itself was floating in a space that was filled with love. Within and without I was surrounded by the love of Christ and the love of God in one all-embracing, overwhelming Love.

One day I was sitting on the kitchen window seat waiting for my steamy mug of morning tea to cool when the love of Christ and the joy of His coming began to swell into something unexpected. I was struck, for the first time, with a visceral awareness of Christ's suffering and agony on the cross. This was not something I'd ever thought much about, but now, right along with the joy, my heart opened to deep sorrow and pain. Though I did not understand it at the time, I was experiencing—as did Jesus Christ—both sides of the one coin that was God. Within myself I was seeing and feeling both the beauty and the ugliness, the joy and the sorrow, the peace and the struggle of the fully lived human life that was embodied in Jesus Christ. This awareness, both joyful and painful, continued on past my cup of tea and throughout the next day. I was living in a sense of the *whole* Christ—Son of God *and* Son of Man.

I hardly knew what was happening to me, and I spent most of my time at home in awe and in deep silence. Once in a while I'd listen to spiritual music or Christmas carols quietly playing in the background. Hearing Joan Baez's silken, silvery voice singing "O Come, O Come, Emmanuel" brought Christ ever closer. Sometimes it was all I could do to endure the intensity of love in and around me. As in the eye of a tornado, I felt profoundly peaceful yet powerless in the grip of this spiritual mystery. I absolutely knew that I was in the process of receiving the Living Christ into my being, but it was beyond what my intellect could grasp. All I could do was wait for guidance, and keep riding my bike and running in the hills. Cycling through the cool winter air, I'd let myself open to the wind, as if it were Christ flowing through me. As I ran through the green, rain-soaked hills, every footfall called His name

Being so absorbed and directed by the power of love within made it hard to stay grounded enough to deal with the tasks of ordinary life. To a great degree I had to let go of trying to get things "done" as the power of this mysterious force carried me forward. Fortunately, during the holiday season life changes substantially for everyone, so my own strange world was not so out of synch with other people's holiday madness.

In the middle of Advent I picked out a lovely little spruce tree for Christmas and placed it into a perfect corner in the living room. It gave off a light scent of the forest from whence it had come, and in spite of my strict commitment to energy conservation, I adorned it with multiple strings of little white lights. As I hung glittery glass balls on branches and twigs, I repeated a phrase from the church liturgy that expressed my innermost feelings: *For He cometh...For He cometh.* For the first time in a lifetime of Christmases and Christmas trees, I knew this decorated tree was a symbol of the shining, living presence of Christ in my home and in my heart.

My dear friend Reverend Maxine was sitting beside me in a wooden pew at St. Timothy's Episcopal Church near my home. I'd asked if she would accompany me to make sure I did it "right"—this time. The previous Sunday I'd woken up with a strong urge to receive the Eucharist. I hadn't been to a service or taken Holy Communion since high school, and I wasn't even sure what it was about, but I'd followed my inner prompting and arrived at St. Timothy's in time for the service. Unknown to me, the protocol for Communion had been updated—a sip from the chalice of wine was no longer offered to congregants. Waiting with lowered eyes and pursed lips, I'd watched the chalice pass me by and missed dipping my wafer into the Blood of Christ. I'd left feeling embarrassed, incomplete, and sad.

This week Reverend Maxine stood in front of me in line and knelt next to me at the altar. I kept a watchful eye on her as the priest approached with the wafers. Maxine took one and held it in her hand. When the chalice of wine appeared, she dipped the wafer in and put it in her mouth. Following her exact moves, I received Holy Communion calmly and reverently. As I lifted myself up from the kneeler to follow Maxine back to our places, I had the clear, indisputable, absolute sense that I had indeed taken in the Body and Blood of Christ. I sat in a daze as the priest continued the service. I could *feel* Christ *inside* me! My rational mind was snuffed out like a candle by this absolute certainty. I was astonished and deeply moved that a dry wafer and wine could be so transformed.

After the service Maxine and I stood outside in the sun as parishioners filed out of the church.

"Did I tell you I was going to Australia in March?"

"Oh, Ginia, that's wonderful! Where will you go there?"

"I have a Pen Pal I've wanted to meet who lives on the east coast, so first I'll visit that area for a week." In the fall I'd set in motion this trip to meet in person the dear man who had coached me through so many months of training for the Spenco. Alfred probably knew more about me than almost anyone, so the thought of finally meeting him in person was exciting. But I had the feeling there was more to this journey than the rendezvous with Alfred. Once again I was walking into the unknown, just trusting my inner guidance.

"And then I want to travel on my own to other parts of Australia. I'm especially drawn to the desert of Central Australia—Alice Springs and Ayers Rock—it's called the Red Centre, the Red Heart...." My voice trailed off.

Maxine smiled. "Oh, you want to be cradled in the arms of the Infinite."

I had the feeling she knew way more about why I was going than I did. *Cradled in the arms of the Infinite.* It was so poetic and mystical that I didn't want to spoil the image or the moment by asking her what she meant. I let her phrase hang in my heart and imagination like a shiny Christmas ornament.

The closer we drew to Christmas, the deeper my love for Christ grew and the more encompassing the Love that carried me. I was now sure that my trip to the Tetons had been an affirmation of our engagement. I had gone as Christ's bride-to-be, but the marriage had not been meant to take place then. Not at that time. But it *was* to take place. When and where and how were beyond me, but I felt overjoyed, scared, excited—and mystified and awed beyond measure.

Trying to understand what marriage to Christ would mean, I turned to the writings of St. Teresa of Avila. Spiritual marriage, she says, "...is all a matter of love united with love." That resonated with how I was feeling, and I loved reading her meditation about how the "pure and extremely delicate and gentle actions of love" are inexplicable but clearly felt. I was clearly feeling that marriage to Christ would be a matter of the sweet, gentle intimacy St. Teresa describes. Like a young girl secretly engaged to her lover, I carried the promise within me into the new year.

In mid-January I was directed from within to attend the Sunday service at Grace Cathedral in San Francisco, an hour's drive from my home. Grace Cathedral is one of those grand, soaring spaces built in the Gothic style. Like a medieval castle, the church and its adjacent buildings occupy an entire city block, high on the top of Nob Hill. As I neared it, I felt like a pilgrim approaching one of the sacred cathedrals in France.

I entered through a side door, picked up the mimeographed "program for the day's service," and took a seat in the back of the vast church, many pews behind the main congregation. I didn't want to bungle any of *this* church's rituals! I'd never been in Grace Cathedral, and I was enthralled by the cavernous space and the silence echoing within it. My eyes and my heart fully opened to the wonder and spirit of the place. Everything within me was absolutely silent, empty, and full of love.

The program said that today was the Feast of the Baptism of the Lord and that this was one of four services during the year when the cathedral administers the Sacrament of Holy Baptism. I'd been baptized when I was about seven years old—one of those formalities that seemed to be something kids did—but it hadn't meant much to me, then or later. I just figured the ritual had been about being accepted as a new member of the Christian church. But somewhere in my explorations over the previous years, I'd read that baptism also "describes a movement of the Holy Spirit upon and within a believer, usually at or sometime after the person is saved." Since the Spenco 500, I'd been experiencing the wholeness and healing that Tillich describes as salvation. I *had* been saved. Was I now to receive the "movement of the Holy Spirit"?

I heard the distant voice of the priest saying, "I baptize thee in the name of the Father, the Son and the Holy Spirit. Amen." The Holy Trinity. My journey had primarily been driven by and was still deeply rooted in God the Father. Advent had brought the Christ of my journey more fully and actively into my life. Receiving the Holy Spirit would complete the Holy Trinity within me. From where I was sitting, I couldn't see if anyone was actually being baptized at the front of the church, but again I heard the priest pronounce the words, and in that moment I knew that *I* was being baptized, that the Holy Spirit was moving upon and within me. And I knew I was being admitted, now as a fully conscious adult, into membership in the Christian Church, a member of the Body of Christ.

As I sat silently steeped in wonder at the mysterious unfolding of Divine Love in my life, I heard an inner voice speak the words: "The Promised Land." I repeated to myself: *The Promised Land...The Promised Land*, recognizing that this was the truth of the new place inside me. Even though the term sounded so corny, like TV evangelism, this profound feeling of wholeness was indeed what I had sought and longed for. To feel the Holy Spirit moving within me, to feel the fullness of the Holy Trinity, was the passage into that place I'd so deeply hoped was possible to find. *The Promised Land.*

As I settled into accepting and embracing this beautiful new place within me, I felt a sudden and indescribable affirmation that Christ was wholly within my body and my being and that I would never be separated from Him. This confirmation, as the teachings say, surely was the movement of the Holy Spirit within me, although at the time I remember explaining it to myself in more secular terms. I sat under that soaring cathedral vault, feeling like my doctor had just sat down next to me in the pew and said, "Virginia, the Christ implant we gave you—which is much like a transplant—has been accepted by your body. You know, sometimes a body rejects these new organs, so I'm very happy to tell you of this success. There's no longer any danger of infection or rejection. The implant has taken." The metaphor helped me grasp this inexplicable, profound mystery.

I don't know how long I sat there soaking in all of this. I could hear the priest up in front of the Cathedral continuing to administer the sacrament of baptism to what must have been a long line of candidates. And then another confirmation arose within me. Absolutely, without a doubt, I was to be wed to Christ in an actual marriage ceremony, and through Christ I would be united with God. There it was at last—union with God. I was quietly, deeply overjoyed. The fulfillment of my deepest longings was dawning on the horizon like the morning star.

The service was concluding as the priest spoke the final words of the Prayer of Thanksgiving: "Through Jesus Christ Our Lord, who with Thee and the Holy Spirit be all honor and glory, world without end. Amen." In a daze of joy, gratitude and awe, I walked slowly out of Grace Cathedral into the noonday sun. I had been baptized. I had entered the Promised Land. The infusion of Christ into my own body and being had been accepted, and I knew for certain that I was to be wed to Christ and would have union with God. As I drove home, Merton's words came to me again: "...in spite of all your misgivings, you realize that you are going somewhere and that your journey is guided and directed and that you can feel safe."

23

ON THE WAY TO THE WEDDING

"There is only one love affair and that is with God," writes Tessa Bielecki. "Any human love affair is a mirror for the divine love affair." I wouldn't discover her insights until several years after that long process of following my heart where it took me. Only then, in retrospect, would I understand the meaning of my human love relationships. In the midst of them, all I could do was to obey the mysterious and somewhat puzzling promptings I was receiving.

Ever since I'd returned from the Spenco, I'd been in Love. I knew now with certainty the answer to my question, "Am I lover, beloved, Love?" I was all three. And Love was everywhere, within and without. The love I felt inside was bouncing off my interior walls—echoing, resounding, filling, expanding. It unexpectedly spilled over into a growing love for Alfred, my Pen Pal from Down Under. Starting with those seven months of intensified letter writing during my training for the race, our connection with each other had continued deepening. Now that we knew we'd be meeting in person, we'd begun to acknowledge the profound bond that had formed between us.

Our love of cycling had continued to expand into letters talking about the depths and heights of our personal relationships, mine with Paul and his with his wife. And I treasured our ongoing spiritual connection. When I wrote to him about my baptism, he sent me a book entitled *The Gentle Love of the Holy Spirit,* which gave me a deeper understanding of the part the Holy Spirit plays in the Trinity, and was playing in my life. Alfred had carefully put little red "x's" next to passages he thought would be meaningful to me: "The Spirit not only reveals Christ, but He actually brings Him to occupy and abide in the heart." And "The Holy Spirit becomes to us the Spirit of life in Christ Jesus because He imparts to us the life of Jesus." I was grateful to have articulated what I was experiencing.

But now here was the undeniable love I was feeling for Alfred as more than a bicycling coach and spiritual companion. Alfred had told his wife about our connection and my plans to visit, but she wasn't aware of the growing love between us. He was in turmoil about how to acknowledge his true feelings for me and still be loyal to her and his marriage. I was also conflicted. I wasn't about to let my spiritual quest spoil another marriage.

It was not our intention to complicate or disrupt his marriage, but as our long distance relationship grew increasingly intimate and intense, we both began to wonder what God's purpose was in bringing us so strongly together. In one of Alfred's letters, he finally brought up the question of being physically intimate. I wrote back that I didn't know what to do about that and confessed I was also longing to have that ultimate bond with him. We agreed that when we met, we would let God guide us.

Near the end of December, I wrote to him that I didn't want to just sign my letters, "Love," or "Much Love, Virginia." Even though I wasn't intending or anticipating physical intimacy what I really wanted and needed to say was "I love you," which is what I did.

It was late January, and I was in the midst of my daily journal writing ritual—with the usual cappuccino and walnut cookie—at my favorite coffee house. Suddenly I had the strong urge to get up and go to the jewelry store around the corner to buy a wedding ring. Oh. Okay. Sure, I replied silently, skeptically, to whatever internal power was directing me. *Of course. Buy a wedding ring,* as if I did this sort of thing regularly. I got up, told the ladies behind the counter I'd be right back, and headed outside. In a kind of incredulous trance, I walked along the brick path past the bookstore and video shop and turned into the village jeweler. I was immediately drawn to one of a half dozen glass cases. Inside it I instantly spotted a wide gold band carved with roses and dotted with tiny amethysts and diamonds. It looked like it had been waiting for me.

"I'd like that one, please," I said to the jeweler. While I looked on in disbelief at what was happening, he fitted me for ring size.

As he slipped the ring off my finger, he looked up at me smiling. "It'll be ready on Valentine's Day."

In December when I'd told Reverend Maxine about my plans to visit Ayers Rock and the surrounding area, I'd had a vague notion of doing some kind of Vision Quest there. Only slowly had it dawned on me what that solo journey to the Outback was really about. My time in the Red Centre of Australia, "cradled in the arms of the Infinite," would be to finalize and celebrate my marriage to Christ. I'd get butterflies inside me every time I thought about this event: Would I be what He wanted me to be? Would I be enough? Would I be worthy?

Once I realized the huge step I was taking, I began having trouble falling asleep, caught up in anxiety that some kind of "evil" forces would rally to keep me from this culminating step on my path to God. Despite the reassurance I'd felt in Grace Cathedral that Christ was firmly embedded within me, I worried that maybe while I slept an evil spirit would sneak into me and snuff out the soft, glowing life and light of Christ. I stayed awake long hours, watching to be sure no harm came to Him or to me. I put a picture of Jesus under my pillow, and I made a little ritual of opening the front door before I went to bed and shooing out all the evil spirits that might be in the house. Then trying to turn the night's safekeeping over to God, I would say the words of Psalm 121, affirming that God does not slumber. But even then I'd stay awake, waiting, watchful and on guard.

I was lying in bed one morning exhausted after several sleepless nights, when it finally occurred to me that in my watchfulness I was actually doubting that God would take care of us. How presumptuous and prideful was *that*? I was acting as if I were more capable than God to protect me and the new Christ within. This seemed like the ultimate affront to the Almighty One who, as I knew, provided me with everything. I lay in bed, berating myself for not trusting in God. Suddenly I began to panic. Would this lack of faith prove me unworthy of my marriage to Christ? The Almighty could take Himself and Christ away from me for not trusting Him. No wonder characters in the Bible so often expressed "fear of God." I could lose Him, and I would rather be dead than have that happen.

This all seemed to be way more than the usual nerves before a wedding. I confessed my angst to a dear friend, who already knew some of the story of my search for God. Judy suggested we talk to her sister Mary, a former nun. This sounded helpful, since nuns consider their vocation to be marriage to Christ. She would understand.

One sunny morning Judy drove me to her sister's house. Mary greeted us warmly and invited us into her small, cheery kitchen for tea. Even though I was reluctant to share my search for God with most people, I had everything to lose by not telling Mary why I was seeking her counsel. And if she were anything like Judy, she would be accepting, compassionate and helpful. So I launched in, completely honest and open with her. Mary listened attentively as I told her how I was called to be Christ's bride. She nodded sympathetically when I got to the part about worrying He wouldn't want me because I'd doubted God's power. I confessed my fear that the marriage would be called off. Mary laughed gently as she in turn recounted a few of her own similar fears of offending God before she took her vows.

I was incredibly relieved to be having a conversation with someone who really understood. An image from *The Sound of Music* arose in my mind, the scene where the novice, Maria, is confessing her confusion and angst to the Reverend Mother. Just as in the story, the "reverend mother" before me was responding with kindness and love. Mary's voice was soothing and encouraging as she said to me, "I'm sure God understands, and the wedding will still take place." Like the novice in the musical, I had no doubt that I was receiving wise counsel, and I rejoiced in the reassurance that I was still on the right path. I left feeling once again at peace. Even though I still felt caught up in a great mystery, I knew now that I could proceed with my wedding plans.

In the same incredulous but matter-of-fact way in which I'd picked out my wedding ring, I began making preparations for what I would wear at the wedding. I called Linne, whose talent with needle and thread even surpassed her counseling skills. Her art was making things with cloth, beads, buttons, feathers, ribbons, lace, and found objects, turning ordinary scraps and trinkets into magical and beautiful clothes, furniture coverings, wall hangings, lampshades, picture frames, purses...anything. Without explaining exactly why I needed to see her, we made a date, and one Saturday I drove to her home in Sacramento.

After we settled in, I began a little awkwardly to tell Linne that I was getting ready for a spiritual marriage and wanted a few special things for the wedding ceremony. In the same uncanny way that she had known I was talking about God when I'd described my dream of Hal Holbrook seven years earlier, Linne seemed to know exactly what this was about. I'd brought parts of my "trousseau" with me—a pair of simple yoga-style cotton pants in royal purple and a cream-colored peasant blouse. She suggested ways she might decorate them and promised that everything would be ready in a couple of weeks.

At the appointed time, I returned to find that Linne had transformed those simple elements into a beautiful and festive wedding outfit. She'd adorned the blouse with silk ribbons and beads, and she'd decorated an earth-colored shawl with beads, shells and Milagros—Mexican tin charms—mostly angels and hearts. And she'd created a wreath for my head of dried flowers and ribbon streamers. As I looked over these beautiful, and very real, parts of my impending marriage, I felt excitement as well as a lot of butterflies gathering in my stomach.

Linne had also put together a bridal bouquet of delicate white lace, with thin silk maroon and white ribbons dangling from it—more suitable for this formal occasion than the weathered bouquet of faded and frayed ribbons that had accompanied me to the Tetons. That first bouquet now had a special place on my altar at home. She put the bouquet into a small box that she had lined and covered with blue velvet and a fabric of Aboriginal designs. Handing me the box and the clothes neatly hung on hangers, Linne hugged me deeply, and I left with all these gifts cradled in my arms. This wedding was real. I was going to be married.

Then there was music to select. I chose three of the pieces I most loved listening to by the Japanese electronic music artist, Kitaro. Only after I'd already picked them did I pay attention to the titles. Reading them, I burst into tears. They expressed the full spectrum of my journey. *Dreams Like Yesterday* reflected the amazing and mysterious process that had actually begun with a dream. In the title of the second piece, I could hear Christ and God saying to me, *Never Let You Go*, which moved me to deeper tears of gratitude and joy. The music of the third selection, *Earth Born*, was mysterious and ethereal, dramatic and majestic. I had always deeply loved the earth, so this reference to Mother Earth felt perfect for me. Later, in the Red Centre, I would find out how telling this piece was of the deep connection I would make with the land there.

I still had no idea what the marriage would look like, or when I would play this music, or where the ceremony would take place, or what it would all be like. I just prepared what I could and packed a few special essentials, including the little hurricane lamp that had accompanied me as I traveled to the Tetons betrothed to Christ. The inscription from *Yentl* meant even more to me now: "May the light of this flickering candle illuminate the night the way your spirit illuminates my soul."

My wedding trousseau

On Valentine's Day I picked up my ring. After making sure the fit was right, I put the ring into its little velvet box and placed it in my purse. As I continued with my errands, I kept reaching in to touch the box. *This is my* wedding *ring. This is happening.* I'd encountered no obstacles in picking up the ring, and I felt a deep sense of rightness in having it. *The next time I put it on will be at the ceremony. Not until then.* Mary had been right—I wouldn't be rejected by God or Christ, and the marriage would indeed take place.

I'd selected March 25 as the date for the ceremony, because that was the night of the full moon. I still had no idea where I would be at that time, but the moon at its fulfillment seemed a good witness to this long awaited marriage. The date also happened to be the Feast of the Annunciation, the day when the angel of the Lord announced to the Virgin Mary that she would conceive a child who would be the Son of God. This work of the Holy Spirit in the Christ story added another dimension of mystery to contemplate in my own.

One evening as I was browsing the TV channels, I happened upon *The Wizard of Oz.* Every time I'd seen this film before, I'd dissolved in tears while watching Dorothy on her quest to find her way back home. I had been that little girl, setting out on "the Yellow Brick Road" ten years before, desperate to find my way. And like Dorothy, I *had* found my way home. This time my tears were not filled with anguish but with laughter and relief and gratitude. My search was over. I marveled at how far I'd had to go to reach home when it had always been right here within me.

Even though Sunny wasn't going with me to Australia, I wasn't about to leave him out of the celebration. I wanted us both to be made new. Because I felt we had been carried on the wings of eagles along our journey together, I had a black eagle on a gold sun background painted on his headset post and seat tube. With his new, hard-earned wings, every day Sunny and I flew along the same roads where I had raged and cried just a few months earlier. My rides now were prayers, which always ended with an "Amen." One of my prayers was to be able to bear the fire within my heart, and to be big enough to contain and share the abundance and great love that was growing ever greater within it. Another prayer was simply, "You Alone," which related to the book I was reading at the time entitled *God Alone*, by Sri Gyanamata, a disciple of Paramahansa Yogananda. Yes, absolutely, God alone was my greatest love.

As preparations for the ceremony unfolded my thoughts turned to a Guest List. I wanted a few close friends to be with me in spirit when I picked up my bouquet and marched down "the aisle" wherever that would be in the Red Centre. I could count on one hand those who knew about my spiritual journey. Besides them, no one had any idea that the past ten years of my life had been devoted to my search for God. It was so personal and hard to explain that I was quite nervous and uncertain about how to go about sharing this secret part of my life with other close friends. Because I could still hear the mocking and demeaning voices of my father and my brothers, I carefully chose to include only those I knew would be accepting of my story. However, more than I feared humiliation or embarrassment, I wanted to share my great joy about this amazing and mysterious experience.

I set about writing a short account of my story, a "confession" of what my life had been about for the past decade. This little book, which I entitled *Holy Days,* would be my wedding announcement. I briefly described my long search for God, and its completion. In noting that I would be in the Australian Outback for this ceremony, I quoted Thomas Merton: *More than we fear, we love the holy desert, where separate strangers, hid in their disguises, have come to meet, by night, the quiet Christ.* Although Merton is referring to those who enter a monastery, I loved the image of meeting the quiet Christ by night in the holy desert. Merton calls his ordination to the priesthood "the one great secret for which I had been born...." For him, following his vocation had been "a matter of life and death." I revealed to my "guests" how my own quest for union with God had also been a matter of life and death. *Holy Days* was my testimonial, and I stated that by the grace of God, of Christ, and the Holy Spirit, I had found life.

I said also that my "coming home" by conversion to Christian life was not what I'd expected, given a minimal Christian background and an eclectic pursuit of other spiritual teachings. Yet because it was Christ, the intercessor to God, who was taking me to be His bride, I had to believe that I was now "a Christian," even though I didn't particularly want to be part of any church's flock. I only wanted to be part of God's flock. "I have reached the Promised Land," I concluded in my announcement. "I have come home. And, like Dorothy in the Wizard of Oz, I can say, 'There's no place like home!'"

I found a blank greeting card with a perfect image on it—a single rose in a porcelain vase sitting on a windowsill with the window thrown open to the view of a magic land of cliffs and quiet water. All the colors were pale except for the bright red rose. I stapled the few pages of my story into the card and placed one into each envelope along with a nylon feather of many colors that I asked my guests to fly on the night of March 25, joining me under the full moon.

Everything was in place. While making travel plans, I discovered that the US Postal Service had issued a special pre-stamped airmail envelope with a picture of Halley's Comet on it and an image of Mark Twain—Samuel Clemens. Of course I thought of Hal Holbrook, who impersonates Mark Twain, and the elegant, handsome man of my dream that had set me on the search for God. The comet would only be seen this year, 1986, in the southern hemisphere. For me this was a sure sign that Australia was the right place to go for my marriage.

In one week I would be aboard a plane carrying me into a great unknown adventure. I would meet Alfred. And I would travel alone into the Outback, drawn there to complete the spiritual journey I'd been on for so long. I was excited, scared, and calm all at once.

USPS Halley's Comet

One morning, a week before my scheduled departure, there was an unexpected knock at the door, and a young man handed me a telegram. In abbreviated Western Union lingo, Alfred said his wife had found my letters with our "extreme secrets," and that not only could we not meet, but he would have to end our relationship altogether. I was stunned. I sat down hard on the cushioned bench beneath the kitchen window. Staring at the telegram, I tried to digest this news.

Meeting Alfred was supposed to be my first step on the way to the great unknown of the Red Centre. I'd so looked forward to meeting this man whom I loved and felt so close to. And I'd counted on him being a kind of anchor for me while I was in a strange country on my own. It had all seemed part of a divine plan. And now this. As I watched my plans fall apart, I grew increasingly upset and scared. Did this mean the entire plan was wrecked? If my wedding ceremony didn't happen in Australia on March 25, would it ever take place...and where? I'd been certain I was to go to Australia for my marriage. I'd been certain that this wedding ceremony would commemorate and celebrate my bond and commitment to and with Christ. Without it, would I lose Him? I was overwhelmed with fears and sadness.

I moped around for another day in my lost and shattered dreams, assuming that if I wasn't going to see Alfred, I wouldn't go to Australia at all. He was the tangible human connection that had led me to that far country. How could I arrive alone in a strange and distant land, and proceed with only vague plans to go into the Outback, which I gathered could be a harsh and dangerous environment? I needed that link to Alfred, and his guidance.

I tried to sort things out by talking to a couple of close friends. One reminded me that I was a courageous and independent woman who did unusual things and that I could very well still go if I wanted to. Another wise friend tried to help me understand the panic that Alfred must have felt when the reality of my coming was imminent. As we talked I began to suspect that he might have unconsciously allowed my letters to be found because he was so conflicted about his love for me and his loyalty to his marriage. This realization helped me come to terms with the sudden loss of our connection, but I was still heartbroken at the thought of losing him.

Over the next two days, I thought of all the pieces I'd put in place—my ring, my outfit, the music I'd selected, my *Holy* Days testimonial, the past ten years of my life consumed with my search for union with God. I had gone ahead with those steps, just as I had gone into the unknown time and again on this journey. How could I *not* follow through with celebrating and honoring the great love and gifts from God that had brought me to this point? And what about "You alone?" If I really meant that, then my plans for Australia were for "God Alone," and no mere mortal was going to interfere with those plans.

I also began to feel, to *see*, that even though we might not be able to meet in physical form, Alfred and I could still damn well meet in spirit. Just because he had backed out of our rendezvous didn't mean that I had to stop loving him. This realization was a huge lift to my spirits. The knowledge of my being "lover, beloved, and Love" could continue filling my days. The abrupt break in the continuum of the love with Alfred had thrown me temporarily, but Love was prevailing. I saw that the most important thing of all was to increase the quantity of love in the world; personal desires were not as important as expressing God's love.

My sense of boundless love returned. So did my energy. I pulled my suitcase out from under the bed and began a list of what to pack. I rearranged a few hotel and airline reservations to make more time for myself in the Red Centre, and once again proceeded with my preparations for Australia.

Three days after the first Western Union message, within hours of my decision to go forward with my own plans, Alfred telegrammed me with a phone number where I could reach him. He had left home to stay for a while with his son who lived near Melbourne. I called immediately. We had never spoken to each other before, so hearing his voice added a new dimension to what I knew of him. It was a calm conversation, without the passion that filled our letters. After reckoning with the crisis that led to the call, we just kept on talking about whatever came to mind, like old and dear friends. We talked for four hours, finally saying reluctant, tired goodbyes at four o'clock in the morning my time. We left open the possibility of connecting in Melbourne, but we agreed that I would call when I arrived to see if meeting was something we could or wanted to do. I hung up the phone relieved. Maybe my willingness to let go of him and remain committed to my spiritual journey had allowed him to come back into my life in a new way.

When I look back now, I see how my love for both Paul and Alfred had called me forth on my spiritual journey. My inner and outer lives had reflected each other and worked together to support my deepest longing. "There is only one love affair and that is with God." These men were a gift, nurturing and mirroring my divine love affair.

By the end of the week I felt ready to jump off another cliff into an unknown adventure. Taking many deep breaths, I boarded my Qantas flight for the eighteen-hour trip to Melbourne, Australia...for God Alone.

24
HONEYMOON

The huge city of Melbourne spread out below me as the Qantas flight descended into Australia. The butterflies in my stomach began to do cartwheels, and my heart fluttered. I was really scared. *I don't think I can do this.* I was far away from home, alone, *and* intending to drive myself on the "wrong" side of the road into the Outback. In that sparsely populated and wild territory I was supposed to be married to Christ. And Alfred—would I be meeting him or not? Until the plane landed and I could get to a phone, I wouldn't know. The thought of actually seeing him filled me with a combination of love, eagerness and apprehension.

After picking up my bags and making my way through immigration, I climbed into a taxi, feeling grateful that at least in this foreign country I spoke the same language. As soon as I checked into my hotel in downtown Melbourne, I phoned Alfred at his son's house. He did want to meet. More butterflies. We decided on a small park not far from the hotel.

My heart pounding, I stepped outside and set off for the short walk. It was easy to spot him from the photographs we'd exchanged. After five years of corresponding, what an extraordinary experience it was to finally meet face to face with the person I'd gotten to know and come to love! After the tension and the passion we had generated over the previous couple of months, it was with relief and gratitude that we greeted each other and simply embraced as two dear friends who hadn't seen each other for a very long time.

We sat down side by side on a stone bench in the park. Alfred wanted to know how my long flight had been; I wanted to know how he was doing during this time at his son's house, and how things were going with his wife. He said it was a day-by-day situation; I could see he was distressed. We took a stroll along the meandering paths through the lush park, watched kids playing on the swings and people throwing balls for their dogs. We walked back to my hotel, settled into a quiet corner of the lounge, and talked into the afternoon, getting to know each other beyond the limits of two-dimensional photographs and letters. Clearly we both felt as gratified in each other's presence as we had been through our correspondence.

We talked about how we were coming to the end of a chapter in our relationship, and we didn't know if there would be more chapters to write. We both hoped there would be, but everything was uncertain. With such affinity for each other, it was hard to part after only a few hours together, and I was grateful that I could phone him at his son's house during my time in the Outback. As we hugged goodbye in front of the hotel, Alfred couldn't hide the tears. "It'll be okay," I said as he closed the door of the cab. As they drove away, I turned back toward the hotel, knowing that somehow, no matter what happened, it *would* be okay.

I spent the next day walking about Melbourne, trying not to dwell on the daunting reality of being on my own in a huge, strange city, nor on the emptiness I felt. I missed Alfred, and there was still much that was unclear about my plans for the days ahead. At one point sounds of celebration interrupted my thoughts. I turned a corner, and a grand procession with horses and carriages, flourishing flags and rousing music, was passing along one of the main streets. Her Majesty, the Queen of England, was in town. I joined the crowds on the sidewalk to watch, feeling like I'd been dropped into the eighteenth century.

After the spectacle had moved on, I turned down a side street and wandered into the Northern Territory Travel Bureau looking for ideas about places to stay in the Red Centre. I had already booked a flight to Alice Springs, the main town in the area, and a hotel for a week at Yulara, a resort about 300 miles beyond that would give me a base for exploring the Olgas and Ayers Rock. But other than these popular sites, I was hoping to find a special place where my marriage ceremony could happen. It looked like there was really only one likely option—a low-key "resort" with cabins, called the Ross River Homestead, about an hour from Alice Springs, in the opposite direction from Yulara. While I was making these reservations, the agent mentioned that seven people had died of exposure in the area two weeks earlier. It was a sobering picture about where I was headed all by myself. All I could do was remember that God was leading and watching over me. I left the bureau in a daze. I'd actually chosen a site for my marriage to Christ. The dream—the mystery—was unfolding.

My little rental car in Alice Springs was an Astra, which I also thought was a nice name for her. Over the next three weeks Astra and I would put in 1,200 miles together. Leaving the airport, I drove on the wrong side of the road for a quarter of a mile before getting it straight that the "right" side was on the left. The five-hour drive to my hotel in Yulara was on a partially paved, two lane remote and unpatrolled highway. There was so little traffic I could actually count the cars I passed—an average of only six vehicles each hour. The isolation made me pay close attention to the ubiquitous "bulldust" at the edge of the road. I'd been warned about the possibility of going into a slide and ending up bogged down in the thick red sand. This seemed highly probable when my old friends, the 18-wheelers, came along. Hauling two additional trailers of the same size, these "roadtrains" would come roaring past, forcing me to navigate the narrow corridor of danger between the tremendous suction of the truck wheels on one side and the bulldust on the other. I felt like I was riding Sunny again as each truck left us swerving in our lane. I did have one slide, which I managed to drive out of, but the journey was stressful and a real lesson in Outback hazards.

I also learned how important water was. The temperature was somewhere between 90 and 100 degrees, and I got so drained by the heat that I finally had to turn on the air conditioner. After that first trip I never went anywhere without a gallon of water in the car, and I bought a small shovel in case I had to extricate myself from bulldust.

The next day I braved the road with a bit more confidence, bouncing along the narrow unpaved, sandy, thirteen-mile washboard on my way to the Olgas. As I came in sight of those astonishing rounded shapes rising above the desert floor like full breasts, I understood why the Aborigines call them *Kata Tjuta*, meaning "many heads." Covering an area of about eight square miles, the Olgas are a collection of thirty-six undulating domes, some as high as 1,800 feet. I had read some of the Aboriginal stories of this magical place—about Mudjura, the red lizard of the sandhills; Mingari, the rodent mice who play beneath the mulga trees; Dying Kangaroo Man; and Wananbi, the great serpent that lives inside Mt. Olga. Knowing these stories brought Kata Tjuta alive for me.

I set out on the two-mile hike up the Lookout Trail to the top of one of the domes overlooking the Valley of the Winds. I was entirely alone on the long upgrade—except for the flies. Sweaty from climbing and constantly swatting, I finally reached the Lookout, some 1,000 feet above the desert. Instantly all my discomfort was forgotten. The raw red desert spread before me in every direction as far as I could see. That immense power and radiant beauty slammed into me, as though I'd been hit with an invisible force field of energy. I knew I had come face-to-face with God.

This absolute realization had happened to me once before—on the bluff overlooking the five volcanoes in eastern Washington. At that time, I'd been knocked down and overcome. I'd turned away, unable to stand the extreme power and beauty. But this time I did not turn away. I *wanted* to see, to feel, to be blown away by *this* face of God. As I stood in awe beholding the scene before me, I realized there was a new strength and power within me now that made it possible for me to withstand this force. I stayed for a long time, taking it all in.

Though reluctant to leave, I urged myself to get back to my car before dark. By the time I arrived in the parking area, Astra was the only car there. Feeling dreamy, I pulled onto the bumpy road for the drive back to Yulara. Like a child giddy with joy, I let my voice bounce with the washboard road: "Uh...uh...uh...uh...uh." It was fun and funny to listen to it.

In the arms of the Infinite

I drove on through the growing dusk, captivated by the vast desert surrounding me. "Where am I?" I asked the Holy Spirit aloud. "I know I'm no longer on the Yellow Brick Road. That was when I was in search of God. But now that I have found God, I don't know where I am." I looked ahead at the bright, rust-colored road.

"I'm on a *red* road, that's for sure. A red *brick* road? A red *carpet* road?" Then it came to me. "The Holy Red Road! Yes! That's it. The Holy Red Road." Later I would learn that this is actually a term used by Native Americans to describe the spiritual path. It was the perfect name for my own new road, and I knew it was winding through the Kingdom of God. The Holy Red Road ran through the Promised Land. At this recognition, my spirit erupted in sheer joy and fullness of delight in the Holy Spirit who had brought me here. I felt thrilled by a sense of great adventure. I didn't care where this road or the adventure took me, because it was all in the Kingdom. I was infinitely and intensely glad to be on it and in it. I was a part of the very road I drove on, and it was a part of me. I laughed and sang and jiggled with the Holy Spirit the whole way home, playfully dreaming up a travel agency called "Holy Spirit Tours."

The Holy Red Road

The next day I set out for Ayers Rock, that island mountain 500–600 million years old. To the Aborigines, *Uluru*, as they call it, is a sacred site. That is undeniable when you see it. Robyn Davidson, who in 1977 traveled 1,700 miles across the desert from Alice Springs to the west coast of Australia with four camels and her dog, writes of her first glimpse of Uluru: "I was thunderstruck. I could not believe the blue form was real. It floated and mesmerized and shimmered and looked too big. It was indescribable...I had not expected anything quite so weirdly, primevally beautiful." I was equally astonished as I beheld this immense rock from a distance. No wonder it is called "the Cathedral of the Desert," a house of God—like Grace Cathedral—right here in the Outback!

A sign at the base of the rock warns that the ascent to the top is "not for the unfit." That was a thoughtful understatement. The grades can be as much as forty percent, almost halfway vertical. However, along with the many other adventurers that day, I was irresistibly drawn upward along the marked and sometimes roped one-mile route toward the high point of 1,142 feet. The wind at the top was every bit as strong, even stronger, than the gale that had blasted Sunny and me on the Umatilla Bridge over the Columbia River. I sat on top of this mighty creature, feeling no bigger than a speck of dust and yet saturated with power. Below me the Red Heart, or Red Centre, of Australia spread out in every direction, endless, flat and unbroken by any other forms. Wherever I looked, the flaming orange-red landscape ignited my spirit and filled my vision with intense, unimaginable beauty. How could such a phenomenal landscape come to be? I felt the same awe and wonder I had known when staring into the starry sky in Montana on my Vision Quest. I was again saturated with the intimacy and immensity of the Love that pervades all. And to think that I had been drawn here to this spectacular place to celebrate union with that Love!

My body ached the next morning from the exertion of the climb up Uluru. But I was determined to continue my immersion in this place where I'd been called to meet my Beloved. This day I would explore more of the mysterious domes of Kata Tjuta, particularly the Olga Gorge. The early European explorers of the late 1800's wrote about "the tremendous life and power" of this "organic heart of Australia." One said, "… surely all the winds and moods and storms of the continent find birth in the Olga chasms." That was where I wanted to be, the birthing place.

From the open desert, towering domes arise to form the Gorge. They drew me into them as if inviting me into the cleavage between two gigantic, sensuous red breasts of the Earth Mother. As I neared the entry to the Gorge, the power of the place was palpable. Two great rocks, like living beings, guarded the entrance. I felt compelled to ask permission to go forward into the narrowing passage. Once again, I was alone in this heart-gripping, mysterious place.

After walking a mile or so along the sandy level wash, I was surprised to arrive at a wall of boulders. This was apparently not a walk-through hike—in one end and out the other—as I had anticipated. I guess I hadn't paid attention to or had forgotten what the tourist information said about the Olga Gorge Walk. A sign at the base of the boulders warned of flash floods, but nothing else indicated that this was the end of the intended hike for visitors. The vast sky was a clear blue so I wasn't worried about a flash flood. I looked up at the stack of boulders rising abruptly from the ground at a near-vertical angle. I couldn't see where the crest was, but I decided to go for it. There had to be a way over and out.

I started upward eagerly, but as I climbed it became harder and harder to find a way over the boulders.

Whoa, now I know what rock climbing is all about! This was more than I'd bargained for. Unnerved, I stopped and looked behind me to assess my situation. The sun was striking the wall on my left, lighting up the orange face like fire. Truly, the rock was glowing from within! Fire inside and fire on the face. Transfixed, I couldn't help but think of Moses and the burning bush, and I had to willfully pull my gaze away from the burning rock to attend to the reality of my situation.

I couldn't see a way back down—falling looked inevitable. I knew now that I was not supposed to be where I was, but it was too late to turn back. I was surely caught between a rock and a hard spot. I was scared. I didn't know if I could do what I had to do, but I crept upward. I would manage to advance a foot or two and then stop, searching desperately for some niche to next put a hand or foot into. Often I was stranded. Then suddenly a crack would appear, as if by magic. I swear God made hand and footholds where there were none, "made a way out of no way." Time after time I was shown the next step, and in this way I made my way finally to the top. The climb must have taken an hour.

Sitting on the topmost boulder, I looked out over the vast valley of orange-red sand dotted with scrub brush and spinifex, the spiky, yucca-like plants growing low to the earth. It was beautiful but not another human being was in sight. I was completely alone. The specter of those seven people dying of exposure was suddenly very real. Below me was another intimidating scramble of boulders. Retreat was unthinkable. There was nothing for it but to go forward. Slowly, one step and one handhold at a time, I managed to let myself down over huge rocks and precipices that looked impossible to navigate. I was very aware of God's continued help and deeply thankful when I reached the bottom.

I moved out into the open space of the desert and looked around to get my bearings. It was pointless to think about the fact that no one knew where I was. I was pretty sure which direction I needed to go to get to the car, but there were no recognizable landmarks. If I was wrong, the first ones to find me would be the vultures. I had no idea how far I had to go or how long it would take me. Trusting in God's help, I set out cross-country over the desert floor.

I had almost a full quart of water in my backpack, along with my ID and camera. I hadn't expected to be out very long, otherwise I would have carried twice the water. The heat from the red sand penetrated the soles of my sneakers. The midday sun beat down on my head and bare shoulders. I wished I'd realized how useful a hat was in preserving hydration. I kept reassuring myself that I was in good physical condition and that I had a decent sense of direction, but the hot, empty desert also kept reminding me that dying of thirst was a sobering reality.

I walked at a steady pace for about an hour, swatting flies all the while, rationing my sips of precious water. *I should have told the hotel where I was going.* But I'd gone beyond the normal trail. *They wouldn't think to look for me way out here.* I glanced back toward the boulder wall I'd descended, now distant but still visible across the flat desert. At least that would be a way I knew would get me back to the car. *No, I can't possibly get up and down that again.* Trying to do that climb might more likely assure my death than following this unknown but best-guess route.

Immediately the old *I can't* chorus sprang to life. Maybe I was in a die-or-die situation. I stopped walking, tempted to let the wave of panic overtake me. I could just slump down on hot sand between spinifex bushes, drink all my water, and wait for the wild birds and beasts to finish what dehydration and heat would not. It would be so easy. There they were again, those forces of defeat that had come upon me during my bike trip when my life had felt threatened.

But I'd managed to get through those crises. My inner warrior had risen up and smothered those forces. I could feel that will to live surging again within me. As I gazed into the empty, trackless desert ahead of me, I reminded myself that in the last ten years I'd gone into the unknown time and time again; I'd always managed somehow and God had never let me down, had always led me on and kept me safe. *Why should it be any different now?* I looked at the distant horizon—somewhere between here and there Astra was parked. And I started walking again in the direction I believed would lead me to her.

After just a few steps, I felt a presence behind me and turned around.

Kangaroos! Real kangaroos!

Three of these exotic icons of the Australian Outback were coming toward me about fifty yards to my right. They weren't hurrying to get anywhere but rather seemed to be enjoying a bounding "stroll" across the desert, stopping occasionally to nibble sparse grass. If I hadn't been so intent on keeping my forward momentum, I would have gotten my camera out for a picture of these exciting creatures before they floated past. Seeing them roused my energy and gave me encouragement to keep going. I didn't feel so alone anymore. Looking back, I'm sure that God sent them along to ease my justifiable fears and to buoy up my trust in myself and in Him. An hour later my heart leapt when I spotted Astra in the distance.

As I bounced and jiggled back to Yulara, it occurred to me that I had just undergone a kind of initiation. My faith had been tested, and I had passed. I could almost hear God saying to me, "Now you know an important thing about the Promised Land. It means putting more and more of your trust and faith in me, as you have just done."

That evening on the phone I eagerly told Alfred about my Olga Gorge adventure and how it had felt like an initiation. He was relieved that I was okay and proud of me for placing my trust in God. About half the time during the three weeks I was in the Red Centre, I had access to a phone, and Alfred was the anchor I had hoped he might be. I'd tell him about my experiences, and sometimes we'd read each other passages from inspirational spiritual texts. He told me that between phone calls, he made notes to himself of things he wanted to ask me. During one of our conversations, his question was: "What is your purpose in the coming year?" I hadn't thought about that until then, and I responded that mainly I wanted to become more solid in my new internal foundation of being with God and Christ. Feeling a bit awkward, I added…"in the Promised Land." When I told him that sounded a little corny to me, he immediately countered that he understood what I meant and assured me that for him too the Promised Land was real.

Alfred was never unable or unwilling to respond to whatever I'd bring up, and for that alone I cherished him and our conversations. I wanted to share everything with him. He said he loved to hear me laugh. For my part, I loved his accent and how he always said "whilst" instead of "while." His mellow voice filtered into my being in a soothing way. I truly loved him. As Tessa Bielecki says, "In human love we can touch and feel and experience the divine, the sense of oneness, the sense of there not being an 'other.'" During our phone conversations, Alfred and I shared so much of ourselves with each other that it seemed there were no boundaries between us, no sense of other. We were so in harmony that I lost my sense of self, what I think of as "I," and the lines of separation between us blurred. As with Paul, I knew I was experiencing the divine through this human love.

As well as being a touchstone in a foreign country, loving Alfred kept me in touch with being a human being at a time when I was intensely in love with Christ and God and inclined to lose touch with my earthly existence. One spiritual teacher whose work I had read talked about people having three basic tendencies, one of which was an inclination to drift off into the ethereal and spiritual realms and leave the earthly realm behind. I didn't want to find myself again in that painful conflict between the divine and human, heaven and earth, where spirit was superior to matter. I'd already gone through that when I fell in love with Paul. My conversations with Alfred whilst in the Red Centre kept me balanced and also connected to my human reality. I had finally understood that Christ, whom I had come here to marry, fully held within Himself both the divine and human natures. That was the model I aspired to.

Day after day I opened to the holy desert —and she to me—like newfound lovers. And each day I took in more of this nurturing, welcoming, powerful, and glorious land. The Red Centre was a feast for all senses: the tangy, pungent aroma that filled the air around the groves of eucalyptus trees; the weird unfamiliar calls of wild exotic birds, like the parrot and red-tailed cockatoo; the piercing howls of the dingos; the precious taste of Red Heart water found in scarce pools nestled into the rocks; the vast display of reds, golds, pinks, and purples of the rocks, mountains and desert floor; the oceans of spinifex grasses blanketing the red earth in all shades of blue- and yellow-greens; the white-barked ghost gum trees; and the vibrant, orange-red earth itself.

Australian artist Lloyd Rees wrote: "All great wilderness areas, all great cathedrals and other places of worship, and all great works of art which man has fashioned in the image or in homage to a natural creator, have the same quality of virginal beauty—virginal not in a moralistic but in a spiritual sense." The Red Centre was pristine, radiant with its wild, unspoiled beauty. My inner state mirrored the beauty I saw around me. I felt the way I looked in the photograph celebrating my year-old birthday—open, loving, full of wonder. At thirty-five I felt like a new being. In this wondrous wilderness cathedral, all I could do was worship God within and without. My Beloved was all in all.

Before setting out for the Ross River Homestead, which would be my "home" in the Red Centre and the area where my marriage ceremony would take place, I returned to Alice Springs to explore the ancient lands surrounding the little city. The MacDonnell Ranges were over 1,000 million years old, and while they didn't make me feel as if I'd been dropped onto Mars the way Uluru and Kata Tjuta did, they had a unique character and power of their own.

My first day in the MacDonnells, Simpsons Gap took me into its arms. Walking barefoot along a sandy wash toward a gorge, I chanced upon a pool of Red Heart water. Looking like a small kidney-shaped swimming pool, it shimmered beneath the high rock walls. I waded ankle-deep through the cool water and pressed my body against the solid, rough warmth of the rock face. The orange-red heat beamed into me, irradiating every cell. After a long embrace, I reluctantly pulled myself away and splashed back across the pool. I could have stayed all day, but there was so much more of this mysterious land that I wanted to see and taste and feel. I said goodbye to the pool and the rocks and started back toward the car.

I was halfway to the parking area, a half mile away, when one of the ghost gum trees in the wash seemed to reach out to me. I'd been finding these particular trees, members of the eucalyptus family, particularly enchanting. They and their relations, the river red gums—elegant and refined and colorful—are the primary tree inhabitants of Central Australia. Set against the red earth and the blue sky, they are vibrant and resplendent. Unable to resist this one special beauty, I went straight to her. Her chalk white skin was silky and soft to my touch. I ran my fingers slowly along the waves and ripples of her trunk. Her elegant arms reached out in every direction. Her leaves waved and pointed in the wind. I bent to kiss her, and ran my lips along her ripples so that I could feel with this most sensitive and delicate part of my body the smooth satiny waves of hers. How extraordinary and beautiful it was to make love with a tree. When I left, I was overflowing with the love that poured in and out of me, and I knew I was now carrying this stately being within me.

The following day I set out to explore another facet of my Beloved, the narrow passageway of Standley Chasm. Named after Ida Standley, the first white woman to walk through the cleft, this stunning formation is nine yards wide and almost the height of a football field. By the time I arrived at noon, other visitors were already within the passage. Taken with awe and wonder, we watched the high noon sun light up the crystalline quartzite walls, making the cliff faces glitter and sparkle like twinkling stars, like flashing strobe lights in a dark theater. It was a dazzling spectacle, but also a little scary. During the few minutes it took to walk the length of the chasm, I kept imagining a huge chunk of rock breaking loose like a calving iceberg and falling down on top of us. Or if not that, maybe the walls might suddenly close like a vice grip.

Relieved to be at the end of the chasm, I noticed a rocky trail heading upward. This climb was obviously meant to attract hikers. I made my way up the switchback path a half-mile to where it ended at a ledge. I was surrounded by a complex of crystalline cliffs of fiery reds and oranges, craggy and pulsing with energy. It felt as if the majesty and power of these astonishing rock mountains were surging directly at me, overwhelming and intoxicating and humbling. Ignoring the jagged rocks poking into my butt, I sat transfixed once again by the face of God.

These magical days with my Beloved in the MacDonnell mountains were crowned with one more divine experience. Floating in a hot air balloon several hundred feet above the red desert, I beheld Halley's Comet. The brilliant white core of the comet appeared in the pre-dawn, pale, royal blue sky, with a stream of dust and vapor flaring out behind it like a kite tail. Halley's Comet...Mark Twain...Hal Holbrook...my dream of God. In my inner world these symbols spoke to me in the special language of my spiritual journey. I had come full circle. I gazed in wonder at the rare spectacle of the radiant comet and felt deep gratitude for the ten-year journey that had taken me into this living dream.

After each day spent absorbed in "the holy desert," I would once again "meet, by night, the quiet Christ." I'd spend the twilight hour sitting on the small porch off my Yulara and Alice Springs hotel rooms, where no lights or noise could intrude on this time of quiet communion. As I watched the light fade and the stars appear, I'd whisper love and awe and gratitude to God and Christ and the Holy Spirit. I directed all my thoughts and prayers to the Southern Cross, or at least what I thought was the Southern Cross. But I was so immersed in Christ that every constellation looked like a cross to me, and each seemed to shine His presence on me.

One night I had a dream of Him. *I am riding bareback. My mount seems very small, but my feet aren't dragging, and the animal seems able and willing to carry me. The only bridle is like that of an Indian pony, a light rope looped through the animal's mouth. I dismount and stroke its face with both hands, a face small enough that my hands can almost embrace the whole of it. Then I see that the face is actually that of a lamb—small floppy ears, a soft nose, and large black eyes that look at me with complete trust. I realize how easily the lamb has carried me. He clearly needed no direction from me; I had only to go with him.* When I woke, I knew the dream had been about Christ, the Lamb of God. The way the Lamb and I moved together as one reminded me of how I felt with my horse Blaze as we raced across the fields in perfect union of movement and spirit.

The next night at twilight I asked God, "Is it presumptuous of me to think I can be one with your Son, Jesus Christ?" The question hung quietly in the night space as if it would be answered some other time. The following evening I again prayed into the blanket of evening stars: "Lord, let me dance as one with your Son, Jesus Christ, from this day on. Let my dance be always for you, to sing your praises. When I dance up mountains, let it be for you, because it is you who makes it possible for my body and being to live and do everything it does."

I was naked to the love of God, and I spoke to Him as if I were whispering into the ear of my Beloved: "When I count my endless blessings right now—the greatest is that I *see* you, hear you, am touched by you, *loved* by you." I felt caressed by the warm, gentle wind, loved infinitely by millions of stars. I nestled into the gentle and passionate breast of Christ where I was held as tenderly as one would cradle a newborn puppy, as lovingly as I would be held in the arms of a man who feels and sees me as the most beautiful being he has ever beheld in his life.

In the midst of that vast wilderness cathedral, I had been taken into the heart of God. I felt absorbed into the depths of God as though I were sinking to the bottom of a beautiful, radiant and warm ocean. I welcomed the drowning. Yet I was not in an ecstatic or rapturous state. It was more a quiet intoxication of Love, as though my whole being was infused with a powerful herb laced with a sweet liqueur. This entire time in the Olgas and in the chasms and glory of the McDonnell range had been my honeymoon, a time which had prepared me for my wedding ceremony.

As well as being deeply in love with God and Christ, I was also having a kind of love affair with myself. Ever since I had accepted my failure to accomplish my goal of finishing the Spenco 500, and had loved myself in spite of it, that sense of wholeness had remained in me. I was on my way to celebrating a "double marriage"—one with Christ and one with myself.

25
WITH THIS RING

I was on a magical highway in heaven—a single lane, somewhat paved road running parallel to the Eastern MacDonnell Ranges, and I was driving the fifty miles from Alice Springs to the Ross River Homestead. It was one week before my wedding date, and I felt several levels of excitement and calm, all at the same time.

After about an hour I arrived at what looked and felt like the kind of camp I'd gone to as a kid. There were ten cabins scattered around a main lodge. When I checked in, I was assigned to Cabin #5, a small wooden bunkhouse with a cement floor, two single metal-frame beds with lumpy mattresses on squeaky springs, a little closet, and a tiny sink. The outhouse was next door. The lodge was a simple building featuring a good-sized, well-stocked bar, a pool table, small lounge area, and a no-frills kitchen.

During that first day, I was introduced to the entire staff—two cooks, the barman, the owners and their teenaged grandson, and three or four hands, including a camel man. Ross River Homestead had four camels, a couple of donkeys, three dogs (Fat Gundy, Little Dog, and Spotted Dog), chickens, and a flock of wild, iridescent parrots and red-tailed cockatoos that made the site their home territory. From time to time a small band of skittish horses passed through camp. I was told they were semi-wild and had been turned out into the desert to fend for themselves during the drought season

I was the only tourist there. Other than connecting to the animals, I felt like a real outsider. Without access to a phone line, I couldn't reach Alfred to hold down the human-contact side of the triangle. It was only the Lamb of God and me, which was quite enough though to keep my heart and soul wide open to why I had come to this far outpost of Australia.

After unpacking and checking out the outhouse, I turned to fulfilling my primary task—finding a place for my marriage ceremony. One of the Homestead hands, not knowing my deeper interest in wanting to see the surrounding desert, took me out on his ATV for a look around. Jack was a wiry, deeply tanned and weathered man in his fifties. His blue eyes sparkled, and he was easy to be with. Sitting behind him on what he called his "trike," my hands lightly holding onto his hips, I could feel through his thin T-shirt his warm and boney backside.

Jack first showed me The Sphinx, an unusual, narrow rock formation that stood out from the flat desert like a sleeping tiger, about two stories high, half a city block long. I walked along it to see if there was a protected cave-like space around its perimeter where I would feel safe, even welcome. But the craggy walls were so jagged and fragmented that even touching them cut into my hands. Wanting somehow to get more of a sense of its spirit, I picked up a rock and struck the looming side. It clanked like metal. *No, this is not the place.* I got back on the trike and we drove on.

A grove of ironwood trees looked like another possibility until I saw old bones scattered about. I didn't give it a second look. As we bounced along over the desert floor, I remembered a time on my bike trip when I'd found a possible campsite for the night but rejected it when a number of whitened bones revealed that something had lost its life there. I hadn't wanted to sleep where the spirit of death lingered, and even less did I want to celebrate my marriage in such a place.

On the way back to the Homestead, we passed a lean-to shelter with a leaf roof, about thirty feet from the road. Inside were a couple of camp cots like the ones in my cabin. Jack said it was called "The Hotel," because tourists sometimes camped out there. I craned my head to study it as we drove by, sensing it was worth another look. Later in the afternoon I walked the half-mile back to check out The Hotel more carefully. I liked that it had a back wall so I wouldn't be totally exposed to the open desert. Ghost gum trunks, probably cut from the trees growing all around the area, supported the leaf roof. A couple of gum trees next to the shelter gave it shade and a sense of protection. Once I'd tidied up a bit—raked up a little trash, smoothed the ground, righted the small table, straightened and dusted the cots, I felt it would be a good place for the ceremony.

Later that afternoon, I was invited to join the staff for "teatime," their lovely afternoon ritual in which almost everyone's "tea" came frothy and amber-colored out of a spigot behind the bar. Though during those first hours, I'd felt awkward, lonely and a bit insecure at the Homestead, tea time broke the ice. After that, I became an accepted member of this gathering. By the time of my departure ten days later, I would also be a regular, helping out in the kitchen and hanging out with my new friends.

In my other life as a bride-to-be, I was feeling surprisingly calm, especially now that I'd chosen and prepared the wedding site. But I was still amazed to be going forward with, and into, such an unbelievable mystery. Was I really going to be Christ's bride at last? It had been two years since I'd carried a bouquet on my solo journey to the Grand Tetons, and I'd come halfway around the world for this incomprehensible event. At one point I'd asked God if this idea was outrageously presumptuous, and I hadn't received a negative response. But it seemed to me it was best not to think too much about what I was doing, lest my rational mind accuse me of insanity, foolish fantasy, or religious zealotry. Instead, with most of the preparations for the ceremony in place, I set out to do more exploring of the spectacular places in this part of the MacDonnell Ranges.

"Just a closer walk with Thee, Grant it, Jesus, if you please." The voice of Joan Baez singing that traditional gospel song kept running through my mind. Palm Sunday was approaching in a few days, and I was immersed in the story of Jesus' triumphant entry into Jerusalem. During this holy season, I wanted to be with Him as best I could; I wanted symbolically to walk in His footsteps. So I decided that on Friday I would walk the seven miles from N'Dhala Gorge back to the Homestead on an off-road track Jack had told me about. When the staff gathered at teatime Thursday afternoon, I asked if someone could drop me off at N'Dhala the next day. One of the guys said he was going to town and would take me.

Friday morning I was about to get into Tom's car for the trip when Jack appeared. "Are you sure you want to do this?" he asked, his eyes intense and especially blue under the bright sun. I could tell he was genuinely concerned, which I found touching. Over the previous three days at the Homestead, with only intermittent encounters, Jack and I had become quite fond of one another. We were attracted to and intrigued with each other—cultured California girl meets rugged Outback guy. We were both curious about how the other lived. I told him I was sure I wanted to go.

"Do you have enough water? It's going to be very hot."

I showed him the gallon jug I had with me.

"If you're not back in four hours, we'll come looking for you. It's a long way."

"Okay," I said, smiling, and got into the car.

"Tom, make sure she knows what direction to head for home," he called after us as we pulled away.

N'Dhala. The name sounded to me like "I love you." As I walked between the craggy rock faces into the narrow canyon, the place exuded a nurturing, protective warmth that had nothing to do with the hot temperature. In contrast to the smooth, rounded, sensuous boulders of the Olgas and of Ayers Rock, the rocks of N'Dhala were rugged, fragmented, and fractured. But they glowed from within every bit as brightly. I stared in wonder and admiration at the little ghost gum trees that grew out of solid rock. They were diminutive compared to their large, robust relatives that inhabited more nourishing parts of the desert, but these were much braver, more resilient, and determined.

There was not another soul in sight—N'Dhala did not draw tourists the way some of the other more dramatic gorges did. I sat down next to one of the brave little ghost gums and let the beauty, love, and gratitude I was feeling overwhelm me. As tears flowed down my cheeks and onto the dry rock, one of the most beautiful poems I knew came to mind. In a few lines of "Unexpected Manna," Gary Holthaus, an Alaskan poet, captures the essence of gratitude that was bursting from my heart and soul for God and for Christ.

So you,
Falling on my days
Like unexpected manna,
Alter every image
And rearrange my mind
So wholly
I am rendered silent
Gathering in my self
So quietly
That what you do for me
Remains unnamed.

"Dear God," I whispered, "I jumped off a cliff and into your arms. You have protected me all along my journey and taken such loving care of me. You have showered me with wondrous gifts. I humbly accept every one of them, though I am unworthy of so many favors. All I can give you in return is my tears."

N'Dhala drew me into the intimacy and beauty of her space, her protective walls, her warm earth-body, as though she were folding me into her arms with great and deep mother-love. I could feel myself dropping deep roots into this earth place. So powerful was her effect on me that for a long while after I'd returned to California I truly believed, but for biological fact, that I had actually been given birth by and in N'Dhala. During my time there, I came to understand why I had chosen the Kitaro piece, *Earth Born*, as part of my wedding music.

It was around noon, and I'd already been gone a couple of hours. Though I was reluctant to leave, I knew I had to get back before the others worried something had happened to me. Knowing I would always keep N'Dhala inside me, I headed for the dirt track which Tom had made sure I'd seen before he dropped me off. As I passed through the parking area, I pulled out the bag I'd brought along for collecting trash. I'd intended to pick up stuff as I walked back to the Homestead, but by the time I'd gathered up the plastic bottles and wrappers, crumpled paper, and tin cans left around in that small area by tourists, the bag was so full I left it there to get later.

The midday heat was like a furnace, and I was aware of being very alone as I walked, my feet sinking into the dry, sandy wash as though I were walking on a beach. Except for occasional groves of sparse ironwood trees and isolated, skimpy ghost gums, the red landscape was parched and bare. And quiet. No wind. No insect or bird sounds. No exotic kangaroos to assure me all was well. I felt very small and vulnerable in this remote, empty, desert wilderness, and I began to feel scared again. Even though I'd passed my test of faith after the Olga Gorge the thought of those seven tourists dying of exposure kept invading my mind. *Why do I keep putting myself in these situations?*

As if I could outrun the specter of death from heat exhaustion and dehydration, I started to walk faster, my heart beating with fear. The faster I walked, the faster my heart raced, the more afraid I became. This suddenly reminded me of bicycling in the intense heat in eastern Washington and in Death Valley. *What had a learned about fear then? Slow down and act like I'm not afraid, like I'm just taking a leisurely stroll through a lush forest filled with little streams and dripping ferns.* I knew a calm rather than frantic state of mind was more likely to get me safely to the Homestead.

Every certain number of steps, I allowed myself five swallows of water, hoping to have enough to last. Closing the cap on the bottle after those few gulps took great restraint. After a couple of hours, with relief I began to recognize areas I'd previously explored around the Homestead. But I knew I was still about a half-mile from camp when I took the last swallow from the jug. Trying not to feel how dry my mouth was, how thirsty and nervous I was, I focused on walking—one foot calmly in front of the other.

When I finally arrived at the Homestead, what a welcome sight to see Jack and Tom! They were in a pickup just on their way out, and they stopped to tell me they were going to see about pulling a cow and calf out of a bog—did I want to come along? I climbed in with them and Spotted Dog, and gratefully downed a half-gallon of their water. I could see that Jack was especially relieved to see me.

We arrived at the bog to find the poor beast up to her neck in thick black mud. Her calf had gone under. Jack roped her horns, and the truck slowly pulled her out. She looked like she'd been in an oil spill. It broke my heart to see her utterly exhausted and traumatized by her struggle and the loss of her calf. In her I saw not only one creature but all the innocent and gentle animals who suffer, either by happenstance or by neglect and disregard. This precious life had been at the mercy of forces greater than herself. Tom and Jack agreed that there was nothing to do but leave her in hopes she would recover. We drove off in a somber mood.

That night, before going to bed, I climbed up onto the ridge overlooking the Homestead. In spite of the lingering sadness I felt for the cow and her baby, I was flooded with gratitude to God for bringing me to this beautiful desert and to the beautiful place within me. The words of the thirteenth century, German mystic Mechtild of Magdeburg came to mind:

Of the heavenly things God has shown me,
I can speak but a little word,
no more than a honeybee can carry on its foot.

In the moonlight I sang "Amazing Grace" over and over. The words—especially "I once was lost but now I'm found"—moved me so much I could not stop singing. By the time I returned to my cabin in the early hours of Saturday morning, the moon had almost set. It was two days before the wedding

The next morning, tired after my long day walking and all night singing, I stayed in my cabin later than usual, glad to be out of the sun for a while. About mid-morning a light knock came on my door. It was Jack, come by to see if I was okay—and to ask if I wanted to come along to check on the cow. Even though I was reluctant to leave my shady rest, I jumped at the chance to be with him. Not only did I enjoy his company, but feeling so carried away in spiritual mystery, I knew I needed some kind of close human connection. Out of contact with Alfred, I felt God had given me Jack to keep my heart open and feet on the ground.

I climbed onto the back of the trike, and despite the nature of our mission, I happily wrapped my arms around him. At the bog we found the cow where we'd left her. She hadn't moved at all, her head hung to the ground and her breathing was labored. She was clearly not going to live. Jack and I stared at her in silence, painfully aware of her suffering, and what had to be done to relieve it. This was not the first time I'd been confronted with euthanizing an animal. In her beautiful, deep eyes I saw every beloved dog, cat, and horse that I'd put to sleep in my life.

Looking at me apologetically, Jack said softly, "I have to do this." He bent down and pulled out a shotgun from beneath the seat of the ATV, and let it rest on his lap.

He looked at me again. "Are you okay?"

I nodded without speaking. I closed my eyes and bowed my head. I sent the cow love as Jack aimed and pulled the trigger. When I opened my eyes, I saw her crumple to the ground without so much as a groan. Perhaps she was grateful for the help to end her suffering.

As Jack started up the trike to leave, I turned to look at her. Tears slid down my cheeks as I waved goodbye. Jack smiled. "You're a real sentimentalist aren't you? Don't ever change." His understanding and acceptance touched my sad heart and made me cry even more than the death of the cow. I leaned against his back, no longer ashamed that he would feel the dampness from my tears.

After my by-now usual dinner with the staff, I walked with Jack to his cabin. I had packed some tiny gifts to give to others on my trip as the Spirit moved me, and touched by Jack and his sweet caring, I wanted to give him some of these mementos. We sat in the swing on his porch with Spotted Dog nearby. He told me that more guests would be arriving soon and that we wouldn't have much more time to spend together. "You know, I believe I love you a bit," he said softly. He told me I was "a nymph, a witch, and a lovely person." I wasn't sure what to make of the nymph and witch part—and didn't ask—but I knew he meant it in a good way. Perhaps he was feeling some of the magical life spirit within me. I brought out the things I had for him—a braid of sweet grass, sacred in the Native American tradition; some tiny shells from California beaches, and "trouble dolls," a Guatemalan version of worry beads.

Jack was intrigued when I told him how the smoke of the lighted sweet grass was used to "smudge" a place or person to clear negative energies, a ceremony I had also done on my Vision Quest. I explained how I loved to throw the little shells out into special places I visited, each shell carrying a prayer, a blessing, or an offering of thanks. I told him I wanted to give him the "trouble dolls" to take away all his worries and fears. He was clearly touched—and a little mystified. "You've changed me," he said. "You've brought some kind of strength and peace to me. I don't really understand why you care for me." I looked into his bright eyes and felt the love I was constantly swimming in swell in my heart. We took each other's hands and in silence went inside. We spent a sweet night making love, and all the love in my heart felt like it was once again finding expression in this human/divine way. Back at my own cabin, I fell asleep feeling peaceful and grateful.

The following morning I drove to Alice Springs for the Palm Sunday service, honoring the day that foreshadowed the imminent death of Christ. I could feel a sorrow rising inside me, a sorrow I'd first felt during Advent the previous December when it became deeply clear to me that Christ's birth would inevitably lead to his suffering and death. I was also saddened by the fact that in just five days, I would be on my way back to California. That would be on Good Friday; Christ and I would both be ending long journeys.

On my way back from Alice Springs, feeling emotional and not yet ready to return to the Homestead, I pulled over at a natural landmark called Corroboree Rock. Having read that this was a place where the aboriginal people had once stored sacred objects, I'd expected to find some comfort in the spirit and beauty of this sacred site. Instead I found discarded plastic cups and bags and shreds of tinfoil scattered everywhere. A huge grief overcame me as I viewed the blatant trashing of this sacred place, the disrespect for Mother Earth and the degradation of all the beauty and life she gives us.

I knew then that the suffering of Mother Earth and the suffering of Christ were inseparable. I also knew that the intensity of the love that had been awakened in me here in the Red Centre was bound together with loss and pain. If I were open to the love of the earth, I would also have to open to her suffering. If I loved anything or anyone, suffering would be part of my experience.

In the midst of the glorious Australian Outback, I'd witnessed the suffering and death of the cow and her calf. Under the power of the sun and its intense heat, I'd felt the danger of my own death. When I was searching for a site for my marriage to Christ, I'd turned away from the bones in one of those potential places. Yet at Grace Cathedral, I'd been baptized into Christ's life as well as His death. I knew the Resurrection would follow and be the ultimate truth of His journey, but I was learning to embrace the whole story of the Son of God, Son of Man. And part of what I would affirm in this coming union would be the reality of birth and suffering and death in Christ's story, and that I would share in that with Him.

Louisa Jacques, a twentieth century mystic born in South Africa, says, "love and suffering are inseparable." She records God saying to her, "Love without suffering does not lead to my heart." I had been learning this all through my long journey. The Red Centre was finally letting me take this in. But I had more to learn about this.

When I returned to the Homestead, the gloom and deep pain in my heart persisted. Why, just the day before my wedding, was this pain so deep? Had something gone wrong? My insights about love and suffering began to give way to worry and fear. As I sorted through the swirl of my thoughts, trying to understand, I struck upon my intimate night with Jack. At the time I hadn't felt any misgivings or hesitation about being with him, but now I hurt so badly that it was the only thing I could think of to explain why my heart would feel like it had a knife in it. Had I somehow offended God by being with Jack? Once again I was overcome by that devastating thought that there might be no marriage, that the union with God I had so longed for might not come to pass. I might have blown everything I had prepared and longed for, just when it was so close to fulfillment.

The only remedy I could think of was to go see Jack at his cabin and tell him I thought I'd given too much of myself to him, and that I wanted to reclaim some of what I had left with him. As I sat with him on the swing and told him my trouble—leaving out the part about God—he hugged my head to his chest. By the time I left, I felt a little better, at least comforted, but back in my cabin, questions and fear took over my mind and heart. *I was about to be united in Holy Matrimony to Jesus Christ, the Highest of All Beings, and I had slept with a mere mortal two days before my wedding!* If this were a human marriage, my husband-to-be would surely, and understandably, call the whole thing off. Would Christ do that?

Maybe it was intended that I give myself only to Christ, and that my marriage to Christ and union with God meant that I needed to be celibate. Nuns married to Christ were celibate. *Why hadn't I thought about that sooner?* Yet human and divine love did not seem separate to me, and learning something about this mystery had seemed to be part of my journey. I felt utterly confused and pulled apart. I had fully accepted and embraced Christ's love for me, and His desire to take me as His bride. But was that still true? Now maybe I was utterly unworthy of such a union. How could I reconcile within me any of these things I couldn't understand? I lay on my cot in anguish. There was so much physical pain in my heart that I wondered if I might be in the midst of a heart attack.

I didn't want to assume that the marriage was still on, so as I got ready for bed, I stripped off all my jewelry, including my "engagement ring." I felt I was, and had to be, "naked" to the will of God. Holding Puppies to my heart, and placing the little lamb doll I'd brought from home under my pillow, I cried myself to sleep, fearing I had ruined everything.

When I woke the next morning, I lay very still for a long while, my attention hovering over my heart like a physician with a stethoscope bending over a heart patient, listening intently. It was March 25, the full moon, the day I had announced and prepared for. I listened inside to my deepest inner self. Were there any messages about the intended marriage? All was surprisingly quiet—no pain, no tension, no anxiety. No voice saying the wedding had been called off. Looking back now, I believe that my inner crash the day before had led me to a place of final surrender. There had been nothing I could do but let go entirely and surrender to God's will, whatever that was. Now this morning I felt washed clean, empty…and now ready.

I got up, put on shorts and a t-shirt, and went to the kitchen for a little toast and tea. The chief cook asked if I could help prep lunch for a busload of tourists arriving at noon. Grateful for the distraction, I gladly spent the next three hours chopping onions and peeling potatoes. My heart and mind remained blessedly at peace.

Early in the afternoon I drove to N'Dhala to pick up the trash I hadn't been able to carry with me the day I'd walked back to the Homestead. On the return trip, for some reason I swerved for a split-second, and Astra bogged down in the infamous bulldust on the edge of the road. In contrast to the previous day's intensity, this was something I could deal with. I was almost delighted to pull out my shovel. Using that and a piece of ghost gum bark, I extricated my car. I drove the rest of the way back feeling like a real Red Centre native—overlooking the fact that a true native wouldn't have bogged down in the first place.

In the late afternoon I began to prepare for the ceremony. I washed my hair and felt pleased when it turned out the way I liked it, with a little wave and not too flighty in the dry air. I put on my purple yoga pants, the white blouse that Linne had decorated, and dangly pearl earrings from India. I dabbed on a little rose perfume. I placed the wreath for my head and bridal bouquet in the decorative box along with the jewel case containing the ring. I folded up one of the cot blankets and a towel and, careful not to be spotted, put everything in the car so I could slip away when the right time came.

Then I waited patiently in my cabin until seven o'clock, just after sunset, and drove out to my chosen site. The camp had been quiet before dinnertime, so I hoped nobody had seen me leave. I parked behind the shelter so that my view of the desert wouldn't be blocked. I also didn't want moonlight to glint off the shiny metal and give my whereabouts away to anyone who might pass on the nearby road—although traffic was unlikely. From that point on I gave myself over to the mystery, surrendering my mind to the inner knowing of what to do and when.

The risen moon

The moon had already risen, creating a magical, luminous blend of pale, cool white light to the east in contrast to the warm, yellow glow to the west. I hung my little Yentl lantern off a twig projecting out of one of the ghost gum posts holding up the shelter. For an altar, I shifted the little table until it was stable enough on the sandy desert floor, then I covered it with the white towel. On it, I carefully set out the bouquet, the wreath of ribbons for my head, and the little black velvet box with the ring in it. I spread the gray camp blanket out on one of the cots. Then I lay down on the mattress to wait. I knew I would sense when to begin.

In the late evening dusk, the vibrant desert colors were subdued and all was still, as though the desert herself was anticipating "the quiet Christ." As the sky darkened into twilight, I put on the earphones, pushed the on-button of the portable cassette player, and was filled with the magical chords of the first Kitaro piece I had selected for this moment. As I listened to *Earth Born*, my heart swelled with the deep love I felt for Mother Earth, the Red Centre, and especially for my "birthplace," N'Dhala Gorge.

At the end of the piece, I paused the tape and let the stillness of the desert enter me once more. It wasn't yet time...and then it was. The moon cast a soft but not bright light over the desert. A slight wind picked up. I turned on *Dreams Like Yesterday* and, sitting at the edge of the cot, I sank into remembering the dream of God making love to me. Then as if in a sacred trance, I stood up, placed the crown on my head and picked up the bouquet. I slipped the cassette player into my pocket and started the wedding march, *Never Let You Go*. In step with the heartbeat of the music, I began to walk slowly away from the shelter. The music perfectly matched the joyful anticipation I felt at the imminent arrival of my Beloved. Without thinking, I headed toward the main road, toward the place where I sensed I would meet my Bridegroom.

The ribbons fluttered in the warm wind. I felt I was now everything I wanted to be for my Beloved. When I reached the road, I stopped, turned off the music, and removed the earphones. The silence of the desert enveloped me. No more than a minute later, I heard footsteps in the distance. At first they were just a faint sound, and then louder. Not single footsteps but more like small stones tumbling down a slope.

The silhouettes of five horses emerged out of the semi-darkness, approaching me at a walk. A couple of the lead horses startled when they saw me, but they kept coming. An arm's length from me, they stopped. In the soft moonlight I could see that the leader was a buckskin with a thick black forelock and mane. The wind flicked his black mane, as if a hand were whisking down his neck. I reached out and stroked his face.

As they gathered closer around, I whispered, "It's me." I ran my hands over the necks and manes of the brave ones, and we all stood quietly together for a few moments. I knew they had brought my Bridegroom; they had brought Christ to me.

Then I turned and together He and I walked slowly back toward the shelter. Behind us, like escorts, a couple of the horses followed and then they drifted off into the night, leaving us alone. I felt deeply calm and in awe.

The wind had picked up and was blowing strongly now. By the time we reached the altar table, the lantern light had blown out. In the moonlight I opened the black jewel box. My right hand slipped the ring onto my left ring finger. The little diamonds sparkled like stars. I had waited so long...now the dream was reality.

The next thing I knew the wind had dust and streamers and blankets tossing everywhere. I hurriedly packed up, wishing the magical moment could have lasted. But smiling, I thought to myself that no wedding ever seemed to come off without a hitch.

The moon was so bright that I drove back to the Homestead with no headlights. Unseen, I slipped quietly into my cabin. The ring—symbol of my deepest longing and desire—gleamed on my finger with a light of its own. Feeling blessed and peaceful, I removed my wedding clothes and got ready for bed. I lay down on my cot in reverie and reverence, wrapped in the magic and mystery of the night's event. Words of Mechtild of Magdeburg came to me:

In my kingdom thou shalt live as a new bride
there will I kiss thee with a kiss of love
and all my Godhead shall sweep through thy soul.

Before I drifted into sleep, I held up my left hand and kissed the ring. Feeling deeply and completely fulfilled, I rested in the silence and in my Lord.

"...there is a fruit that suffering and love infallibly produce and which men often forget to name when they speak of the way that leads to me. I will tell you, my little daughter; it is *joy*."

—Louisa Jacques

EPILOGUE

Marriage to Christ, and union with God, was the beginning of a new spiritual life for me, though I didn't realize that until some time after my return from the holy desert in Australia. I think I felt, "The story is over. I've found my heart's desire, I have union with God, I have married Christ. All is well. What more is there?"

Even though I was now married to Christ, I was an uncomfortable Christian. I had gone to several church services when I first returned, but found them dry and routine, lacking the richness and energy that matched the depth and reality I was experiencing in the Spirit. It was disturbing to be so disenchanted with the church yet feel that I was a Christian. I didn't know what to do about this.

Then, as always, I was guided to a new and broader perspective. I heard the story of the Mexican divinity, Quetzalcoatl, who so closely resembled Christ that the two were considered by some to be the same being. This discovery of another Christ story, and subsequent readings about the "Cosmic Christ" by Matthew Fox, expanded my sense of what Christ meant to me. Here was Ram Dass's "Christ consciousness" revealed in a new way.

Imagining and reflecting on the Cosmic Christ freed me to continue exploring other spiritualities without a sense of betrayal to my Divine Spouse. I had always been attracted to and influenced by Buddhism because of its insightful, practical guidance for daily living. Ernest Holmes' Science of Mind was very meaningful to me, not only because both my nanny, Ilse, and my friend, the Reverend Maxine, were practitioners of these teachings, but also because it offered a way to put a positive spin on life's difficult circumstances, and always showed me a new perspective. Eventually moving to New Mexico exposed me to Native American spirituality; their deep connection to the earth, reverence for all life, and care of the planet for future generations had deep, inner resonance with me.

Just as my discovery of God continued, so did the unfolding of my personal human life. Paul and I tried one more time to live together and give our deep love a home in daily relationship. We even brought a golden retriever puppy into our lives thinking that would start us off on the road to becoming a permanent family, but the puppy became sick and died, a sad symbol of our own troubled and unworkable relationship. In early summer Paul packed *all* his things into his red station wagon for the final time and pulled out of the driveway. I was in tears as I started off for a run along a fire trail in the hills where I lived. After about a half hour the tears began to dry as I realized it was finally over and I could accept the rightness of that step. At that very moment I spied a glittering object in the bushes. I stepped off the road and pulled out a shiny, deflated Mylar balloon. It read, *Congratulations Graduate.*

The ending of the love that had carried me into and through my long search for God wasn't the only "life school" I'd graduated from. The force of my food addiction had been wearing off over the years of inner work, and the act of self-acceptance and love after my Spenco failure took the remaining power out of it. I can still overindulge in a sumptuous Tiramisu desert, but it is only a fleeting temptation to my sweet tooth to have more than one.

While I did learn to feel kindness toward my mother, I confess that when winter serves up a string of cold, gray days, a deep childhood fear still grips my heart, challenging me to separate my oppressive memories of her from the bone-chilling weather.

As these parts of my life were falling away, new ones were arising. Within six months of my return from the Red Centre, I moved to the high desert of northern New Mexico, drawn by the irresistible power of the vast space and beauty that I loved and that mirrored my own inner landscape. At first I intended to live and work as a cook at the Benedictine Monastery, Christ in the Desert, but ultimately I found a house in a sparsely populated area that served my desire for immersion in solitude and silence. Following my passion for printing and making books, I enrolled in the Book Arts program at Mills College back in California. After a six-month apprenticeship with an esteemed printer in Berkeley, and a bookbinding intensive, I returned to my home in New Mexico with 10,000 lbs. of printing equipment in the fall of 1989.

A year later a master printer from the Pacific Northwest, Clifford Burke, from whom I'd purchased a fabulous type collection and several pieces of equipment from his own shop, joined me in the nurturing peace and beauty of my desert home. We married and as life partners began making unique and beautiful books and fine printed objects at Desert Rose Press. Clifford honors my marriage to Christ and shares my commitment to personal growth and spiritual living. We share our remote area of northern New Mexico with horses, dogs, and a menagerie of wild neighbors—coyotes, rattlesnakes, bears, deer, elk, ravens and wild turkey.

I am still on the Holy Red Road, aware that it is goes on forever in the Kingdom of God. As with intimate human relationships, energy and attention is required to nourish and grow the relationship with one's Divine Beloved as well. And so I continue to nurture and deepen my relationship with Christ and God, each day devoting time to meditation, prayer, reflection, and reading spiritual books.

My journey of self-discovery and transformation continues as I find myself and God on ever-deeper levels. I encounter the same bothersome hang-ups I thought I had taken care of, but meet them in different ways with a new perspective as though I am circling around on a spiral staircase, letting go all the way. It is an endless adventure.

I am still amazed, humbled and uplifted by the experiences I have recounted in this book. My spiritual marriage to Christ—such a mystery!—still fills me with awe and deep joy. I know that from Day One of my life I have been led and guided and supported by God. In spite of my fierce sense of independence I can now freely and even happily admit that I am utterly dependent on God for my well being in body and soul. As I reflect on my journey to God, I see everything as a gift from God, including—and especially—that fateful plate of scrambled eggs. I continue learning to surrender to God's will for me and to trust that everything is for my highest good, no matter how challenging or uncomfortable a situation may be.

As I travel along the Holy Red Road in the Promised Land, I see my journey as being both *to* and *with* God. What best describes how I want to walk along my path now are the lyrics from the musical *Godspell:* "To see Thee more clearly, love Thee more dearly, follow Thee more nearly, day by day."

My hope and prayer is that very soon we humans will recognize that the earth and all who dwell here are interconnected, that all life is sacred, and that we humans are called on to care for and love one another, the earth, and all who dwell here. I invite you to join me on my website, www.virginiamudd.com as we continue the journey to find ourselves and find God, and to share and create the vision of a peaceful, just, and healthy planet for all.

Amen.

ACKNOWLEDGEMENTS

Let me begin my "gratitude pages" with a deep bow to and heartful hug for Shoshana Alexander—editor, teacher, coach, guide, friend. When presented with several hundred pages of my unordered writings, like a sculptor before a block of stone, Shoshana saw the essence of the story and how to shape it to highlight the themes from ten years of my experiences that would interest and inspire a broad readership. Her own experience, spiritual wisdom, stimulating questions, and encouragement led me to a deeper understanding of my experience to bring out the richness of an incredible journey, and describe it more clearly. It was such a great pleasure to work with her that I can honestly say I never tired of the countless rewrites that followed her corrections and suggestions. As a friend, she always cheered me on: "Brava!" she would say whenever I reached another rewrite goal. She is truly a visionary editor, who shaped my story, kept me going, opened me to new spiritual explorations, and incidentally gave me a university education in writing in the course of our work together. It is thanks to her that I have not only come to the end of a long writing project—fulfilling something I always felt called to do—but now begin a new phase of my life with a deeper sense of my own spiritual path. I bow to her again, and give her another huge hug.

It is often awkward, if not impossible, to share our deepest spiritual truths or religious faith with a partner, especially if she or he has a different spiritual home. I am immensely grateful that Clifford was always open and responsive as I explored my Christian path, and shared my work on the book with him. When I needed a consultation, or a hug, he was always there, commiserating, celebrating, and everything in between. His insights and ideas often highlighted my path, pointed me in a new direction, revealed a next step to take, or a new way to see. His participation in and support of my book journey has been a great gift.

I give deep thanks to my former husband, who enriched my life in innumerable ways, but above all I'm grateful for his steadfast, gracious, and loving support of me during our marriage and beyond.

Everyone mentioned in this story (some names have been changed to respect privacy) has had a unique and important role to play in my inner and outer journey. To all of you, I am deeply grateful for your being in my life, and for all your help along my way. And "thank you" only begins to express how blessed I am for all the special friends who are not written about here—you know who you are—who have loved, encouraged, and supported me on my life's journey.

I would like to give special thanks to my cycling companions: to Carol, my cycling "blind date" with whom I shared an incredible cycling adventure across America, and who became a special, treasured, lifelong friend. And to Geri, for her steadfast and enthusiastic support of me and my Spenco journey, and our continued friendship.

Of course, two life-changing, cross country cycling trips cannot be done without great and trusty bicycles, and I will always have a special place in my heart for Little Silver and Sunny, who steadily and nobly carried me over thousands of miles.

I offer my deepest and ongoing thanks to all those modern-day teachers who guide me in becoming a more loving, more aware, happier divine human being, helping me to find myself and find God in new and beautiful ways. Most important for me are Thomas Merton, Fr. Thomas Keating, Matthew Fox, Pema Chodron, Thich Nhat Hanh, Andrew Harvey, Tessa Bielecki, Marion Woodman, Rabbi Rami Shapiro, Rev. Maxine Kaye, Neil Douglas-Klotz, Byron Katie, Ram Dass, Paul Tillich.

And there are too many people to name—and many whose names I don't even know because we were just "passing strangers"—who have not made teaching their life's work but who have guided and inspired and taught me in unexpected and powerful ways. And this goes for the beloved pets and wild critters who have blessed my life in so many ways. I would not be where I am today without each and every one of you.

I want to thank my publishing friends at Sunstone Press. Even more than their editorial, business and artistic expertise, I am grateful for their caring and support for me as a person and an author, and their commitment to helping me manifest my vision for this book. The best way I can describe this wonderful publishing experience is to say that when I first stepped into their office and met them, I felt like I had come home.

I conclude my gratitude pages with thanks to God by quoting thirteenth century German mystic Mechtild of Magdeberg: "Of the heavenly things God has shown me, I can speak but a little word...." The story will speak for itself as to what God has shown and given to me. God's love for me—the greatest of all gifts—ignited my love for Him, a love that only grows stronger. God continues to shower me with gifts of His love and grace, and for all that I can say but a little word.

CPSIA information can be obtained
at www.ICGtesting.com
Printed in the USA
LVOW06s0737040917
547465LV00008B/159/P

9 780865 349971